D0909589

AMERICAN LABOR RADICALISM

TESTIMONIES AND INTERPRETATIONS

WILEY SOURCEBOOKS IN AMERICAN SOCIAL THOUGHT

Edited by *David D. Hall and Daniel Walker Howe*

Daniel Walker Howe	THE AMERICAN WHIGS
Staughton Lynd	AMERICAN LABOR RADICALISM: TESTIMONIES AND INTERPRETATIONS
R. Laurence Moore	THE EMERGENCE OF AN AMERICAN LEFT: CIVIL WAR TO WORLD WAR I
Laurence Veysey	THE PERFECTIONISTS: RADICAL SOCIAL THOUGHT IN THE NORTH, 1815–1860
Donald Worster	AMERICAN ENVIRONMENTALISM: THE FORMATIVE PERIOD, 1860–1915
Alan Trachtenberg	LITERATURE AND SOCIETY IN TWENTIETH-CENTURY AMERICA

AMERICAN LABOR RADICALISM

TESTIMONIES AND INTERPRETATIONS

Edited by
Staughton Lynd

John Wiley & Sons, Inc.
New York • London • Sydmey • Toronto

Library of Congress Cataloging in Publication Data:

Lynd, Staughton, comp.
American labor radicalism

(Wiley sourcebooks in American social thought)
Bibliography: p.
1. Labor and laboring classes—United States—Addresses, essays, lectures. 2. Trade-unions—United States—Addresses, essays, lectures. 3. Radicalism—United States—Addresses, essays, lectures. I. Title. II. Series.

HD8072.L885 331.88'0973 72–13097

ISBN 0–471–55730–7
ISBN 0–471–55731–5 (pbk)

Printed in the United States of America

10–9 8 7 6 5 4 3 2 1

CONTENTS

INTRODUCTION

"With the development of industry the proletariat not only increases in number, it becomes concentrated in great masses, its strength grows, and it feels that strength more. The collisions between individual workmen and individual bourgeois take more and more the character of collisions between two classes. Thereupon the workers begin to form combinations (Trade Unions) against the bourgeoisie; they club together in order to keep up the rate of wages; they found permanent associations in order to make provision beforehand for these occasional revolts . . . .

Now and then the workers are victorious, but only for a time. The real fruits of their battle lie, not in the immediate result, but in the ever expanding union of the workers. . . .

This organization of the proletarians into a class, and consequently into a political party, is continually being upset again by the competition between the workers themselves. But it ever rises up again, stronger, firmer, mightier . . . ."

Thus Karl Marx and Friedrich Engels predicted the development of labor radicalism in their *Communist Manifesto,* published in 1848.

The youthful Marx expected that as industry developed, the class struggle would deepen, labor organizations would become more and more militant, and their outlook would become increasingly political. Spreading out as it progressed, embracing entire industries instead of separate factories and finally speaking for the working class as a whole, the labor movement would collide with government authority at every step. Life itself would organize a class aware of the common interests of all who toil, and dedicated to the transformation of capitalism into socialism.

A half century's experience in Europe called this forecast into question. In England, Sidney and Beatrice Webb published studies of trade unionism in that country where industrialization first began, and showed that English trade unions had adjusted to capitalist management of industry and were interested in piecemeal pragmatic gains rather than in social transformation. Lenin translated the Webbs' work while sentenced to Siberia. Soon after his release, he published a pamphlet entitled *What Is To Be Done?* (1902), which came to the same conclusion. Lenin wrote:

> "The history of all countries shows that the working-class, exclusively by its own effort, is able to develop only trade-union consciousness, i.e., it may itself realize the necessity for combining in unions, to fight against the employers and to strive to compel the government to pass necessary legislation, etc."

But socialist consciousness—recognition of the necessity for replacing the system of private property itself—could only be brought to the working class "from without," Lenin insisted.

Whereas Marx believed that life itself would develop radical consciousness in the labor movement, Lenin concluded that radicalism would have to be introduced into the labor movement by socialist agitators. Thus Lenin's analysis supported the thesis of nonsocialists who argued that as labor organizations mature they exhibit less (not more) tactical militancy, less (not more) rank-and-file participation in decision-making, less (not more) concern for the oppression of working people everywhere, and, especially, less (not more) will to challenge the validity of the system as a whole.

Capitalism still being with us, the jury is of necessity still out on this question. Those who agree with the Webbs and Lenin cite the fact that in the century and a quarter since the publication of the *Communist Manifesto* there has not been a single socialist revolution in a highly industrialized nation. Those who agree with Marx cite phenomena like the occupation of factories in France in May–June 1968 as proof that the industrial working class has not been domesticated, and may yet lead a socialist transformation.

This book provides evidence for assessing this question as it presents itself in the history of the American labor movement.

Labor radicalism was very much in evidence in America during the period between the depression of 1873 and World War I. A number of labor organizations that sought to replace the capitalist system with a cooperative or socialist system were formed in these years, among them the Knights of Labor (which favored producers' cooperatives, not socialism), the Socialist party, and the Industrial Workers of the World (IWW). The last, especially, with its famous preamble proclaiming that the working and employing classes have nothing in common, seemed an incarnation of Marxist prophecy.

Individual working men and women experienced just such a radicalization as the *Communist Manifesto* envisioned. Eugene Victor Debs, who twice polled close to a million votes as Socialist party candidate for United States president, came to socialism step by painful step. Only after several years as officer and editor for railwaymens' craft unions did he perceive the necessity for one industrial union of all railroad workers. And only after forming such a union, and leading it into a strike against the railroad corporations, and seeing the local and federal governments blatantly intervene on the side of the employers to break the strike, did Debs conclude that labor required its own political party, too.

Yet other working people passed through a transition that took them to the Right, not to the Left. Samuel Gompers was president of the American Federation of Labor (AFL) from its founding in 1886 until his death in 1924. A cigar maker, he was at first influenced by the socialist ideas common among German workers in New York City. But the violence that accompanied the depression of 1873 caused him to reconsider. Gompers held radical agitators partially responsible for a police riot in New York City's Tompkins Square in 1874, which he personally witnessed. Thereafter, he emphasized more and more a "job conscious" or "business" unionism. Gompers and the AFL came to be identified with the belief that workers should build craft unions to defend their immediate economic interests and not permit themselves to be diverted by the political utopias of middle-class intellectuals.

At least in the short run, history vindicated Gompers rather than Debs. The IWW failed to establish itself as a competitor to the AFL. After 1912, when the IWW won the dramatic textile strike in Lawrence, Massachusetts, for "Bread and Roses" and Debs polled six per cent of the electorate, radicalism in the labor movement began to decline. Both the IWW and the majority of the Socialist party courageously opposed American entry into World War I. They suffered isolation and repression as the result: Debs, for instance, was sentenced to ten years in prison for encouraging draft refusal. A final effort to establish industrial unions in the steel and packinghouse industries in 1919 was defeated, in part because of Red-baiting of the steel strike leader, William Z. Foster.

Historian John H. M. Laslett has probed the reasons for the decline of this first wave of radicalism in American labor history on the basis of a study of six unions in which socialist ideas were strong. There was, he writes, "an increasingly evident conflict between the logic of collective bargaining (which even the most radical trade-unionists came in the end to accept) and the demands of the socialists for separate, revolutionary action on the part of a united working class." In the coal industry, for instance, where the United Mine Workers organized one of the few industrial unions in the AFL and socialist ideas were widespread, "the checkoff system, the need to abide by nationally negotiated contracts, and growing cooperation between the union and the coal operators in imposing order on the anarchic coal market rapidly limited the union's potential for revolutionary change." Laslett's conclusion for the period before World War I applies to other periods in the history of American labor, as well:

"The notion of contract implies a recognition by the union of *its* responsibilities for the enforcement of the agreement, which sometimes placed even radical union leadership in the seemingly anomalous position of having to act against its own constituency, when the contract was violated by members of the rank and file. Thus, the price which the union had to pay for the benefits it received was to become part of the productive system itself, able to modify but not to change in any basic way the nature of the system."[1]

In the 1920s it was natural to suppose that labor radicalism in America had run its course, and that the American labor movement would approximate more and more the model of the AFL. A group of historians at the University of Wisconsin, notably Selig Perlman, John R. Commons, and Philip Taft, published a series of influential books that said just that.

Then came the Depression of 1929.

Local and spontaneous struggles to form industrial unions in the early 1930s were gathered together in the organizing drive of the Congress of Industrial Organizations (CIO), formed in November 1935. In 1936–1937 the CIO involved perhaps half a million workers in sit-down strikes and organized perhaps four million into industrial unions. The optimism of the *Communist Manifesto* once again seemed relevant. But not for long. Len De Caux, first editor of the *CIO News*, recalls:

"The CIO uprising shook up conservative labor theorists, but after 1937 they recomposed themselves. In a first breakthrough to union-

[1]John H.M. Laslett, *Labor and The Left: A Study of Socialist and Radical Influences in the American Labor Movement, 1881–1924*, Basic Books, New York and London, 1970, pp. 297 ff.

ism, they held, it was hard to avoid some disorderly struggle, and some radical guff. But once the law and the employers accepted collective bargaining, order reasserted itself. Union leaders could consolidate their machines, discipline their members, and collaborate in orderly bargaining procedures. The class struggle, if such it had been, was at an end."[2]

Many things combined to bring CIO militancy to an end so rapidly. One was the conservative outlook and authoritarian style of leaders like John L. Lewis, president of the CIO, which proved more influential than the radicalism of the socialists and Communists whom Lewis hired as organizers. Another was the return of prosperity, with defense spending during and after World War II. And a third was the fact, stressed by New Left historians such as C. Wright Mills, Mark Naison, Stanley Aronowitz, Ronald Radosh, and myself, that unionization in the 1930s, sponsored as it was by the federal government and soon acquiesced to by such corporations as United States Steel, functioned as much to discipline rank-and-file action within the constraints of time contracts as to enhance rank-and-file action because of union recognition.

When all these things have been duly noted, however, it is also the case that radicalism did not die a natural death in CIO unions, but was brutally purged.

James R. Prickett has studied the process that ended in the expulsion from the CIO of unions representing between 500,000 and 1,000,000 members, and the harassment of radicals in the unions that remained. Communists operated in the CIO unions in an apolitical manner almost indistinguishable from the conduct of non-Communist liberals, Prickett insists. In the most democratic of the large CIO unions, the United Automobile Workers (UAW), Prickett finds that the Communists passed up the chance to run their own members for top office in 1939 and were never in control thereafter. Communism was not a serious threat to rising CIO bureaucrats like Walter Reuther, according to Prickett, but provided a convenient opportunity for eliminating independent rank and filers of all political views.[3]

[2]Len De Caux, *Labor Radical: From the Wobblies to CIO. A Personal History*, Beacon Press, Boston, 1970, p. 244.

[3]James R. Prickett, "Communism and Factionalism in the United Automobile Workers, 1939–1947," *Science and Society*, Summer 1968; "The NMU and Ambiguities of Anti-Communism," *New Politics*, Winter 1968; "Some Aspects of the Communist Controversy in the CIO," *Science and Society*, Summer–Fall 1969.

Reuther, indeed, came to symbolize the CIO after World War II, as Lewis had symbolized the CIO before the war. Paradoxically, in view of the controversy as to whether unions must restrict themselves to narrow economic goals, Reuther won a reputation for liberalism by espousing progressive measures for the society at large while running his own union in a conventional and heavy-handed manner. But his words seemed empty and far away to men working on automobile assembly lines or struggling to control their local unions (see the selections by Mathew Ward and Harvey Swados).

In *Going Away* novelist Clancy Sigal evoked the mood in 1946–7 when Reuther took control of the UAW, and the CIO of the 1930s was laid to rest for good.

"The people who most hated Hauser [Reuther] were . . . the militants and old-line shop stewards: theirs was the clearest case. These old ones (in the auto industry you are old at thirty-five), with their memories, looked back to the thirties as the high point in their lives because they had a chance, for the first time, to fight back and give the front office the well-deserved works, and now here was Victor Hauser, flanked by teams of social psychologists and campus economists, proposing replacement of this (granted, frequently anarchic) militance with a morbid philosophy of 'sound labor-management relations,' 'centralization of union authority,' 'co-operation,' 'responsibility.' Had a major unemployment crisis hit in '46 and '47 Victor Hauser would have gone down the drain. It didn't. Hauser bet right, we bet wrong. We paid."[4]

Rank-and-file steelworkers, speaking to a community labor history forum in 1970, also looked back with a sense that the CIO had changed things for the better but had not fulfilled the dreams of its organizers. A black Communist cried:

"I wanted a union that would be a watchdog for the working class and guard its interests. If I ever had a chance I was going to turn my dog loose on the steel corporation. I always looked at Mississippi and Alabama. The lynching, Jim Crow, and segregation always stayed on my mind: How could we stop it? . . . [Today, Jesse Reese went on,] we have in our unions a pet dog—what you might call a pet company dog—led by the caretakers; and the caretakers are the leaders of our union. And our dog is being fed Red-baiting and his teeth have been pulled out (that's the strike clause) and your dog don't bark no more

[4]Clancy Sigal, *Going Away: A Report, A Memoir,* Houghton Mifflin, Boston; and The Riverside Press, Cambridge, Mass., 1962, p. 329.

for you. Your dog don't bark at no misery; your dog won't bark no more—he can't hear. Makes no difference how many people they kill, your dog don't say nothing; he ain't the dog of 1937, when that dog turned loose nine boys—the Scottsboro Boys—and freed Tom Mooney. What's the matter with your dog? They have declared war on color, and they're now dancing on the doorsteps of Asia, and your dog don't bark. Because you don't have anything but the pet dog of the steel trusts."[5]

Thus a second cycle of American labor radicalism played itself out. After this second disappointment many Left intellectuals concluded that the working class of advanced industrial societies had been integrated into the establishment, and could no longer be expected to lead a movement for social change.

Yet a third labor upheaval seems to be in the making. Since the mid-1960s there has been a trend toward rank-and-file rejection of nationally negotiated contracts, and local and national strike action in defiance of no-strike clauses and government injunctions. What does it all mean? Where is all this energy going? Will new unions of farm workers, Southern woodcutters, or public employees remain or become social movements concerned with more than wages and hours? Or will they, like so many unions before them, be militant and radical only until recognized by management as bargaining agents, and thereafter become policemen for the boss? Is there a promise of political radicalism in the militancy with which electrical workers, truckdrivers, postmen, teachers, auto workers, and railwaymen defend their real wages? Will corporations, fearful of renewed competition from abroad, press their employees through wage controls or insistence on higher productivity so as to awaken militancy in unions that have long been asleep? Or do expressions of militancy, like the 1972 strike in Lordstown (see below), signify only an "economism" quite consistent with racism toward black and brown fellow workers, sexism toward women, and chauvinism toward the victims of American imperialism around the world?

A frequent answer is that working people in America will be more radical in the next few years than in the decades after World War II, but that their radicalism will not express itself through unions. New forms of organization will have to be improvised, according to this line of thought, comparable to the soviets of 1905 and 1917 in Russia, or the workers' councils of 1920 in Italy and 1968 in France. This way

[5]Jesse Reese, quoted in "Personal Histories of the Early CIO," ed. Staughton Lynd, *Radical America*, May–June 1971, pp. 70–71.

of looking at the matter offers a certain synthesis of the views of Marx and Lenin. Recognizing, with the Webbs, Lenin, and Selig Perlman, the tendency of trade unions to become routinized and conservative when recognized by management, one may still insist on the possibility of radicalism among workers themselves—radicalism that will express itself through forms other than unions.

A good deal of recent radical thought converges on this hypothesis. For example, in 1952 Martin Glaberman, an auto worker and a member of a Trotskyist group in Detroit, published a pamphlet entitled *Punching Out* about the constrictions of the contract and the dilemma of a good man who becomes a shop steward. Glaberman stated flatly: "The union and the contract have outlived their usefulness. The union is no longer a place where the worker can express his views." Twenty years later in 1972 Stanley Aronowitz, a former steel and oil worker, published an article in *Liberation* magazine called "Which Side Are You On? Trade Unions In America." He wrote with equal explicitness: "The trade unions serve corporate interests in America today. Their role as an organ of struggle has virtually expired." Despite their skepticism toward trade unions, however, both Glaberman and Aronowitz are optimistic about the radical potential of working people themselves.

One thing seems clear. If there is a new wave of American labor radicalism in the 1970s, it will reflect the libertarian spirit of the student and civil rights movements of the 1960s. It will be a radicalism more concerned with control of the work process than in the past. Workers' control is not a political demand in the sense of reaching out to problems beyond the factory. It is a demand directed at what happens inside the factory, a demand that asks something new and even more political: it asks that working people not only receive benefits, but also begin to take part in decisions about the work process.

The leading theorist of workers' control is the French writer André Gorz. In one of his articles, Gorz stresses the unexpressed and almost unknown potentialities of laboring men and women:

"A potential of frustration and of revolt permanently lies dormant within the working class and, in so-called *normal* periods, no one knows how deeply the working class feels oppressed, exploited, frustrated. No one knows: neither the union leadership nor the workers themselves. Their feelings and awareness about their conditions are normally repressed because they have no opportunity and no words to express them, to speak about them, to make themselves heard. It is because of this repression that expression of discontent always comes as a surprise and always takes the form of violent outbreaks, of so-called spontaneous wildcat strikes.

The recurrence and growing number of wildcat strikes all over the advanced capitalist world presently demonstrate that the basic assumption on which modern trade unionism was built no longer holds true: this assumption was that improved wages could compensate the workers for the changes that technological innovation was making in their lives. In other words, unions as well as management took to considering workers as commodities that could be bought into submission if the price offered for their labor was high enough. Workers were held by union and management alike to care for their wages only, and all the union's bargaining power was concentrated on quantitative demands. Potential qualitative demands were left aside."[6]

In Gorz's view the radicalism of working people will ask increasingly for "meaningful, enjoyable, enriching, healthy work and working conditions," and for an economic system that permits workers to put their hearts into work without putting themselves out of a job.

[6]André Gorz, "Workers' Control," *Socialist Revolution,* November–December 1970, pp. 22–23.

Part One

THE POSSIBILITY OF RADICALISM: KNIGHTS OF LABOR AND IWW

1

Mother (Mary) Jones
EARLY YEARS

Mother Jones (1830–1930) was one of the outstanding woman organizers in the history of the American labor movement. In these opening pages of her autobiography she tells of the loss of her husband and four small children to yellow fever in 1867, and her subsequent dedication to the work of the Knights of Labor. Mother Jones was the only woman on the committee that planned the founding of the Industrial Workers of the World (IWW) in 1905. She was particularly active among the bituminous coal miners of West Virginia and other Appalachian states, where her memory is still cherished. In 1919, at the age of almost ninety, she played a vigorous role in the steel strike that foreshadowed the industrial unionism of the Congress of Industrial Organizations (CIO).

I was born in the city of Cork, Ireland, in 1830. My people were poor. For generations they had fought for Ireland's freedom. Many of my folks have died in that struggle. My father, Richard Harris, came to America in 1835, and as soon as he had become an American citizen he sent for his family. His work as a laborer with railway construction crews took him to Toronto, Canada. Here I was brought up but always as the child of an American citizen. Of that citizenship I have ever been proud.

After finishing the common schools, I attended the Normal school with the intention of becoming a teacher. Dress-making too, I learned proficiently. My first position was teaching in a convent in Monroe, Michigan. Later, I came to Chicago and opened a dressmaking establishment. I preferred sewing to bossing little children.

However, I went back to teaching again, this time in Memphis, Tennessee. Here I was married in 1861. My husband was an iron moulder and a staunch member of the Iron Moulders' Union.

SOURCE. *Autobiography of Mother Jones*, ed. Mary Field Parton, first published in 1925 and reissued in paperback in 1972 by the Charles H. Kerr Company, 431 South Dearborn Street, Chicago, Illinois, pp. 11–16.

In 1867, a yellow fever epidemic swept Memphis. Its victims were mainly among the poor and the workers. The rich and the well-to-do fled the city. Schools and churches were closed. People were not permitted to enter the house of a yellow fever victim without permits. The poor could not afford nurses. Across the street from me, ten persons lay dead from the plague. The dead surrounded us. They were buried at night quickly and without ceremony. All about my house I could hear weeping and the cries of delirium. One by one, my four little children sickened and died. I washed their little bodies and got them ready for burial. My husband caught the fever and died. I sat alone through nights of grief. No one came to me. No one could. Other homes were as stricken as was mine. All day long, all night long, I heard the grating of the wheels of the death cart.

After the union had buried my husband, I got a permit to nurse the sufferers. This I did until the plague was stamped out.

I returned to Chicago and went again into the dressmaking business with a partner. We were located on Washington Street near the lake. We worked for the aristocrats of Chicago, and I had ample opportunity to observe the luxury and extravagance of their lives. Often while sewing for the lords and barons who lived in magnificent houses on the Lake Shore Drive, I would look out of the plate glass windows and see the poor, shivering wretches, jobless and hungry, walking along the frozen lake front. The contrast of their condition with that of the tropical comfort of the people for whom I sewed was painful to me. My employers seemed neither to notice nor to care.

Summers, too, from the windows of the rich, I used to watch the mothers come from the west side slums, lugging babies and little children, hoping for a breath of cool, fresh air from the lake. At night, when the tenements were stifling hot, men, women and little children slept in the parks. But the rich, having donated to the charity ice fund, had, by the time it was hot in the city, gone to seaside and mountains.

In October, 1871, the great Chicago fire burned up our establishment and everything that we had. The fire made thousands homeless. We stayed all night and the next day without food on the lake front, often going into the lake to keep cool. Old St. Mary's church at Wabash Avenue and Peck Court was thrown open to the refugees and there I camped until I could find a place to go.

Near by in an old, tumbled down, fire scorched building the Knights of Labor held meetings. The Knights of Labor was the labor organization of those days. I used to spend my evenings at their meetings, listening to splendid speakers. Sundays we went out into the woods and held meetings.

Those were the days of sacrifice for the cause of labor. Those were the days when we had no halls, when there were no high salaried officers, no feasting with the enemies of labor. Those were the days of the martyrs and the saints.

I became acquainted with the labor movement. I learned that in 1865, after the close of the Civil War, a group of men met in Louisville, Kentucky. They came from the North and from the South; they were the "blues" and the "greys" who a year or two before had been fighting each other over the question of chattel slavery. They decided that the time had come to formulate a program to fight another brutal form of slavery—industrial slavery. Out of this decision had come the Knights of Labor.

From the time of the Chicago fire I became more and more engrossed in the labor struggle and I decided to take an active part in the efforts of the working people to better the conditions under which they worked and lived. I became a member of the Knights of Labor.

One of the first strikes that I remember occurred in the Seventies. The Baltimore and Ohio Railroad employees went on strike and they sent for me to come help them. I went. The mayor of Pittsburgh swore in as deputy sheriffs a lawless, reckless bunch of fellows who had drifted into that city during the panic of 1873. They pillaged and burned and rioted and looted. Their acts were charged up to the striking workingmen. The governor sent the militia.

The Railroads had succeeded in getting a law passed that in case of a strike, the train-crew should bring in the locomotive to the roundhouse before striking. This law the strikers faithfully obeyed. Scores of locomotives were housed in Pittsburgh.

One night a riot occurred. Hundreds of box cars standing on the tracks were soaked with oil and set on fire and sent down the tracks to the roundhouse. The roundhouse caught fire. Over one hundred locomotives, belonging to the Pennsylvania Railroad Company were destroyed. It was a wild night. The flames lighted the sky and turned to fiery flames the steel bayonettes of the soldiers.

The strikers were charged with the crimes of arson and rioting, although it was common knowledge that it was not they who instigated the fire; that it was started by hoodlums backed by the business men of Pittsburgh who for a long time had felt that the Railroad company discriminated against their city in the matter of rates.

I knew the strikers personally. I knew that it was they who had tried to enforce orderly law. I knew they disciplined their members when they did violence. I knew, as everybody knew, who really perpetrated the crime of burning the railroad's property. Then and there I learned in the early part of my career that labor must bear the cross for others' sins, must be the vicarious sufferer for the wrongs that others do.

These early years saw the beginning of America's industrial life.

Hand and hand with the growth of factories and the expansion of railroads, with the accumulation of capital and the rise of banks, came anti-labor legislation. Came strikes. Came violence. Came the belief in the hearts and minds of the workers that legislatures but carry out the will of the industrialists.

2

Selig Perlman
LABOR AND CAPITALISM IN AMERICA

A Theory of the Labor Movement, *published in 1928 by University of Wisconsin economics professor Selig Perlman (1888-1959), is the single most influential interpretation of American labor history. Perlman generalized from the experience of the American Federation of Labor (AFL), founded in 1886, and its president Samuel Gompers. He argued that radical ideas enter the labor movement from the outside and that left to themselves working people will develop the kind of apolitical trade unionism represented by the AFL. In the United States, according to Perlman, this universal tendency was helped along by certain additional influences: the property orientation and lack of class consciousness in American society and, paradoxically, the teachings of Karl Marx.*

A. The Basic Characteristics of the American Community

The following pages point to aspects of American society that have worked against class-conscious trade unionism, an independent labor party, and socialism. Even those who disagree with Perlman's conclusions concede his assertion that the United States has been an exceptionally difficult situation for the radical organizer.

THE STRENGTH OF THE INSTITUTION OF PRIVATE PROPERTY

A labor movement must, from its very nature, be an organized campaign against the rights of private property, even where it stops short of embracing a radical program seeking the elimination, gradual or abrupt, "constitutional" or violent, of the private entrepreneur. When this campaign takes the political and legislative route, it leads

SOURCE. Selig Perlman, *A Theory of the Labor Movement,* The Macmillan Company, New York, 1928, reprinted by Augustus M. Kelley, Publishers, 1951, 1964, 1966, 1968 and 1970, pp. 155–169, 192–198.

to the denial of the employer's right to absolute control of his productive property. It demands and secures regulatory restrictions which, under American constitutional practice, are within the province of the "police power" vested in the states and granted by specific authority to Congress; only they must, in every case, square with "public purpose," as that term is interpreted in the last analysis by the United States Supreme Court. When the same campaign follows the economic route—the route of unionism, strikes, boycotts, and union "working rules"—the restrictions on the rights of property are usually even more thoroughgoing and far-reaching, since unions are less amenable to judicial control than are legislatures and Congress. A third form of the labor movement seeks to promote cooperative production and distribution—neither of which is practiced appreciably in this country. This co-operative movement sets out to beat private capitalism by the methods of private business: greater efficiency and superior competitive power. To the advocates of the rights of private property, this third mode of the labor movement is the least offensive.

Because the labor movement in any form is a campaign against the absolute rights of private property, the extent to which the institution of private property is intrenched in the community in which a labor movement operates is of overwhelming importance to it. In England, the advent of industrial capitalism synchronized with an agrarian revolution which uprooted and set adrift hundreds of thousands of her peasant yeomanry to join the urban proletariat. Thus eventually the urban capitalists in the fight for their rights were denied the vital and valuable support which might have come from a land-owning peasantry. England, therefore, permitted more drastic inroads into property rights than France, where the Great Revolution created peasant proprietors on a scale far vaster even than that on which the contemporary English Enclosure movement destroyed them. The same holds for newer countries. Property rights are safer from infringement in Canada, settled by farming homesteaders, than in Australia, where, until recently, the desirable lands were owned in large holdings, by capitalistic pastoralists.

The enormous strength of private property in America, at once obvious to any observer, goes back to the all-important fact that, by and large, this country was occupied and settled by laboring pioneers, creating property for themselves as they went along and holding it in small parcels. This was the way not only of agriculture but also of the mechanical trades and of the larger scale industries. Thus the harmony between the self-interest of the individual pursuing his private economic aim and the general public interest proved a real and lasting harmony in the American colonies and states. This Adam Smith saw in 1776, his eye on the frugal and industrious class of masters of workshops still on the threshold of their elevation by the industrial revolution yet to come. Every addition to the total of the privately held wealth was at the same time an addition to the productive equipment in the community, which meant a fuller satisfaction of its wants and a higher level of the general welfare. Moreover, being held in small parcels, wealth was generally accessible to whomever would pay the price in industry, frugality, and ingenuity. Furthermore, this condition had not been destroyed even with the coming in of modern "big business," combinations, mergers, and "trusts." For, too often does the grandeur of business on its modern gigantic scale, the magnitude of billion dollar corporations completely hide from one's view those other millions of small businesses. These, here and now, may be forced to struggle hard for existence, perhaps only to fail in the end. But failing, still others will take their place and continue to form a social layer firm enough to safeguard against even a possible revolutionary explosion from below. The earnestness with which judges will rush to stand between legislatures and menaced property rights; the rigor of their application of the injunction to keep unionists and strikers from interfering with those rights in their own way; the ease with which a typically American middle class community may work itself up, or be worked up, into an anti-radical hysteria, when Soviet missionaries or syndicalist agitators are rumored to be abroad in the land; and the flocking to the election polls of millions to vote for the "safe" candidate—all are of one piece, and are to be explained by the way in which the American community originated and grew.

This social and economic conservatism, bred in the American community from the beginning, has been tested repeatedly by sections of the American labor movement—now wittingly, now unwittingly, and invariably the test has evoked the same and identical reaction. It began in 1829, when the Workingman's Party of New York, moved by the desire to frighten employers lest they add to the recently won ten-hour day, officially endorsed the crude communistic "Equal Division" program of Thomas Skidmore. A whole generation had to pass before the recollection of this brief indiscretion had faded from the public memory and ceased to plague the labor movement. Another such test of the public mind was the unplanned, but virtual anarchy of the destructive great railway strikes of 1877, from Baltimore to San Francisco. It was then that the judiciary, watching the paralysis which had seized the democratically chosen sheriffs and governors, and remembering well the Commune of Paris of 1871, resolved to insure society against a labor revolution by dint of the injunction, the outlawing of the boycott, and like measures. Nine years later, the

Chicago "Anarchists," with a full-blown program of revolutionary syndicalism in all but the name itself, were made to feel the ferocious self-defense of a gigantically growing and self-satisfied community against those who would import the methods of the class struggle of Russia and of Spain. Still later, in the Pullman strike of 1894, the labor movement saw how the courts, the Federal Executive, and the ruling forces in the country could be counted on to act as one in crushing any real or fancied industrial rebellion. The treatment of the Industrial Workers of the World in the Western States, the anti-"Red" hysteria of 1919 and 1920, and the great godsend which the syndicalist past of William Z. Foster proved to the employers in defeating the great steel strike in 1919, which he led—are of too recent occurrence to necessitate detailed discussion. The state of Kansas, a representative American farming and middle-class community, furnishes perhaps the most telling illustration of the typical American reaction to industrial radicalism. That state, which was in 1912 a stamping ground for Roosevelt progressivism, just as it had been the heart of the "Populism" of the nineties, showed no hesitancy, in 1919, when the coal miners' strike had endangered the comfort of its citizenry, at enacting a law depriving of the right to strike, labor in public utilities and in other industries supplying food, fuel, and clothing, which the law classed as public utilities for that purpose.

Briefly, if the century-long experience of American labor as an organized movement holds any great lesson at all, that lesson is that under no circumstances can labor here afford to arouse the fears of the great middle class for the safety of private property as a basic institution. Labor needs the support of public opinion, meaning the middle class, both rural and urban, in order to make headway with its program of curtailing, by legislation and by trade unionism, the abuses which attend the employer's unrestricted exercise of his property rights. But any suspicion that labor might harbor a design to do away altogether with private property, instead of merely regulating its use, immediately throws the public into an alliance with the anti-union employers. Before the Russian Revolution had intensified this fear of revolution, reform movements were probably helped by pointing out to the public that unless that and other reforms in industrial conditions were effected, a revolution might take place. But with revolution no longer a mere remote abstraction but a very lively going concern in Europe and Asia, such a threat becomes a boomerang and enthrones reaction. This is especially so because American organized labor lives in a potentially hostile environment. The American public has tolerated the labor movement, or has even aided it, as the miners were aided in their strike of 1902 against the anthracite coal combination. But a misstep can easily turn sympathy into hostility. Gompers' reiterated denunciations of communism in the disturbed years immediately following the Russian Revolution, which have been continued by his successor, seem to have been prompted at least partly by the realization of the ease with which the environment of the American labor movement may be turned into a hostile environment. And this same realization that, in the American community, labor is in a minority, and is facing a nation of property holders, actual or potential, is at the bottom of American labor's distrust of government authority which is so puzzling to Europeans. Experience has taught American labor leaders that, whatever may have been the avowed purpose when powers were extended to the government, and whatever may have been the express assurances given to labor that such powers would never be used against it, it is all in vain when a crisis breaks, like a threatened strike in a vital industry, and when the powers that be feel that with some stretching perhaps, the law might be applied to handle the situation. It is enough to recall that the Sherman Anti-Trust law was applied for the first time in the Debs case arising from the Pullman strike, and that the War-time Lever Act, intended against food and other profiteers, was made the basis, one year after the Armistice, of an injunction against striking coal miners.

THE LACK OF A CLASS CONSCIOUSNESS IN AMERICAN LABOR

The overshadowing problem of the American labor movement has always been the problem of staying organized. No other labor movement has ever had to contend with the fragility so characteristic of American labor organizations. In the main, this fragility of the organization has come from the lack of class cohesiveness in American labor. That American unions have appreciated the full gravity of this problem, whether or not they have also consciously connected it with a weak class cohesiveness, is shown by several practices, which they have carried to a much farther extent than unionists in other countries. It would seem as though, through these practices, they have tried to make up for the lack of a spontaneous class solidarity, upon which European unions could always reckon with certainty. These practices are ways of ruthlessly suppressing "dual" unions and "outlaw" strikes.

An "outlaw" strike is a strike by local groups, usually one or more local branches, undertaken without complying with the regular procedure prescribed in the constitution of the national union, and against the wishes of the national officers. Such strikes are invariably defeated by the national officers themselves, who, if need be, and especially if a breach of a trade agreement with the employer is also involved, will not only expel the "outlaws," but will even go to the extent of recruiting from among out-of-town members in sufficient numbers to fill the places of the strikers. In Great Britain, on the contrary, when national leaders have been thus defied by their own local branches, they have refused, to be sure, to put the strikers on the strike benefit rolls, but, on the other hand, they have never thought of visiting upon these "outlaws" anything like the reprisals employed in America. We find a similar contrast between England and America in regard to the treatment of "dual" unions. A "dual" union originates in the secession of a disaffected faction from an established union, or else it may arise as a brand new organization; in either case, it competes with the old union for membership in the same craft or industry. In America, "dual" unions are ruthlessly exterminated by the combined strength of all the unions in the American Federation of Labor. But British union leaders will view dual unionism with a complacency that seems utterly incomprehensible to American union officers. The American procedure, both in regard to outlaw strikes and dual unions, has often been decried as a bold and shameless manifestation of union "bureaucratism" and of boss-control. Much can be said in favor of this interpretation. Yet a different interpretation is equally in point. This ruthlessness, while making full allowance for the tyranny and ambition to rule by union "bosses," is at the same time a device for self-protection hit upon by labor organizations operating under conditions in which everything and everybody seem engaged in a conspiracy to undermine their solidarity within. British unions, luckily for themselves, have their internal solidarity presented "on a silver platter," as it were, by the very organization of the society in which they work. British society, with its hierarchy of classes, keeps labor together by pressure from the top. Accordingly, British workers act together in strikes, notwithstanding the rivalry between their unions. But the experience of American unionism has been that, with some few exceptions, easily explained, whenever "radical" or merely impetuous local leaders defied their own union constitution with an "unauthorized" strike, or where factions have broken away to form a more "progressive" rival to the old union, the resulting fratricidal war, including mutual "scabbing," has always led to an all around defeat for labor, and to a total collapse of organization.

The cause of this lack of psychological cohesiveness in American labor is the absence, by and large, of a completely "settled" wage earning class. Sons of wage earners will automatically follow their fathers' occupations in the mining districts, which, because of their isolation, are little worlds in themselves. The Negroes in industry are, of course, a hereditary wage earning group. And apparently such a class has developed also in the textile centers. To be sure, the great mass of the wage earners in American industry today, unless they have come from the farm intending to return there with a part of their wages saved, will die wage earners. However, many of these do not stay in a given industry for life, but keep moving from industry to industry and from locality to locality, in search for better working conditions. Moreover, the bright son of a mechanic and factory hand, whether of native or immigrant parentage, need not despair, with the training which the public schools give him free of charge and with whatever else he may pick up, of finding his way to this or that one of the thousand and one selling "lines" which pay on the commission basis; or, if his ambition and his luck go hand in hand, of attaining to some one of the equally numerous kinds of small businesses, or, finally, of the many minor supervisory positions in the large manufacturing establishments, which are constantly on the lookout for persons in the ranks suitable for promotion. It is, therefore, a mistake to assume that, with the exhaustion of the supply of free public land, the wage earner who is above the average in ambition and ability, or at least his children, if they are equally endowed (and the children's opportunities color the parents' attitude no less than do their own), have become cooped up for good in the class of factory operatives. For today, the alternative opportunities to being a lowly factory hand are certainly more varied and entail less hardship than the old opportunity of "homesteading" in the West and "growing up with the country."

But, in a sense, the opportunity of the "West" has never ceased. In this vast country, several historical industrial stages are found existing side by side, though in demarcated areas. There is, therefore, the opportunity to migrate from older to newer and less developed sections, in which a person without much or any inherited property may still find the race for economic independence a free and open race. The difference between a section in the United States which is still underdeveloped economically and a similar one in a European country, is the difference between a navigable stream with some obstacles in its bed still waiting to be removed, and a stagnant pool without an outlet. In the former, opportunities are plentiful, multipliable by effort, and only waiting to be exploited; in the latter, the few extant opportunities are jealously monopolized by their incumbents.

If the characteristically American fluidity of economic society has preserved and created opportunities for the non-propertied individual of not much more than average ability, those with a higher ability and a gift for leadership have found their upward progression smoother still. Participation in political life in America has never been reserved to the upper classes, as until recently in England, nor to those with a higher education, as in France, but is open to all who can master the game. In the past, before the trade unions became stabilized, capable of holding both their leaders and their membership, considerable leadership material drained away from labor into politics. However, at that time industry had not yet come to appreciate the "political" talent of handling men as a valuable business asset. But in the present era of "personnel management" and "industrial relations" departments, of "Welfare capitalism," and of efficiency by "inducement" and "leadership," there is room for that sort of talent, at least in the largest establishments. For the present, business men look to college trained men to fill these positions. But it is not at all precluded that what otherwise might have been union leadership talent, is being drawn into this sort of activity.

Another cause of the lack of "class-consciousness" in American labor was the free gift of the ballot which came to labor at an early date as a by-product of the Jeffersonian democratic movement. In other countries, where the labor movement started while the workingmen were still denied the franchise, there was in the last analysis no need of a theory of "surplus value" to convince them that they were a class apart and should therefore be "class conscious." There ran a line like a red thread between the laboring class and the other classes. Not so, where that line is only an economic one. Such a line becomes blurred by the constant process of "osmosis" between one economic class and another, by fluctuations in relative bargaining power of employer and employee with changes in the business cycle, and by other changing conditions.

Next to the abundant economic opportunities available to wage earners in this country, and to their children, immigration has been the factor most guilty of the incohesiveness of American labor. To workers employed in a given industry, a new wave of immigrants, generally of a new nationality, meant a competitive menace to be fought off and to be kept out of that industry. For, by the worker's job consciousness, the strongest animosity was felt not for the employer who had initiated or stimulated the new immigrant wave, but for the immigrants who came and took the jobs away. When immigrants of a particular nationality acquired higher standards and began rebuilding the unions which they destroyed at their coming, then a new nationality would arrive to do unto the former what these had done unto the original membership. The restriction of immigration by the quota system has at last done away with this phenomenon, which formerly used to occur and recur with an inevitable regularity.

American labor remains the most heterogeneous laboring class in existence—ethnically, linguistically, religiously, and culturally. With a working class of such a composition, to make socialism or communism the official "ism" of the movement, would mean, even if the other conditions permitted it, deliberately driving the Catholics, who are perhaps in the majority in the American Federation of Labor, out of the labor movement, since with them an irreconcilable opposition to socialism is a matter of religious principle. Consequently the only acceptable "consciousness" for American labor as a whole is a "job consciousness," with a "limited" objective of "wage and job control"; which not at all hinders American unionism from being the most "hard hitting" unionism in any country. Individual unions may, however, adopt whatever "consciousness" they wish. Also the solidarity of American labor is a solidarity with a quickly diminishing potency as one passes from the craft group—which looks upon the jobs in the craft as its common property for which it is ready to fight long and bitterly—to the widening concentric circles of the related crafts, the industry, the American Federation of Labor, and the world labor movement.

B. From the Knights of Labor to the AFL

As Perlman saw it, the Knights of Labor represented all that a mature labor movement needed to outgrow: an interest in working-class political action, an inclusiveness so broad that solid bases of power in the skilled crafts were neglected, and—the point stressed in this selection—the dream of eventually replacing the wage system with cooperative enterprises owned by the producers themselves. He argued ingeniously that Marx, because of his hostility to utopian schemes promoted by middle-class intellectuals, helped to create the very pure and simple unionism associated with Gompers and the AFL.

The Order of the Knights of Labor, because the lineal descendant and at the same time the most grandiose culmination of the American labor movement—which, since its beginning in the thirties, had continued as characteristically American in outlook as the Declaration of Independence—by their wholesale experiment and failure in the eighties permanently discredited the whole idea of producers' co-operation. This failure sent the native American labor movement to school to a body of foreign-born "job" and "wage conscious" trade unionists, who had already achieved a stability for their organizations and an enduring success for their efforts, which no American labor organization—excepting a few trades in a privileged position, like the locomotive engineers, iron puddlers and rollers, and glass workers—could as yet boast. Moreover, it is more than questionable whether, if it had not been for the contribution of these foreign speaking, mostly German, groups of wage earners, the rise of a stable trade unionism might not have been delayed still further, until, at least, the turn of the century—when the arrival of prosperity in agriculture had at last taken the ground away from under all "populistic" anti-monopoly movements.

These foreign workingmen had the advantage of being protected by their immigrant origin and upbringing from two serious dangers to the stability of their trade union organizations. Foreign to the American individualistic ideal of self-employment, they were free from the temptation to make their trade unions over into mere nurseries for co-operative shops which should fulfill that ideal. Second, their imperviousness to the call of "anti-monopoly" political movements, to which the native American labor movement usually responded so enthusiastically, kept from their organizations the risk of internal dissensions or of an infiltration of professional politicians. Moreover, it may be doubted whether even these wage earners, notwithstanding their different origin and different inherited social tradition, might have withstood any better than their native American brothers the potent sweep of the waves of "anti-monopoly" politics, had they not been fortified in advance by a philosophy of their own, which was antagonistic to the "anti-monopoly" philosophy, and which interpreted their own previous experience as a part of a European subject class with a clarity and a logic as compelling to them as was the clarity and logic of the "anti-monopoly" philosophy to the individualistic American "producer." This philosophy was the "class-conscious" philosophy of the International Workingmen's Association, which was founded by Marx in London in 1864. It was out of this class-consciousness associated with Marx, that there has grown the trade union "job and wage consciousness" of the American labor movement of today.

Before this imported socialistic class-consciousness became deep-rooted in American soil, a wage consciousness of native origin made its first appearance in the eight-hour philosophy of Ira Steward, which had its greatest vogue in the sixties. In substance, however, Stewardism was only a half-way station between the "anti-monopoly" individualism of the past and the self-confident trade unionism of the future. Stewardism shared with the "anti-monopoly" philosophy a fundamental depreciation of trade union action and a complete reliance on political action, although Steward, like George Evans of the homestead movement, twenty years earlier, did see clearly the futility of an independent labor party. He was convinced that a well-organized labor movement with a single-minded purpose to get the eight-hour day by law, could confidently use the old party politicians without being used by them instead. Second, Stewardism still saw, at the end of its shorter-hour rainbow, the old pot of gold of individualistic producers' co-operation. Where Stewardism actually anticipated the mind of modern trade unionism was in regarding as the paramount objective of the labor struggle the reform of the wage system, instead of a quick escape from it, as the "anti-monopoly" programs did. To Steward, the eight-hour day, by increasing leisure, would increase the wants of the wage earner, and by increasing his wants, lead inexorably to higher wages. "Reducing the day will increase the pay."

The socialistic class-consciousness of the immigrant labor movement was expressed in both the Lassallean and the Internationalist formulations. The Internationalists were the older immigrants, not a few of them having sojourned in England on their way. Thus they were familiar both with trade unionism and with the pitfalls of American politics. The Lassalleans, here as in Germany, held to political action exclusively. True to their idea of the importance of trade unions as an indispensable first and long step towards an eventual struggle for socialism, the American followers of the International threw themselves into organizing trade unions in their own trades. In their own immigrant circle, especially among the Germans, they succeeded. When, however, they tried, at a national labor convention in 1876, to impress their program of class-consciousness plus trade unionism upon those remnants of the general American labor movement which had survived the depression and the preceding venture into politics, they found that that convention, as befitted a convention that carried on the established tradition, chose to succumb once more to the greater lure of "anti-monopoly" and of "greenbackism." In the following year, the Internationalists lost control even in the socialist movement, which now rushed into immediate political action. The majority of the socialists had grown impatient with a program which confined them to their trade unions until the day, which seemed remote, when these could effectually be superseded by a revolutionary political movement. Thereupon the Internationalists withdrew from all active part in the socialist movement, and devoted themselves all the more earnestly to their trade unions.

In these small but promising trade unions, the future builders of the American Federation of Labor, like Strasser and Gompers of the Cigarmakers and McGuire of the Carpenters, studied the labor question both theoretically and experimentally. They studied Marx and the other European socialists, but they were also constantly testing to see what appeals were "taking" with the workingmen so that they came in as permanent members, and what appeals had only an ephemeral effect. It was in this unusual school, in which theory was mixed with direct experience, that they discovered that the union card was the only real bond that held wage earners together—not politics, whether "greenback" or socialist. They found that a labor movement became proof against disintegration only when it was built around the job. These discoveries did not at first estrange them from socialism as a program for the future. But as time went on and they became engrossed in their "job unionism," which eschewed politics and every other quick social panacea; as they watched their organizations grow from nothing to something like the large and stable British "Amalgamated" unions, from which the International Cigar Makers' Union, reorganized by Strasser and Gompers, copied its comprehensive benefit features and centralized financial management; and as they observed with pride how their organizations, small though they still were, held together and grew steadily, in defiance of the alternating tides in business conditions so fatal to the labor organizations which had preceded theirs; then the original socialistic class-consciousness of these "philosophers-organizers" gradually paled if not shriveled, and in its place flourished a robust trade unionist "job and wage consciousness."

It was indeed a new species of trade unionism that was thus evolved. It differed from the trade unionism that the native American labor movement had evolved earlier, in that it grasped the idea, supremely correct for American conditions, that the economic front was the only front on which the labor army could stay united. From this it followed that when a business depression or a powerful combination of employers made the chances for advance on that front unlikely for the time being, the correct strategy was not, as the unions before them had done, to shift the main strength to the political front, because that front seemed weakly held by the enemy. On the contrary, this unionism reasoned that, during depression, labor's strategy should be thoroughly to dig in on the same economic front, awaiting the next opportunity, which was certain to come, for advancing further; in the meantime using every device, like benefit features, to keep the membership from dropping out. For the American labor movement, which, during the first half century of its existence, had been doing exactly the opposite, that is, abandoning trade unionism for the lure and excitement of "anti-monopoly" politics, this discovery was as pivotal a discovery as that by the Rochdale pioneers was for the world co-operative movement. But this discovery, it should not be forgotten, could neither have been hit upon nor later exalted into the cardinal principle of the American labor movement, if the class-consciousness of these "philosopher-organizers" had not, from the beginning, rendered them immune against being swept off their feet by the "producer consciousness" of the individualistic panaceas of the native American labor movement, and thus kept them at their "study-experiment" in their own trade unions. In this circuitous way, therefore, the class-conscious International of Marx was the cause of the least class-conscious labor movement in the world today.

3

Melvyn Dubofsky
FROM "PURE AND SIMPLE UNIONISM" TO REVOLUTIONARY RADICALISM

Far from bringing to an end the effort to form radical labor organizations, the founding of the AFL was followed by the most radical period in American labor history. Another depression began in 1893. At the U.S. Steel mill in Homestead, Pennsylvania, strikebreakers and National Guardsmen were used to crush what had been the strongest craft union in the country. In 1894 federal troops broke a nationwide strike by an incipient industrial union, the American Railway Union (ARU). The ARU's president was the great socialist and labor leader, Eugene V. Debs (1855–1926). Convinced by the experience of the Pullman strike that trade union action alone was insufficient, Debs helped to organize the Socialist party in 1900 and the Industrial Workers of the World in 1905. His strongest allies were Western metal miners in the Western Federation of Miners (WFM), whose evolution toward radicalism is described in the following selection.

The Westerners' radicalism derived directly from their economic and social environment. With other individuals and groups pushed by corporate capitalism to the bottom of the ladder, Western miners asserted their claim to more decent treatment and a better place in the American system. To gain control over their situation Western workers joined the Knights of Labor, crusaded with Populists, and eventually united with Eastern socialists. Nurtured on the utopianism of the Knights, their hopes stoked by the promise of Populism, and victimized by the corporations, they refused to accept the labor program expounded by Samuel Gompers, who drifted from militant, class-conscious unionism in the 1890's to "pure and simple unionism" in the 1900's.

SOURCE. Reprinted by permission of Quadrangle Books from *We Shall Be All* by Melvyn Dubofsky, copyright © 1969 by Melvyn Dubofsky, pp. 58–74.

By the mid-1890's Western workers, then, had absorbed the spirit of solidarity and the anti-capitalist ethic of the Knights of Labor, the industrial unionism of the WFM, and the politics of Populism. Though most miners probably joined the Knights simply to gain better conditions or job security, many just as likely became imbued with that organization's spirit of solidarity. Certainly, the WFM continued the Knights' belief in the unity of all workers, regardless of skill; or as Haywood put it: "All for One, One for All." These same union members learned their political lessons in Populist schools, for Populism in the Mountain West was a working-class movement. Labor organizations there courted farmers. In Montana, for example, the major Populist newspapers were labor journals, and state labor conferences and Populist conventions generally met simultaneously in the same city and were attended by the same delegates. The Silver Bow (Butte) Trades and Labor Assembly called upon the farmers to "join hands with the wage earners. . . . The People's party," it said, "is organized by those from the humble walks of life to destroy monopoly and give equal and exact justice to all." The Montana Populist State Committee chairman was an official of the American Railway Union, and party candidates in Silver Bow County were mostly union members. And in Idaho's Coeur d'Alenes, local labor groups were indistinguishable from the Populists: Ed Boyce was a power in both the union and People's party, serving as a Populist representative in the state assembly. At its 1895 convention, during the depths of depression, the WFM not unexpectedly endorsed "the party [Populist] advocating the principles contained in the Omaha platform."

Western miners, like farmers elsewhere, learned that politics paid. Across the Mountain West, mining districts elected candidates to local office on labor or, more usually, Populist tickets. Silver Bow County in Montana, Lake and Teller Counties in Colorado, and the major cities in each of these counties were dominated politically by the People's party. On occasion working-class Populists even held the balance of power in statewide elections.

Western workers created a radical Populism which was the industrial counterpart of the rural agrarian type. Moutain States Populists endorsed all the usual party planks, including free silver and nationalization of telephones, telegraphs, railroads, and mines. But they also emphasized specific labor reforms. They demanded legislative enactment of the eight-hour day; sanitary inspection of workshops, mills, and homes; employers' liability laws; abolition of the contract system of public works; and abolition of the sweating system. Western workers wanted no part of an ideology which allowed the marketplace and the so-called law of supply and demand to determine the conditions of their existence. Instead they proposed to guarantee that supply and demand, instead of bringing unemployment and misery to the many, brought a decent standard of living to all, not just the fortunate few.

No wonder, then, that after the Populist party coalesced with the Silver Democrats in 1896, and William Jennings Bryan lost that year's presidential election, WFM President Ed Boyce, speaking at his union's 1897 convention, denounced the free-silver fraud and Populism in words recalling those uttered by socialist revolutionary Daniel DeLeon. Capitalism, Boyce had discovered, was indivisible; if Wall Street was the enemy, so was the Colorado Springs Mining Exchange; if John D. Rockefeller was to be fought, so was John Hays Hammond, the Western mining enterpreneur. Boyce demanded from his union followers more intelligent and effective political action, a request which could lead in only one direction—toward socialism.

So, at the end of the nineteenth century, just as the AFL turned away from socialism and independent political action to follow the narrower path of "pure and simple" trade unionism, the Western Federation moved toward socialism, political action, and the broader road of radical unionism.

Having begun as an open, inclusive union, the Western Federation became even more so. This highly democratic labor organization devoted itself to the open-union concept and the universal union card, accepting any member of a bona fide union without initiation fee upon presentation of his union card. The WFM never demanded a closed shop or an exclusive employment contract. It supported no apprenticeship rules, having no intention of restricting union membership. It wanted jobs for all, not merely for the organized few. As Boyce said in 1897: "Open our portals to every workingman, whether engineer, blacksmith, smelterman, or millman. . . . The mantle of fraternity is sufficient for all." Three years later he expanded his concept of fraternity: "We will at all times and under all conditions espouse the cause of the producing masses, regardless of religion, nationality or race . . ." Boyce's successor, Charles Moyer, urging better-paid and more skilled miners to support smelter and mill hands, warned that labor is only as strong as its weakest link. "The unskilled now constitute [the] weakest link in the chain of the labor movement. It is our duty and interest to strengthen it." He also put his argument in moral terms, strange perhaps to an AFL member, but not to a former Knight or to a follower of Eugene Debs. Moyer insisted that the true trade unionist was his brother's keeper and that it was the *obligation* of the highly skilled to use their power to aid the less skilled.

The WFM's belief in solidarity and fraternity went deeper than platform oratory. The organization practiced it: recall the Colorado labor war of 1903–1904 and its origin in the WFM's decision to call out skilled miners in order to protect the mill hands' right to organize trade unions and bargain collectively. This commitment to industrial unionism and solidarity led the Western organization into conflict with the American Federation of Labor. In 1896 the WFM had affiliated with the AFL; a year later it let its affiliation lapse. In the interval, during the unsuccessful WFM struggle at Leadville, Boyce had pleaded in vain with Gompers and the AFL for financial assistance. In company with another executive board member, Boyce even attended the 1896 AFL convention to carry the WFM's appeal for aid directly to the American Federation's membership. But the convention proved a grave disappointment to the WFM delegates, who subsequently lost what little interest they had in the AFL.

By 1896–1897, though Gompers and the AFL had won their battle against the Knights of Labor, they were not without labor critics outside the confines of Western labor. Foremost among the opponents of the AFL within the labor movement was Eugene Victor Debs, the martyr of the 1894 Pullman strike, whose name was soon to become synonymous with American socialism. In 1896 Debs allied with Ed Boyce, and the two men worked closely during the final stages of the Leadville strike. Sometimes with Boyce, and sometimes on his own, Debs moved toward dual unionism, socialism, and finally to the creation of the Industrial Workers of the World.

The son of Alsatian immigrant parents, Eugene Debs was born in 1855 and grew up in Terre Haute, Indiana, in respectable, if not affluent, circumstances. His should have been a typically nineteenth-century bourgeois life. Debs hardly seemed cut out for the career, or more properly crusade, he chose to lead, which would eventually find him five times Socialist party candidate for President and twice imprisoned for challenging the authority of the federal government.

Young Debs at first accomplished much within the American tradition of success. Although he left school at fourteen to work as a railroader, he rose rapidly in the esteem of fellow workers and his native townsmen. In 1875 Debs founded the first local lodge of the Brotherhood of Locomotive Firemen, but later, despite his activities as a "labor agitator," he was elected city clerk and then to the state legislature. Unsatisfied by his activities as a grocery clerk, city official, and Democratic legislator, Debs returned to the labor movement, becoming in 1880 grand secretary and treasurer of the Brotherhood of Locomotive Firemen as well as editor and manager of the *Firemen's Magazine* (both at a substantial salary). As secretary-treasurer of a successful national trade union he could lead the life his wife so much desired. They built a lavish home in a fine Terre Haute neighborhood and stuffed it with expensive Victorian bric-a-brac.

Behind Debs's respectable American Victorian facade, a radical conscience rested uneasily. No man could serve the American labor movement in the 1870's and 1880's without a nagging concern over its future. Beginning in 1877 as a defender of the existing order and foe of that year's railroad strikers and rioters, over the succeeding fifteen years Debs became an opponent of unjust laws and the enemy of an iniquitous social order. Between 1877 and 1894 he discovered that the labor movement served only some workers, not all. He had witnessed members of the Railway Engineers break a strike waged by Firemen; and then he had seen the Firemen do the same, helping the Burlington Railroad break the 1888 Engineers' strike. Deciding that divided unions could not combat united employers, Debs tried to unite the separate railroad brotherhoods. When the unions rejected solidarity, he resorted to a different course of action. In 1893 he resigned his positions with the Locomotive Firemen, sacrificed his $4,000 annual salary, and went where his conscience directed. He determined to establish a new labor organization that would open its doors to all railroad workers—operating and nonoperating, skilled and unskilled. Thus was born the American Railway Union (ARU), an industrial organization for all railway workers. Thus Eugene Debs took his first giant step on the road to radicalism.

Not only unskilled railroad workers flocked to the new union, but also many of the skilled, seeing in solidarity their best hope for betterment. In its first strike the ARU challenged and defeated James J. Hill's Great Northern Railway by compelling that corporation to rescind a recent wage cut. Success brought in more members from all over the nation, including the South.

But Debs had still to learn the lesson that Boyce and the Western miners were discovering: unions fought not only employers but also the state. In the summer of 1894 the ARU found itself in a battle it had not sought: the Pullman strike. Debs knew his infant union should not strike in sympathy with Pullman employees who had recently affiliated with the ARU, and he advised against it. But Debs and fellow delegates at the ARU's 1894 Chicago convention could not close their hearts to the sufferings recounted by George M. Pullman's workers. So Debs and the ARU committed their total resources to the ensuing labor struggle. But Pullman had more resources to commit, including the support of the united Midwestern railroads and the power of the federal government. When President Grover Cleveland intervened on behalf of the boycotted railroads, the end of the Pullman strike was no longer in doubt. The ARU was destroyed, and Debs spent six months in a Woodstock, Illinois, prison.

It has been said that "Debs entered Woodstock Jail a labor unionist, and . . . came out a Socialist . . ." Debs himself maintained that it was in prison he first read Laurence Gronlund, Edward Bellamy, and especially Karl Kautsky, whose writings converted him to socialism. But it must have been a strange conversion, for in 1896 he campaigned for William Jennings Bryan, and a few years later, after publicly declaring for socialism, he beseeched "Christian Gentleman" John D. Rockefeller for a contribution to aid in establishing the Co-operative Commonwealth. Rockefeller naturally refused.

Debs's own Social Democratic party, established in the summer of 1897, was anything but Marxist. Far from seeking to revolutionize American society, the Social Democrats proposed to go off into the wilderness (preferably to some unsettled Western territory) and establish the perfect society, thereby setting an example others would irresistibly follow. Still espousing the "utopian socialism" that Marx fifty years earlier had so savagely ridiculed, as a socialist Debs still had much to learn.

But by 1897 he had come a long way as a radical, and was prepared to go much further. Debs had already moved from craft unionism to militant industrial unionism; now he was ready to move from utopian to Marxian socialism—which he did in 1901 when his Social Democrats united with Morris Hillquit's and Job Harriman's Socialist Labor party insurgents to form the Socialist Party of America. (These insurgents were Socialists dissatisfied with Daniel DeLeon's dogmatic control of the Socialist Labor party, and his war with Gompers and the trade unions.) Five times the new party would nominate Debs for President, including 1920 when he was once again in prison, this time for opposing America's involvement in the First World War.

For a quarter of a century Debs personified American socialism and radicalism. Not because he was socialism's best theorist or most creative organizer; quite the contrary. Although a great orator and a stirring personality, Debs had a shallow intellect and proved a poor party organizer. Too often at Socialist party conventions, or when sectarianism threatened to split the party, Debs was at home, sick or drunk. But he had unusual credentials for an American socialist. In a party dominated by German immigrants and Jewish lawyers and dentists, Debs was American born and, though a professed nonbeliever, a Christian almost by instinct. Debs Americanized and Christianized the socialist movement. By doing so he made it acceptable, respectable, almost popular. For many followers who still retained traditional religious beliefs, Debs personified the essence of the Christ figure: the simple, humble carpenter who sacrifices himself to redeem a corrupt society. Standing on the speaker's platform, tall, gaunt, balding, slightly stooped, his eyes expressing years of suffering, his haunting voice piercing his audience's emotions, Debs played this role to the hilt. He once expressed this role in these words:

". . . I did not believe that Christ was meek and lowly, but a real living, vital agitator who went into the Temple with a lash and a knout and whipped the oppressors of the poor, routed them out of doors and spilled their blood-got silver on the floor. He told the robbed and misruled and exploited and driven people to disobey their plunderers! He denounced the profiteers, and it was for this that they nailed his quivering body to the cross and spiked it to the gates of Jerusalem, not because he told men to love one another. . . . I did the same thing in a different way . . . but I fared better than Christ. They nailed him to the cross and they threw me in here [Atlanta Penitentiary]."

Among those with whom Debs agitated for a better society were Ed Boyce and his associates in the WFM. Both Debs and Boyce had discarded the limitations of craft unionism for what they saw as the greater possibilities of industrial unionism; both also came to see that industrial unionism alone was not enough to bring a new society into existence. Sharing the experience of unhappy relations with Gompers and the AFL, Debs and Boyce decided to create a new federated labor organization.

Immediately after his disillusioning experience at the 1896 AFL convention, Boyce visited Debs in Terre Haute. Early the following January, Debs arrived in Leadville, and for the next three months he and Boyce spent a considerable amount of time together. Although no records or papers describing these meetings exist, it seems reasonable to assume that they discussed the state of labor, its apparent weakness in the face of corporate capital, and the utter inability of the AFL to comprehend the evolving American social and economic order. From their discussions both labor leaders probably came away convinced that a new national labor organization was needed to accomplish what the AFL could not or would not do, and that this new labor organization must pledge itself to the destruction of American capitalism.

At the same time, Boyce was engaged in bitter correspondence with Samuel Gompers, who feared the threatened emergence of a rival national labor organization. On March 16, 1897, Boyce wrote to a worrried Gompers to deny that the WFM intended to leave the AFL. But the tone of Boyce's letter could hardly have allayed Gompers' anxieties, for Boyce criticized the AFL for talking about conservative action while four million idle men and women tramped the highways. These unemployed, said Boyce, were victims of a vicious system of government which would continue to repress them "unless they have the *manhood to get out and fight with the sword* or use the ballot with intelligence." Still more threateningly, Boyce declared: "You know that *I am not a trade unionist*; I am fully convinced that their day of usefulness is past." Gompers pleaded with Boyce to remember the importance of labor unity and to keep the WFM within the fold. He further reminded Boyce that the American labor movement rejected force and revolution as the means to achieve a better life, and angrily advised him to become a loyal trade unionist or leave the movement. Boyce took Gompers' advice. Reaffirming that he was not a trade unionist by Gompers' definition, Boyce assured him that Western miners would not take hasty action calculated to injure the labor movement, but coldly concluded: ". . . Now, as ever, I am strongly in favor of a Western organization."

Boyce went to his own union's 1897 convention eager to put his increasing militancy into effect. First, he advised delegates that the WFM should purchase and operate its own mines because only then would miners achieve equality and freedom. Second, Boyce warned that if employers and the state continued to use military force to subjugate strikers, miners should assert their constitutional right to keep and bear arms. "I entreat you," he proclaimed, "to take action . . . so that in two years we can hear the inspiring music of the martial tread of twenty-five thousand armed men in the ranks of labor." Significantly, Boyce asserted that American workingmen would never regain their full rights through "trades unionism." "With this knowledge and the bitter experience of the past [Leadville, for example]," he concluded, "surely it is time for workingmen to see that trades unionism is a failure." The WFM delegates took their president's advice. Voting to stop per capita payments to the AFL, they laid preliminary plans for the creation of a Western labor organization.

By 1897, as we have seen, Western labor interests had merged with those of other radical reformers and labor leaders. Debs, for example, convened a national labor conference in Chicago in September 1897, whose participants included, along with Boyce, J. A. Ferguson, president of the Montana State Federation of Labor, and Daniel MacDonald, representing the Silver Bow Trades and Labor Assembly. The next month the Montana State Trades and Labor Council acted to bring Western trade unionists into a new coalition. And in December 1897 the WFM's executive board invited all Western unions to attend a meeting in Salt Lake City to found a new organization.

On May 10, 1898, Boyce watched labor union delegates from Montana, Idaho, and Colorado meet in Salt Lake City. The next day they voted to organize the Western Labor Union, and on May 12 they elected Dan MacDonald president of the new organization. A loyal AFL man in attendance described the new Western federation to Gompers as "only the Western Federation of Miners under another name. . . . Boyce dominated everything. . . . Boyce's influence with the miners is unquestionably strong. The majority believe him sincerely, and all of them fear to oppose him."

What manner of man was this Ed Boyce whom Western workers both respected and feared? As with so many other labor leaders, little beyond the barest facts are known about Boyce's life—and of these only a few details can be known with any certainty. He was born in Ireland in 1862, the youngest of four children whose father died at an early age. Educated in Ireland, Boyce arrived in Boston, the Irish immigrants' "Promised City," in 1882, but Boston attracted him only briefly. Less than a year later he went west, first to Wisconsin, and then to Colorado, where in 1883 he went to work for the Denver and Rio Grande Western Railroad. The railroad job brought him to Leadville, where he worked in the mines and first made contact with the labor movement; in 1884, he joined the local miners' union, then a Knights of Labor affiliate.

Like so many other Western workers, Boyce continued to drift from place to place and from job to job, seeking better conditions and greater opportunities, until in June 1887 he settled in the recently opened Coeur d'Alene mining district. There he became a local union leader and a key participant in the 1892 strike—a role which led to his arrest, imprisonment, and blacklisting. Released from prison early in 1893, Boyce attended the WFM's founding convention. By 1894 he was back at work in the Coeur d'Alenes, where he was the leading official of the Coeur d'Alene Executive Miners' Union as well as an influential figure in statewide Populist politics. Only two years later, still working in a local mine, Boyce was elected WFM president, an office he held until his voluntary retirement in 1902.

Boyce, in short, grew up with the Western mining industry and its labor movement. Like most miners he had even prospected on his own. Unlike most miners, however, he succeeded grandly in whatever he chose to do; he even struck it rich while prospecting! But even after he acquired wealth and retired, Boyce never rejected the labor movement that had nurtured him, the union men who had befriended him, or the socialist movement that had promised him a better world.

Haywood remembers Boyce in 1897 as tall and slender, with a fine head of thin hair, good features, and prominent buck teeth, caused, according to Big Bill, by years of handling quicksilver in Idaho's quartz mines. Others remember him as energetic and fearless, intelligent but never above conversing in the lingo of the miners, a man who wrote more fluently than he spoke, and a natural leader who was undaunted by the powerful mine owners with whom he negotiated.

Under Boyce's aggressive leadership, the differences between Western labor and the AFL intensified. The Western Labor Union became more, not less, radical. Even those Western workers who retained sympathy for the AFL's position did so as missionaries for the Western point of view, not as true believers in Gompers' version of the labor movement. Although some Westerners realized that labor should unite in the face of united capital, they insisted that "we must try to teach our benighted brothers in the 'jungles of New York' and the East what we have learned here in the progressive, enterprising West." Underneath the whimsy lay a perfectly serious conviction.

Western workers were careful to spell out their points of difference with Gompers. Where the AFL emphasized skills and crafts, the Westerners demanded a policy "broad enough in principle and sufficiently humane in character to embrace every class of toil . . . one great brotherhood." Where the AFL stressed the national craft union and complete union autonomy, the Westerners favored the industrial union, free transfer from union to union, and labor solidarity. Where the AFL sought to close America's gates to immigrants, the Westerners welcomed most newcomers, except Asians. Where the AFL preferred to seek betterment through the use of strikes, boycotts, and collective bargaining, the Westerners initially claimed that industrial technology and corporate concentration had made those tactics obsolete, leaving the working class but one recourse: ". . . the free and intelligent use of the ballot."

Boyce's rhetoric, which his followers relished, neatly incorporated their view of American society. "There can be no harmony between organized capitalists and organized labor. . . . There can be no harmony between employer and employee; the former wants long hours and low wages; the latter wants short hours and high wages . . . ," Boyce told Butte's miners, whom he also reminded: "Our present wage system is slavery in its worst form. The corporations and trusts have monopolized the necessities of society and the means of life, that the laborer can have access to them only on the terms offered by the trust." He ended by proclaiming, "Let the rallying cry be:

'Labor, the producer of all wealth, is entitled to all he creates, the overthrow of the whole profit-making system, the extinction of monopolies, equality for all and the land for the people.' "

A great many Western workers echoed Boyce's indictment of the American system. Testifying before a congressional committee investigating industrial conditions in 1900, one worker asserted: ". . . Our present social system is based upon a fundamental injustice, namely, private ownership of land . . ." Another said: "The great principle of [labor] organization is to remove the wage-earners from competition with each other, substitute the cooperative system for the competitive system, and remove the wage-earners from the competitive state to the cooperative state." Yet another ordinary miner testified simply that the answer to America's ills was unlimited government ownership of the means of production.

To achieve their better society, Western workers at first preferred political to economic action, the ballot and the statute to the strike and the boycott. As a Gibbsonsville, Idaho, miner wrote to the *Miners' Magazine:* ". . . The majority of our members are beginning to realize . . . that strikes and lockouts are ineffectual weapons to use against capital. They are firm believers in political action. . . . Let labor break loose from the old parties and make itself a party of pure social democracy. Let its principles and purposes be, the earth for the people; to every man according to his needs and for every man the product of his own labor; products for all, but profits for none." A Declaration of Principles adopted at the WFM convention in 1900 proposed, among other items, public ownership of the means of production and distribution, abolition of the wage system, and the study of socialist political economy by union members. Agreeing with these principles, a union member in Granite, Montana, commented: "In government ownership we have a remedy for the trust which will minimize its evils and maximize its benefits; a remedy which will make the largest projects in the industrial world the most beneficial and will cause the inventive genius of the centuries to be applied for the benefit of all instead of for the benefit of the few."

The 1900 presidential election saw the *Miners' Magazine* endorse the Socialist party unity candidates, Debs and Harriman, who, as Boyce noted, "come nearer representing the views of the Western Federation of Miners as expressed in its set of principles" than any other candidates. Only a year later, the WFM's adopted child, the Western Labor Union, publicly denounced the American government, "the very foundation of which is crumbling to decay, through the corruption and infamy of the self-constituted governing class . . ." In addition, the Western organization professed its readiness to spill every drop of its members' blood at bayonet point before submitting to further capitalist aggressions. Revolutionary pronunciamentos increasingly filled Boyce's speeches and the columns of the *Miners' Magazine,* culminating in a demand by delegates at the 1901 WFM convention for "a complete revolution of present social and economic conditions . . ."

Boyce's 1902 farewell address to the WFM convention summarized what by then had become the Western organization's guiding philosophy. Conceding that the major purpose of the union, like that of all labor organizations, was to raise wages and lower hours, Boyce nevertheless cautioned that permanent improvements would not come until miners recognized that pure and simple trade unionism would inevitably fail. The only answer to labor's predicament, he stressed, was "to abolish the wage system which is more destructive of human rights and liberty than any other slave system devised."

In keeping with Boyce's advice, the convention delegates voted to unite their organization with the Socialist party of America. Early the following year the union's executive board under its new president, Charles Moyer, reaffirmed the WFM's radicalism by promising to make the union "an organization of class-conscious political workers that constitute the vanguard of the army that is destined to accomplish the economic freedom of the producers of all wealth."

The growing radicalism of Western labor overjoyed some American radicals. "I have always felt that your organization is the most radical and progressive national body in the country," Debs wrote Boyce in January 1902, "and . . . in my mind . . . it is to take a commanding part, if it does not lead, in the social revolution that will insure final emancipation to the struggling masses."

The conflict between Western workers and the AFL was not primarily because of the Westerners' radicalism or socialism. Gompers and the AFL would have tolerated socialism in the West if it had been divorced from the labor movement, or if it had found a home within the AFL. What irked Gompers was the WFM's decision not only to go it alone but to establish a rival labor center in the West. At the WLU's birth in 1898 the AFL was still a fragile institution just over ten years old, a mere infant which Gompers desperately wanted to survive beyond childhood. If the WFM managed to live and thrive outside the AFL, other large national labor organizations, such as the United Mine Workers, might also choose to leave. It was to combat what he conceived to be dual unionism, not to destroy radicalism, that Gompers fought Western labor's radicals.

After 1900, AFL organizers suddenly appeared in the previously neglected Mountain States to compete with their WLU-WFM counterparts. Gompers' agents in the West attempted to convince workers that the future of the American labor movement was with the AFL, not the WLU. When AFL men failed thus to win over Western Labor Union locals, they tried to wreck them by organizing dual unions of their own, even offering employers inducements to deal with the AFL rather than the WLU.

The Westerners, by contrast, maintained that they had no quarrel with the AFL. Their fight was with employers, not with other workers. Emphasizing its attempts to organize the unorganized within its territory, the WLU's executive board informed the AFL that Western labor was too occupied battling corporations to seek a fight with another labor organization.

But AFL officials were firmly convinced that the American nation was unable to support two labor movements, however noncompetitive. Hence the AFL demanded that the WFM (which it held responsible for all Western separatism) disband all "dual unions" in Denver, abolish the WLU, and reaffiliate with the AFL. To accomplish those ends, Gompers sent two representatives to the WFM convention in 1902. But, far from submitting to what amounted to an AFL ultimatum, Western workers only became more aggressive. Cataloguing the indignities which the WFM had borne with patience, they warned: ". . . There comes a time in the history of all such imposition when patience ceases to be a virtue, and this juncture for the Western Federation of Miners has now arrived." The *Miners' Magazine* informed Gompers' two emissaries: "The Western Federation . . . and the Western Labor Union are ready to join forces with any labor organization that offers a remedy, but they don't propose to be led like sheep into a slaughter pen to await the butcher's knife without a struggle."

Instead of dissolving the WLU and returning to Gompers' waiting arms, the WFM transformed the Western Labor Union into the American Labor Union and embraced socialism more firmly than before. In part, this action was a tacit recognition that the WLU had never amounted to much, that, apart from locals among a handful of restaurant workers and other minor city trades, the organization had almost nothing to show for five years' effort. Conceding the failure of the WLU as a regional labor organization and letting it die an unmourned death, Western workers now decided to carry their challenge directly to the AFL by forming a national labor body—the American Labor Union—which would compete with the AFL for members on a nationwide basis.

The ALU began where the Western Labor Union left off—but with one important difference. The ALU sent organizers east into traditional AFL territory and invited AFL affiliates, especially the Brewery Workers, to join the new national labor center. Although ALU leaders proclaimed their desire to live in peace with the AFL, they had every intention of weakening, if not destroying, the older national labor organization.

What did the American Labor Union offer workers that could not be obtained through AFL membership? First, the ALU offered its members unswerving loyalty to socialist principles and to the Socialist party. Second, it offered members a constitutional structure more democratic than that of the AFL, one under which basic principles and policies would be established by membership referendum rather than by "irresponsible" officers. Third, it promised Western workers the assistance the AFL so often in the past had denied them. Most important, however, the American Labor Union opened its membership to those neglected by the AFL: the semi-skilled and the unskilled in America's basic industries, women, and immigrants ignored by the established labor unions.

Dan MacDonald, the ALU's president, argued the case for the unorganized, whose "position . . . is more exposed to the influence of unjust conditions and subject to greater impositions and greater burdens than the organized." D. C. Coates, labor leader, former lieutenant governor of Colorado, and later an IWW founder, put the ALU's case for the unorganized more directly and precisely:

"We find there is no need of aristocratic unions standing aloof from the common laborer as the craftsman is fast passing away . . . our aim is not so much to help the fellow on the inside, but to help every wage worker. . . . Our plan is progressive, it will help every child and woman worker; in fact, it will solve the labor problem by capturing the government for the workers."

Haywood summarized the ALU's advocacy of industrial unionism and its critique of the American Federation of Labor. He emphasized that the AFL was merely a council of loosely affiliated trade unions representing a small minority of workers who, inculcated with the spirit of craft selfishness, continually engaged in jurisdictional warfare to monopolize union benefits for the favored few. In times of crisis, he said, the AFL had always proved impotent to aid its affiliates, usually sacrificing them on the "sacred altar of contract." To Gompers' impassioned defense of craft unionism, trade autonomy, and exclusive jurisdiction, Haywood retorted:

"The diversity of labor is incapable of craft distinction; thus pure and simple trade unions become obsolete. The machine is the apprentice of yesterday, the journeyman of today. But [the] industrial union is the evolution of the labor movement, confronting and competing with the strides of the machine in industrial progress . . . it is also the open door of organized labor. . . . With twenty millions of unorganized wage earners the material presents itself for a progressive, compact, militant organization, the local unions of which will be lyceums for the discussion of political economy, teaching the working class to understand their position in life."

In keeping with its emphasis on industrial unionism, the ALU, though employing the rhetoric of political socialism, stressed the primacy of economic action—which the IWW would later label direct action. The ALU, for example, never required political conformity on the part of its members; in fact, it allowed each man to ride his favorite political hobby horse to exhaustion. Moreover, the organization's constitution barred any member from holding union office if he also held political office, regardless of party affiliation. ". . . The ALU is not a political organization. . . . With regard to its political character, it amounts to this: it simply recommends to the worker what to do and how to do it," claimed ALU officials, seeking to distinguish their organization from Daniel DeLeon's dual union, the Socialist Trades and Labor Alliance, which made membership in the Socialist Labor party a requisite for membership. The ALU, its spokesmen maintained, would concentrate on the industrial field, leaving politics to other organizations.

From the first, the ALU cherished the two tenets most characteristic of the post-1908 IWW: the primacy of economic over political action and a belief in the syndicalist organization of the new society. As the ALU *Journal* expressed the organization's philosophy:

"The economic organization of the proletariat is the heart and soul of the Socialist movement. . . . The purpose of industrial unionism is to organize the working class in approximately the same departments of production and distribution as those which will obtain in the co-operative commonwealth, so that if the workers should lose their franchise, they would still retain an economic organization intelligently trained to take over and collectively administer the tools of industry and the sources of wealth for themselves."

Western workers adopted still another principle later characteristic of the IWW: opposition to time contracts. Moyer, for example, informed WFM convention delegates in 1903: ". . . It behooves us at all times to be free to take advantage of any opportunity to better our condition. Nothing affords the majority of corporations more satisfaction than to realize that they have placed you in a position where you are powerless to act for a period of years." The WFM and the ALU by 1903–1904, like the IWW thereafter, believed that no agreement with employers was legally or morally binding, and that workers could achieve their objectives only by remaining free to strike at will.

Clearly, then, what later would become the distinguishing traits of the IWW had been formed in the American West by 1903. The combination of industrial unionism, labor solidarity, political nonpartisanship, direct economic action, and syndicalism, so characteristic of the IWW, had already been subscribed to by the WFM and its offspring, the American Labor Union. Contrary to what some historians have asserted, neither a Daniel DeLeon, nor an Algie Simons, nor a William Trautmann, nor European labor radicals provided the ideological framework for the IWW. True, European radicals in France and Italy—and to a lesser extent in England and Germany—were moving at the same time toward syndicalist principles; granted that DeLeon, Simons, and Trautmann were familiar with continental developments and European radical ideology, and propagandized about them in America; nevertheless, it was primarily the experiences Western workers had lived through in America—the failure of Populism, bloody industrial warfare, capital's use of the state to repress labor—that created among the more radical their belief in industrial unionism, solidarity, and syndicalism.

Part Two

CIO

1

Jeremy Brecher, Henry Kraus, and Kermit Johnson
SITDOWN

In the early 1930s rank-and-file workers in the mass production industries once again tried to organize industrial unions. Sometimes they used existing AFL craft unions; sometimes they took over company unions; sometimes they created independent industrial unions in a particular plant or mill. The sitdown strike was a favorite tactic. In a sitdown strike, workers stop work but remain in the workplace rather than leaving and picketing outside.

When the CIO came into being in late 1935 this rank-and-file ferment was already going on. The CIO assisted local activists with money and organizers, and played an important role in inducing huge corporations like General Motors and U.S. Steel to sign collective bargaining agreements. But there was often conflict between the goals of the rank and file and the goals of CIO officers like John L. Lewis. The CIO wanted union recognition and a signed contract. The rank and file wanted these things, but also wanted control over their conditions of work, for example, the speed of the assembly line in the rubber and auto industries.

A. Sitdown In Akron

There had been sitdown strikes before the 1930s both in the United States and abroad. The tactic seems to have been rediscovered by rubber workers in Akron, Ohio, without knowledge of its earlier use. Basing his work on contemporary accounts by Louis Adamic and Ruth McKenney, Jeremy Brecher describes the development of a sitdown strike tradition in Akron and the successful use of the sitdown against the Goodyear Rubber Company early in 1936.

SOURCE. From *Strike!* by Jeremy Brecher. Published by Straight Arrow Books. Reprinted by permission. First published as Root & Branch Pamphlet No. 4, "The Sitdown Strikes of the 1930's."

One day in 1936, a reporter named Louis Adamic visited the rubber capital of America, Akron, Ohio. A new kind of strike called the sitdown had just started hitting the headlines, and Adamic tried to find out how they had begun. The first Akron sitdown, he was told, was not in a rubber factory but at a baseball game, where players from two factories refused to play a scheduled game because the umpire, whom they disliked, was not a union man. They simply sat down on the diamond, while the crowd cheered and yelled for a new umpire, until finally the old one was replaced. Not long after, a dispute developed between a dozen workers and a supervisor in a rubber factory. The workers were on the verge of giving in when the supervisor insulted them and one of them said, "Aw, to hell with 'im, let's sit down." The dozen workers turned off their machines and sat down. Within a few minutes the carefully organized flow of production through the plant began to jam up as department after department ground to a halt. Thousands of workers sat down, some because they wanted to, more because everything stopped anyway. What had happened, workers wanted to know? "There was a sitdown at such-and-such a department." "A sitdown?". . . "Yeah, a sitdown; don't you know what a sitdown is, you dope? Like what happened at the ball game the other Sunday."

Adamic describes the response:

"sitting by their machines, caldron boilers, and work benches, they talked. Some realized *for the first time how important they were in the process of rubber production.* Twelve men had practically stopped the works! Almost any dozen or score of them could do it! In some departments six could do it! The active rank-and-filers, scattered through the various sections of the plant, took the initiative in saying, 'We've got to stick with 'em!' And they stuck with them, union and non-union men alike. Most of them were non-union. Some probably were afraid not to stick. Some were bewildered. Others amused. There was much laughter in the works. Oh boy, oh boy! Just like at the ball game, no kiddin'. There the crowd had stuck with the players and they got an umpire who was a member of a labor union. Here everybody stuck with the twelve guys who first sat down, and the factory management was beside itself. Superintendents, foremen, and straw bosses were dashing about. . . . This sudden suspension of production was costing the company many hundreds of dollars every minute. . . . In less than an hour the dispute was settled—full victory for the men!"

Between 1933 and 1936 the sitdown gradually became a tradition in

Akron, with scores of sitdowns, the majority probably not instigated even by rank-and-file union organizers, and almost invariably backed by the workers in other departments. It became an understood principle that when one group of workers stopped work everyone else along the line sat down too. . . .

Late in 1935, Goodyear announced that it was shifting from the six- to the eight-hour day, admitting that 1,200 men would be laid off and that other companies would follow suit. The announcement created shock in Akron—unemployment was still high and six hours under speed-up conditions were already so exhausting that rubberworkers complained "When I get home I'm so tired I can't even sleep with my wife." As the companies began "adjusting" piecerates in preparation for introducing the 8-hour day, a wave of spontaneous work stoppages by non-union employees forced a slowing of production.

January 29, 1936, the truck tirebuilders at Firestone sat down against a reduction in rates and the firing of a union committeeman. The men had secretly planned the strike for 2:00 A.M.; when the hour struck,

"the tirebuilder at the end of the line walked three steps to the master safety switch and, drawing a deep breath, he pulled up the heavy wooden handle. With this signal, in perfect synchronization, with the rhythm they had learned in a great mass-production industry, the tire-builders stepped back from their machines.

Instantly, the noise stopped. The whole room lay in perfect silence. The tire-builders stood in long lines, touching each other, perfectly motionless, deafened by the silence. A moment ago there had been the weaving hands, the revolving wheels, the clanking belt, the moving hooks, the flashing tire tools. Now there was absolute stillness, no motion anywhere, no sound.

'We done it! We stopped the belt! By God, we done it!' And men began to cheer hysterically, to shout and howl in the fresh silence. Men wrapped long sinewy arms around their neighbors' shoulders, screaming, 'We done it! We done it!' "

The workers in the truck tire department sent a committee around the plant to call out other departments, another to talk with the boss, and a third to police the shop. Within a day the entire Plant No. 1 was struck, and when, after 53 hours, the workers at Plant No. 2 announced they had voted to sit down in sympathy, management capitulated completely. Two days later, pitmen at Goodyear sat down over a pay cut, were persuaded to return to work by the company union, sat down again and were again cajoled back to work, sat down a third time and returned to work under threat of immediate replacement by the Flying Squadron, a special strikebreaking force in the plant. February 8 the tire department at Goodrich sat down over a rate reduction. The strike spread through the rest of the plant, stopping it completely within six hours, and management rapidly capitulated to the sitdowners. The sitdown had shaken each of the big three within a ten-day period.

The crisis finally came Feb. 14. A few days before Goodyear had laid off 70 tire-builders and the workers assumed that this was the signal for introducing the 8-hour day. At 3:10 A.M., 137 tirebuilders in Dept. 251-A of Goodyear's Plant No. 2—few if any of them members of the union—shut off the power and sat down. The great Goodyear strike was on.

Akron workers had developed the sitdown strike largely because the union had failed to control the speed-up. It had called strikes and then called them off at the last minute, called them again and then reached a settlement which management described accurately as "no change in employee relations," after which rubber workers had stood on street corners tearing up their union cards. But by now the United Rubberworkers Union had changed its course, replaced union professionals with former rubber workers in office, and allied itself with the new CIO industrial union movement. With each sitdown, the union signed up the participants, and now workers flooded back into the union halls. The initiative for the sitdowns, however, did not come from the union; indeed, as labor historian Irving Bernstein pointed out, "The URW . . . disliked the sitdown." Thus URW officials now persuaded the Goodyear sitdowners to leave and marched them out of the plant. Goodyear offered to take the laid-off men back, but by now the rubber workers of the entire city were up in arms, determined to make a stand against the 8-hour day. 1500 Goodyear workers met and voted unanimously to strike, but four days later the president of the union local was still saying the strike was not a URW affair.

Meanwhile, the workers began mass picketting at each of the 45 gates around Goodyear's 11-mile perimeter, putting up 300 tarpaper shanties to keep warm. The men elected picket captains who met regularly, coordinated strike action, and set the strike's demands. Inside plant No. 1 hundreds of men and women staged a sitdown until a union delegate marched them out. At the union hall, "committees sprang up almost by themselves" to take care of problems as they arose. A soup kitchen developed out of the sandwich- and coffee-making crew, staffed by volunteers from the Cooks and Waitresses Union. On the 6th day of the strike the CIO sent in half-a-dozen of its top leaders to Akron, and the URW executive board sanctioned the strike.

The company now tried to break the strike by force. It secured an injunction against mass picketting, which the workers simply ignored. The sheriff put together a force of 150 deputies to open the plants, but 10 thousand workers from all over the city gathered with lead pipes and baseball bats and the charge was called off at the last possible second. Next a Law and Order League was organized by a former mayor with money from Goodyear which claimed 5,200 organized vigilantes. Word spread that an attack was planned for March 18. The union went on the radio all that night while workers gathered in homes throughout the city ready to rush any place an attack was made. The Summit County Central Labor Council declared it would call a general strike in the event of a violent attack on the picket lines. In the face of such preparations, the vigilante movement was paralyzed.

President Roosevelt's ace mediator, Ed McGrady, proposed that the workers return to work and submit the issues to arbitration. To this and other proposed settlements the workers at their mass meetings chanted "No, no, a thousand times no, I'd rather die than say yes." After more than a month Goodyear capitulated on most of the demands. . . .

B. The General Motors Sitdown: Skirmishes

The decisive struggle in the CIO organizing drive was the sitdown strike against General Motors in January–February 1937. The center of the strike was Flint, Michigan, where GM owned several assembly plants. During the summer and fall of 1936, UAW organizers Wyndham Mortimer and Bob Travis patiently built the beginnings of a union in Flint. A successful sitdown strike in November, described below, encouraged auto workers to join the union. This account was written by Henry Kraus who edited the GM strike newspaper.

Three days after Travis' meeting with the union's volunteer organizers, a situation such as he had anticipated arose. The day before the supervision had removed one worker from a group of "bow-men."[1] Two of the men were brothers, typical farm boys from mid-state,

[1]The "bow" is a supporting angle-iron that is welded across the top of the roof structure of the auto body.

SOURCE. Henry Kraus, *The Many & the Few. A chronicle of the dynamic auto workers*, The Plantin Press, Los Angeles, 1947, pp. 47–55.

named Perkins. Another was a little Italian-American, full of guts. None of them were in the union but they had been reading about the Bendix strike so they simply stopped working. The foreman and the superintendent came over and begged them to get back to work, they were holding up the line. A long discussion took place over the increased production required due to the removal of the one man.

"The day crew is doing it, why can't you?" the superintendent asked. It was perhaps the billionth time this argument had been repeated in an industrial plant.

They sat gabbing that way till there was a job-gap of twenty jobs. And then the workers got a little disturbed to see it. It made them nervous to be responsible for such disorder on the production line. Finally they agreed to go back to work, to continue putting out for that night. But tomorrow they'd talk to the day shift fellows about it! Before they got back to work, however, the whole department had become interested in the argument. At shift-end the excitement overflowed. Everybody talked about the sitdown of the "bow-men." So that's what a sitdown was! Nothing to it, really! The men felt awfully pleased about it somehow.

When the two Perkins boys came to work the next evening they found their cards missing from the rack. In their places were tell-tale notices: "Report to the employment office." They went and sure enough there was their money waiting for them. But the union had anticipated this contingency. The committee had talked the situation over with Travis the night before, after the end of the shift. It was decided that this would be an excellent opportunity to come out into the open. If anyone was victimized over the little stoppage the entire "body-in-white"[2] department must be closed down.

When the two brothers showed Simons and the other committee members their red cards the latter ran up to the department and spread the word:

"The Perkins boys were fired! Nobody starts working!"

The whistle blew. Every man in the department stood at his station, a deep, significant tenseness in him. The foreman pushed the button and the skeleton bodies, already partly assembled when they got to this point, began to rumble forward. But no one lifted a hand. All eyes were turned to Simons who stood out in the aisle by himself.

The bosses ran about like mad.

"Whatsamatter? Whatsamatter? Get to work!" they shouted.

[2]Where the main welding and soldering work of the assembly process takes place.

But the men acted as though they never heard them. One or two of them couldn't stand the tension. Habit was deep in them and it was like physical agony for them to see the bodies pass untouched. They grabbed their tools and chased after them. "Rat! Rat!" the men growled without moving and the others came to their senses.

The superintendent stopped by the "bow-men."

"You're to blame for this!" he snarled.

"So what if we are?" little Joe Urban, the Italian, cried, overflowing with pride. "You ain't running your line, are you?"

That was altogether too much. The superintendent grabbed Joe and started for the office with him. The two went down along the entire line, while the men stood rigid as though awaiting the word of command. It was like that because they were organized but their organization only went that far and no further. What now?

Simons, a torch-solderer, was almost at the end of the line. He too was momentarily held in vise by the superintendent's overt act of authority. The latter had dragged Joe Urban past him when he finally found presence of mind to call out:

"Hey, Teefee, where you going?"

It was spoken in just an ordinary conversational tone and the other was taken so aback he answered the really impertinent question.

"I'm taking him to the office to have a little talk with him." Then suddenly he realized and got mad. "Say, I think I'll take you along too!"

That was his mistake.

"No you won't!" Simons said calmly.

"Oh yes I will!" and he took hold of his shirt.

Simons yanked himself loose.

And suddenly at this simple act of insurgence Teefee realized his danger. He seemed to become acutely conscious of the long line of silent men and felt the threat of their potential strength. They had been transformed into something he had never known before and over which he no longer had any command. He let loose of Simons and started off again with Joe Urban, hastening his pace. Simons yelled:

"Come on, fellows, don't let them fire little Joe!"

About a dozen boys shot out of the line and started after Teefee. The superintendent dropped Joe like a hot poker and deer-footed it for the door. The men returned to their places and all stood waiting. Now what? The next move was the company's. The moment tingled with expectancy.

Teefee returned shortly, accompanied by Bill Lynch, the assistant plant manager. Lynch was a friendly sort of person and was liked by the men. He went straight to Simons.

"I hear we've got trouble here," he said in a chatty way. "What are we going to do about it?"

"I think we'll get a committee together and go in and see Parker," Simons replied.

Lynch agreed. So Simons began picking the solid men out as had been prearranged. The foreman tried to smuggle in a couple of company-minded individuals, so Simons chose a group of no less than eighteen to make sure that the scrappers would outnumber the others. Walt Moore went with him but Joe Devitt remained behind to see that the bosses didn't try any monkeyshines. The others headed for the office where Evan Parker, the plant manager, greeted them as smooth as silk.

"You can smoke if you want to, boys," he said as he bid them to take the available chairs. "Well, what seems to be the trouble here? We ought to be able to settle this thing."

"Mr. Parker, it's the speedup the boys are complaining about," Simons said, taking the lead. "It's absolutely beyond human endurance. And now we've organized ourselves into a union. It's the union you're talking to right now, Mr. Parker."

"Why that's perfectly all right, boys," Parker said affably. "Whatever a man does outside the plant is his own business."

The men were almost bowled over by this manner. They had never known Parker as anything but a tough cold tomato with an army sergeant's style. He was clearly trying to play to the weaker boys on the committee and began asking them leading questions. Simons or Walt Moore would try to break in and answer for them.

"Now I didn't ask you," Parker would say, "you can talk when it's your turn!" In this way he sought to split the committee up into so many individuals. Simons realized he had to put an end to that quickly.

"We might as well quit talking right now, Mr. Parker," he said, putting on a tough act. "Those men have got to go back and that's all there is to it!"

"That's what you say," Parker snapped back.

"No, that's what the men say. You can go out and see for yourself. Nobody is going to work until that happens."

Parker knew that was true. Joe Devitt and several other good men who had been left behind were seeing to that. The plant manager seemed to soften again. All right, he said, he'd agree to take the two men back if he found their attitude was okay.

"Who's to judge that?" Simons asked.

"I will, of course!"

"Uh-uh!" Simons smiled and shook his head.

The thing bogged down again. Finally Parker said the Perkins brothers could return unconditionally on Monday. This was Friday night and they'd already gone home so there was no point holding up thousands of men until they could be found and brought back. To make this arrangement final he agreed that the workers in the department would get paid for the time lost in the stoppage. But Simons held fast to the original demand. Who knew what might happen till Monday? The Perkins fellows would have to be back on the line that night or the entire incident might turn out a flop.

"They go back tonight," he insisted.

Parker was fit to be tied. What was this? Never before in his life had he seen anything like it!

"Those boys have left!" he shouted. "It might take hours to get them back. Are you going to keep the lines tied up all that time?"

"We'll see what the men say," Simons replied, realizing that a little rank and file backing would not be out of the way. The committee rose and started back for the shop.

As they entered a zealous foreman preceded them, hollering: "Everybody back to work!" The men dashed for their places.

Simons jumped onto a bench.

"Wait a minute!" he shouted. The men crowded around him. He waited till they were all there and then told them in full detail of the discussion in the office. Courage visibly mounted into the men's faces as they heard of the unwavering manner in which their committee had acted in the dread presence itself.

"What are we going to do, fellows," Simons asked, "take the company's word and go back to work or wait till the Perkins boys are right there at their jobs?"

"Bring them back first!" Walt Moore and Joe Devitt began yelling and the whole crowd took up the cry.

Simons seized the psychological moment to make it official.

"As many's in favor of bringing the Perkins boys back before we go to work, say Aye!" There was a roar in answer. "Opposed, Nay!" Only a few timid voices sounded—those of the company men and the foremen who had been circulating among the workers trying to influence them to go back to work. Simons turned to them.

"There you are," he said.

One of the foremen had taken out pencil and paper and after the vote he went around recording names. "You want to go to work?" he asked each of the men. Finally he came to one chap who stuck his chin out and said loudly: "Emphatically not!" which made the rest of the boys laugh and settled the issue.

Mr. Parker got the news and decided to terminate the matter as swiftly as possible. He contacted the police and asked them to bring the Perkins boys in. One was at home but the other had gone out with his girl. The police shortwaved his license number to all scout cars. The local radio station cut into its program several times to announce that the brothers were wanted back at the plant. Such fame would probably never again come to these humble workers. By chance the second boy caught the announcement over the radio in his car and came to the plant all bewildered. When told what had happened the unappreciative chap refused to go to work until he had driven his girl home and changed his clothes! And a thousand men waited another half hour while the meticulous fellow was getting out of his Sunday duds.

When the two brothers came back into the shop at last, accompanied by the committee, the workers let out a deafening cheer that could be heard in the most distant reaches of the quarter-mile-long plant. There had never been anything quite like this happen in Flint before. The workers didn't have to be told to know the immense significance of their victory. Simons called the Perkins boys up on the impromptu platform. They were too shy to even stammer their thanks.

"You glad to get back?" Simons coached them.

"You bet!"

"Who did it for you?"

"You boys did."

Simons then gave a little talk though carefully refraining from mentioning the union.

"Fellows," he said amid a sudden silence, "you've seen what you can get by sticking together. All I want you to do is remember that. Now let's get to work."

The men got the double meaning of his last words and from that moment the barriers were down at Fisher Body No. 1. Organization shot out from "body-in-white" to the other departments—into paint, trim, assembly, press-and-metal; even the girls in "cut-and-sew" began heeding the call.

And more. The news of the Fisher One sitdown spread through the entire city. The Fisher One boys began bringing friends into the union from Fisher Two, Buick and Chevrolet. The response at Fisher Two was especially good. In one afternoon alone Travis signed up fifty workers in a beer hall near that plant. Shortly after, he rented a store across Fisher One from a union sympathizer and the first open meeting was announced. There was an overflow crowd. Mortimer came back for the meeting, accompanied by Adolph Germer of the CIO.

Dick Frankensteen came up also to bring the greetings of the Detroit workers and to tell of equally exciting things occurring in the motor capitol, the Midland Steel sitdown strike having just begun. As the workers stood outside the open door of the jammed hall, craning their necks for a look, while the applause crashed out repeatedly, there was no one any longer that could doubt that the union had come to Fisher One. . . .

C. The General Motors Sitdown: Taking Chevrolet Plant 4

On December 30, 1936, workers at General Motors' Fisher Body Plant 1 in Flint, Michigan, discovered that the company was loading dies, critical for the making of car bodies, onto railroad cars for shipment to plants elsewhere. Furious, the workers decided to shut down and occupy Fisher Body Plants 1 and 2. The strike spread quickly throughout the GM system.

The first two weeks of the strike were relatively peaceful. Then on January 11 the police attempted to drive the strikers from Fisher Body Plant 2 in a nightlong encounter that became known as the Battle of the Running Bulls. Although the UAW retained control of the plant, Michigan governor Frank Murphy afterwards ordered the National Guard into Flint. The question became: Could the strikers pressure GM to settle before Governor Murphy was pressured to use the National Guard to end the strike?

In an effort to regain the initiative, strikers developed a strategy to occupy another plant, Chevrolet Plant 4. The union pretended to plan to take Chevrolet Plant 9 while a small circle of insiders made the real plan to take Plant 4. There is an unresolved controversy about who played what part in devising this action. What is clear is that it was brilliantly successful. The following is a rare narrative of the event by Kermit Johnson, then chairman of the strike committee in Plant 4. (Kermit Johnson was the husband of Genora (Dollinger) Johnson, who organized the celebrated Women's Emergency Brigade.)

Plant 4 was huge and sprawling, a most difficult target, but extremely important to us because the corporation was running the plant, even though they had to stockpile motors, in anticipation of favorable court action. GM had already recovered from the first shock of being forced to surrender four of their largest body plants to sit-down strikers. They already had the legal machinery in motion that would, within a short time, expel by force if necessary the strikers from the

SOURCE. Kermit Johnson, "Lest We Forget!!" *The Searchlight,* Local 659, UAW, February 11, 1959.

plants. If that happened, we knew the strike would be broken, and the fight for a union in General Motors would be lost. Even the top leadership in the CIO, including John L. Lewis, were seriously worried about the GM situation. When Lewis' right-hand man, John Brophy, approved our plan of action, he did it with great reluctance and a complete lack of confidence. He couldn't conceive of a successful strike in a plant that was less than one-fourth organized.

I was remembering all these things and many others as I walked through the plant gate that afternoon, February 1, 1937. I was doing a lot of thinking. Everything that had happened in the past week was flashing through my mind over and over again. I though about last night's final secret meeting, held deep inside the South Fisher plant. What a farce that had been! I laughed to myself and felt like a conspirator when I recalled all the pretense we'd gone through to arrange a meeting for one despicable man, a stool pigeon. Thirty men had been secretly picked for that meeting by Bob Travis, Organizational Director, and his aide, Roy Reuther, including Ed Cronk and myself from Chevrolet. The four of us who alone knew the actual plans put on a real show that night selling the right guy the wrong bill of goods. It seemed like a dirty trick to dupe so many good men, but to make the big fish swallow the bait we had to have a lot of little fish nibbling. I was sure we had convinced the stool pigeon that today at 3:30 P.M. the men in Plant 9 would stage a sit-down strike. I was sure because he asked so many pointed questions about strategy, and because others, taking a natural part in the discussion, helped to allay any suspicions he might have had.

Now, at exactly 3:10 P.M. I was upstairs in the toilet at the west end of Plant 4. I had nothing to do but wait and hope that everything was moving according to schedule. At this very minute someone was rushing into the mass meeting downtown, yelling, "Trouble at Plant 9!" Bob Travis would be chairing the meeting, and Roy Reuther would be clamoring for the floor to make a motion and an impassioned plea that the meeting be adjourned so that they could all go to Plant 9 and help their brothers in the fight against their common enemy. I could see them now, cheering wildly and singing "Solidarity" as they thundered down the rickety stairs of the union hall. There wouldn't have to be a vote taken; they wouldn't even wait for it, because this was action and that's what they wanted. Who could blame them for having bitterness in their hearts after witnessing the police brutality that had taken place in the past few weeks, No, it wouldn't happen again, not if this army of more than a thousand men and women could stop it.

3:25 P.M. I was down on the main floor, and the minutes were going fast. I was walking slowly in the aisle trying to be as inconspicuous as possible, but I couldn't understand why Ed and his men weren't here; they were long overdue. The next few minutes seemed like hours, and as I ambled toward the door, my previous confidence was rapidly giving way to fear—fear that we'd lost our one big gamble. My thoughts were moving a mile a minute, and I was re-hashing the same plan over and over, but this time all of its weaknesses stood out like red lights. I had never realized before how many if's there were, and how every if was so utterly dependent upon every other if. No wonder John Brophy had been skeptical. Why this was like a mathematical problem without a single known quantity, or like trying to—and then the door burst inward, and there was Ed! Great big Ed, his hairy chest bare to his belly, carrying a little American flag, and leading the most ferocious band of twenty men I have ever seen. He looked so funny with that tiny flag in comparison with his men who were armed to the teeth with lead hammers, pipes, and chunks of sheet metal three feet long. I felt like crying and laughing at the same time.

When I asked Ed where in the hell the three hundred men were that he had guaranteed to bring with him, he seemed dumbfounded. I don't think he'd ever looked back from the time he had dropped his tools, picked up the flag, and started his line plunge to Plant 4. It didn't take a master mind to know that trying to strike a roaring plant of more than three thousand men and almost as many machines with just twenty men was absolutely impossible. We huddled together and made a quick decision to go back to Plant 6 for reinforcements, and if that failed to get out of Chevrolet in a hurry. Luckily we encountered little opposition in Ed's plant, and in a short time we were back in Plant 4 with hundreds of determined men.

Although we didn't know it then, a real war was going on in and around Plant 9, the decoy. Every city cop and plant police were clubbing the strikers and using tear gas to evacuate the plant. In retaliation the men and women from the hall were smashing windows and yelling encouragement from the outside.

Back in Plant 4 a relatively peaceful operation was proceeding according to plan; a little late, but definitely moving now. Up and down the long aisles we marched, asking, pleading, and finally threatening the men who wouldn't get in line. For the first hour the men in Plant 4 were being bullied not only by us, but by management as well. Almost as fast as we could turn the machines off, the bosses following in our wake would turn them on, and threaten the men with being fired. As the lines of marchers grew longer, the plant grew quieter, and finally after two hours every machine was silent.

The men were standing around in small groups, sullenly eyeing members of supervision. No one knew who belonged to the union because no one had any visible identification. We had successfully taken the plant, but we knew that our gains had to be immediately consolidated or we'd face counteraction. We had a few men go through the plant and give a general order that all who didn't belong to the union should go upstairs to the dining room and sign up. While the vast majority were thus taken care of, a few hundred of us were left unhampered to round up the supervisors. It didn't take long to persuade them that leaving the plant under their own power was more dignified than being thrown out. Herding the foremen out of the plant, we sent them on their way with the same advice that most of us had been given year after year during layoffs. "We'll let you know when to come back."

Ed and I were shaking hands, dancing up and down, and slapping each other on the back. We'd won! We'd beaten the hell out of 'em! The plan that couldn't work had worked! Not only had we captured this monster of mass production, but we'd outwitted in a most humiliating way the best brains that General Motors' millions could buy!

D. The General Motors Sitdown: Victory

With perhaps 10,000 workers from many cities surrounding Fisher Body Plant 1 and the National Guard poised to open fire, General Motors beat a strategic retreat. GM agreed to recognize and bargain with the union in the struck plants and promised not to deal with any other organization in those plants for six months. The strikers did not win all their demands. Management retained authority over the speed of the line. Instead of a shop steward system with one elected steward for every twenty-five workers authorized to leave his job to bargain with the corresponding foreman, this and subsequent CIO contracts established a cumbersome and bureaucratic grievance procedure. With the collaboration of the union, the right to strike at a local level was severely restricted.

However, at the time the settlement seemed a dramatic victory even to those most conscious of these unmet demands. Henry Kraus records from personal experience the presentation of the negotiated settlement to those participating in the sitdown, and the evacuation of the plants which followed the presentation.

SOURCE. Henry Kraus, *The Many & the Few. A chronicle of the dynamic auto workers*, The Plantin Press, Los Angeles, 1947, pp. 286–293.

On arriving in Flint that afternoon we stopped first at Fisher One for a prearranged meeting. As Mortimer read the pact and explained the individual points the faces that were glued on his were serious almost to the point of somberness. These men had given too much to be carried away by a gust of enthusiasm. The night before when told of the "settlement" by reporters, Bud Simons had snapped: "This strike isn't over till these boys say so." And now "these boys" fired questions at Mortimer. Did that mean everything else stood where it did when they started? How about the speed of the line? How about the bosses—would they be as tough as ever? "I'll be goddamned if I ain't gonna smack the first one that looks the least bit cockeyed at me!" one chap said and was cheered.

The announced raise was hardly mentioned or even thought of. These other things were what the strike had been fought for. All questions were answered painstakingly. It was not that the men didn't know the answers themselves—they had discussed these things hundreds of times. But it was part of that toughness that had grown up in them, of that new self-reliance that spoke so well for the future, that was reflected in this seeming skepticism. Finally one of them defined the settlement with basic clarity:

"What's the use of kidding ourselves? All that piece of paper means is that we got a union. The rest depends on us. For God's sake let's go back to work and keep up what we started here!"

When the vote was taken not one hand was raised against accepting the pact. Then a great cheer burst from the throats of the sitdowners and demonstrative joy broke through their restraint.

These experiences were repeated at the other plants. After all, none of these men had any criterion to go by to understand exactly what they had won. At Fisher Two the discussion went on for several hours before the pact was ratified. At Chevy 4 there was disappointment among the fellows from the other units who had engaged in the sitdown because the entire plant had not been included in the sole bargaining agreement. But all pledged earnestly not to consider their work completed until the entire Chevrolet division had been completely unionized and had received equal recognition.

The strike whose character in Flint was as much a social upheaval as anything else found its full and immediate vindication in the reaction of the whole people to the settlement. We had outlined an extensive plan for the evacuation ceremonies but the explosive spontaneity of joy and freedom that seized the city late that afternoon and evening made a chaos more glorious and significant than anything mere organization could have contrived.

The evacuation began at Fisher One at about 5 o'clock. All day the plant had been filled with an immense turmoil that was probably not unlike the excited but grave preparations of a pioneer people before a great trek into an unknown land. How did the men feel about leaving this home, scene of the birth of an exciting new freedom? One of them[1] recorded his feelings with beautiful simplicity:

"As the exhilaration of our first union victory wore off the gang was occupied with thoughts of leaving the silent factory which for [forty-four] days had been our home.

One found himself wondering what home life would be like again. Nothing that happened before the strike began seemed to register in the mind any more. It is as if time itself started with the strike.

What will it be like to go home—and to come back tomorrow with motors running and the long-silenced machines roaring again? But that is for the future. . . .

One must pack. Into a paper shopping bag I place the things which helped make my "house" a place to live in: house slippers, extra shirts, sox and underwear; razor and shaving equipment; two books; a reading lamp; and the picture of my wife that hung above my bed. . . .

It is near time to go. Already there is a goodly number of cars and people outside, brother workers who have come to escort us out of the plant. The first victory has been ours but the war is not over. We were strong enough to win over all the combined forces of our enemies and we shall continue to win only if we remember that through *Solidarity* we have been made free.

Now the door is opening."

The factory whistle blew a full blast and the men began marching to the door. The crowd of thousands that was gathered outside let out a great hurrah as Bud Simons appeared heading the line. Following him came the "Bearded Brigade" carrying their placard: "We Shave When Victory Is Ours." Long stogies were in their mouths, a sign of their new prosperity and importance. Every striker toted a big bundle on his back. The lines formed immediately in the street for the two-mile parade to the other plants where the chief celebration was scheduled. Four color bearers with large American flags were in the lead. Tiny flags were carried in every hat. The massive jam of sitdowners, sympathizers and hundreds of autos began their singing, cheering, honking way toward town.

[1]John Thrasher of Standard Cotton, a small feeder plant for Fisher One, whose sitdown closely paralleled that of the major unit.

Night was beginning to close down on Chevrolet Avenue when the Fisher One contingent appeared at the crest of the hill. A combined roar from the two great crowds down the street—one before Chevy 4 and the other in the hollow at Fisher Two—greeted the long-awaited marchers. The Chevy 4 leaders were standing on the high landing above the gate, a tall American flag on each side, and their men were gathered inside the doors. As the Fisher One parade reached the plant, great flares suddenly lit up, confetti flew and the enormous gates of the plant opened slowly.

Lungs that were already spent with cheering found new strength as the brave men whose brilliant coup had turned the strike to definite victory began to descend the stairs. They looked haggard with exhaustion. The mark of suffering was on them. Yet their collective joy and pride submerged all this. As they came out, wives and children rushed to husbands and fathers who had not been seen for ten fear-filled days. Strong, heavily-bearded men were unashamed of tears. Then someone began to sing "Solidarity"

Solidarity forever!
Solidarity forever!
Solidarity forever!
For the union makes us strong!

and as all joined in, the moment was carried beyond its almost unbearable tenseness and emotion.

The crowd was so great at the Fisher Two plant that the thousands coming from up the hill had to stop by the bridge fifty yards away. On the Chevy 2 roof across the street, sixteen National Guardsmen stood watching. The cheering and noise exceeded all the bounds of hearing as the small group of Fisher Two men came out of the plant which they had defended so valiantly against police gas and bullets for the first great victory of the strike. A narrow path had been left open for them and then they were swallowed up in the mass. Hardly anyone paid any heed to the speakers at the sound car. The people needed no further words for their drunkenness.

They surged into Third Avenue bound for the center of the city. It was hardly a parade, it was more like a great migration. And to some who watched from the windows of the ritzy Durant Hotel as the human flood poured into the main street of the city, it must have seemed an ominous invasion. Crossing the river on Saginaw Street right in the heart of the city the parade halted momentarily while four bearded sitdowners solemnly bore a dummy tagged "Boysen" to the parapet and with ex-preacher Homer Martin pronouncing last rites for the deceased, tossed it into the river.

Not a policeman was in sight anywhere yet thousands of people lined the street and—for the first time in Flint—applauded and cheered a union parade. "Come on in!" the men and women shouted. Many responded. Union buttons were visible everywhere along the route.

Passing the Ritz theatre the marchers gave a cheer, remembering the friendliness that Maxi Gealer, the manager, had shown their cause. The nearby Strand theatre on the other hand which had been pronounced "unfair" to the Motion Picture Operators got a salvo of boos. Never had a boycott appeal of an AFL union in Flint received such an impressive approval. It was a first sign of the new union consciousness and solidarity that had been forged in this struggle, a spirit more earnest and profound and far-reaching perhaps than any that had preceded it and which was destined to sweep from coast to coast in the wake of the splendid victory of the auto workers.

The Pengelly auditorium was jammed beyond the last inch of space. The vestibules on all floors and the stairs and the long hall downstairs were packed also and when the crowd couldn't get into the building anywhere the people began to mass outside. And still more came. Sound apparatus was strung down to the second floor from the hall and was hung out of the auditorium windows facing the street. Five thousand people were gathered outside. No one could estimate the number that had crushed and fought their way into the building.

In the hall an original play with two hundred actors, mainly from the Women's Auxiliary, was being given. It had the significant title—"The Strike Marches On." It had been several days in preparation by writers Josephine Herbst and Mary Heaton Vorse and though the players had had the benefit of a final going-over by Morris Watson, director of New York's famous "Living Newspaper," the performance was exceedingly crude.

And yet one did not require a special gift of loyalty to see something there. The mere numbers on the low stage; their exuberant, infectious vitality; the audience prompting and responding across the hardly distinguishable break; the universally-shared rock-bottom terms of the enacted message . . . were these not amply expressive of the class awakening, of a mass soul in birth?

In the general merry-making that went on all night in celebration of the victory one might have found cause to doubt the reality of this significant social fact. Particularly as the heavy drinking that went on everywhere gave the workers' hilarity much of the loose and uninspiring character of a Rotarian shindig or American Legion convention whoopee.

Around two in the morning I was in the Pengelly auditorium. The crowd had thinned out considerably but there were still some dozens of people in the hall, men and women filled by the glamour of the great strike and reluctant to abandon it finally for the humdrum of everyday life. The music dragged on wearily, playing for a handful of indomitable couples. Tired faces were unnaturally flushed, eyes ringed and blinking with immense fatigue.

Leaving, I noticed two young fellows near the door. They had been drinking and one of them was trying to explain something to his buddy. His words came garbled and as though realizing that he was not making himself understood, he shook his head violently several times. Finally, almost tearful, he exclaimed as from the very depths of his being:

"Emmet, you gotta believe me! It ain't me that's talkin', it's the CIO in me!"

E. The General Motors Sitdown: Aftermath

When working people realized that the UAW had defeated General Motors by sitting down, a hundred varieties of sitdowns bloomed across the United States. Auto workers sat down to consolidate recognition in GM plants and to win recognition by Chrysler. Other workers, public aid recipients, prisoners, students, even National Guardsmen, also sat down. The sitdown enabled oppressed persons to exercise power immediately, without the frustrating delays of a grievance procedure, and directly, without transferring trust to an often unreliable representative. Jeremy Brecher has gathered instances of sitdown activity from The New York Times. *He shows that the wave of sitdowns represented an implicit challenge to the right of a handful of nonelected businessmen to rule the economic lives of millions of their fellow citizens.*

In the wake of the GM strike, people throughout the country began sitting down. Even excluding the innumerable quickies of less than a day, the Bureau of Labor Statistics recorded sitdowns involving nearly 400,000 workers in 1937. It would be impossible of course even to summarize them all here, but we can learn something of their range

SOURCE. From *Strike!* by Jeremy Brecher. Published by Straight Arrow Books. First published as Root & Branch Pamphlet No. 4, "The Sitdown Strikes of the 1930's."

and pattern by examining a number of those that occurred in the peak of the wave during and just after the GM sitdown.

The most immediate impact was in the auto industry. The union began negotiations with Chrysler, and the company offered to accept the GM agreement. According to the *New York Times*, at the start of negotiations

". . . the union committee started the discussion on the issue of seniority, but said that the rank-and-file demanded that sole bargaining be put first on the agenda.

Then the various union locals held meetings and passed resolutions ordering the union committee to present an ultimatum demanding a yes-or-no answer from the company on sole bargaining by the following Monday.

When the company replied in the negative, according to the union, the men themselves sat down without being ordered out by their leaders."

The company secured an injunction ordering the 6,000 sit-downers to leave, but as the hour it ordered evacuation came near, huge crowds of pickets gathered—10,000 at the main Dodge plant in Hamtramck, 10,000 at the Chrysler Jefferson plant, smaller numbers at other Chrysler, Dodge, Plymouth and DeSoto plants—30 to 50 thousand in all, demonstrating the consequences of an attempted eviction. "It is generally feared," the *Times* reported, that an attempt to evict the strikers with special deputies would lead to an "inevitable large amount of bloodshed and the state of armed insurrection. . . ."

Governor Murphy warned that the State might have to use force to restore respect for the courts and other public authority, to protect personal and property rights, and to uphold the structure of organized society, emphasizing that the State must prevent "needless interruption to industry, commerce and transportation." He established a law and order committee; when top UAW officials refused to serve on it, "Strikers inside the plant could be seen waving their homemade blackjacks in jubilation. Inside the gate about 150 women who had been serving meals in the company cafeteria engaged in a snake-dance, beating knives and forks against metal serving trays."

Shop committees in the occupied plants voted not to leave the plants until they had won sole bargaining rights for the union. Nonetheless on March 24, John L. Lewis, representing the union, agreed to evacuate the plants on the basis of the GM settlement, which Chrysler had accepted even before the strike began. Many strikers considered the settlement a surrender, but they reluctantly left the plants.

The Chrysler strike was merely the largest of dozens of simultaneous sitdowns in the Detroit area. About 20,000 additional auto workers were out as a result of a sitdown at the Hudson Motor Company. Wildcat sitdowns in General Motors plants . . . occurred by the score during this period, many of them involving tens of thousands of workers at a time; by April 1 there were more than 120,000 auto workers on strike in Michigan. Workers occupied the Newton Packing Co. in late February and, after 11 days, turned off refrigeration of $170,000 worth of meat, stating that they were "through fooling." In early March clerks sat down in the Crowley-Milner department store and in the Frank & Sedar department store. Thirty-five women workers seized the Durable Laundry, as the proprietor fired a gun over organizers' heads "to scare them away." The same day Detroit's four leading hotels were all closed by sitdowns and lockouts, the auto workers providing a mass picket line in one case. Women in three tobacco plants barricaded themselves in for several weeks; in one case residents of the neighborhood battled police with rock-filled snowballs. Eight lumber yards were occupied by their workers. Other sitdown strikes occurred at the Yale & Towne lock company and the Square D electrical manufacturers.

Unable to challenge the giant Chrysler strike, police moved forcefully against the lesser sitdowns. Early in the afternoon of March 20, police evicted strikers from the Newton Packing Company. Three hours later 150 police attacked sitdowners at a tobacco plant.

"Hysterical cries echoed through the building as, by ones and twos, the 86 women strikers, ranging from defiant girls to bewildered workers with gray hair, were herded into patrol wagons and sped away, while shattering glass and the yells of the street throng added to the din."

Such action could clearly be an entering wedge against the auto workers, and the UAW responded by calling a mass protest rally in Cadillac Square and threatening to call a strike of 180,000 auto workers in the Detroit area (excluding those at GM for whom they had just signed a contract) and hinting that it would ask for a city-wide general strike unless forcible evictions of sitdowners in small stores and plants was halted. In the judgement of Russell B. Porter,

". . . it is wholly possible that the automobile workers' union might get the support of the city's entire labor movement, now boiling over with fever for union organization . . . for a city-wide general strike."

Telegrams went out to UAW locals in Detroit to stand by in preparation to strike, but the city quickly halted its drive against the more than twenty remaining small sitdowns.

In the two weeks March 7–21, Chicago experienced nearly 60 sitdowns. Motormen on the 60-mile freight subway under Chicago shut off controls and sat down when the employer decided to ship a greater proportion of goods above ground and laid off 35 tunnel workers; they were joined by 400 freight handlers and other employees who barricaded their warehouses. On March 12, sitdowns hit the Loop, with more than 9,000 men and women striking, including waitresses, candy makers, cab drivers, clerks, peanut baggers, stenographers, tailors, truckers and factory hands. 1800 including 300 office workers sat down at the Chicago Mail Order Co. and won a 10% pay increase; 450 at three de Met's tea rooms sat down as "the girls laughed and talked at the tables they had served" until they went home that night with a 25% pay increase; next day sitdowns hit 9 more Chicago firms.

The range of industries and locations hit by sitdowns was virtually unlimited. Electrical workers and furniture workers sat down in St. Louis. Workers at a shirt manufacturer sat down in Pulaski, Tenn. In Philadelphia workers sat down at the Venus Silk Hosiery Co. and the National Container Co. Leather workers in Garard, Ohio sat down, as did broom manufacturing workers in Pueblo, Colorado. Workers sat down at a fishing tackle company in Akron, Ohio. Oil workers sat down in 8 gasoline plants in Seminole, Okla. The list could go on and on.

Sitdowns were particularly widespread among store employees, so easily replaced in ordinary strikes. Women sat down in two Woolworth stores in New York. Pickets outside one store broke through private guards, opened windows from a ledge 15 feet above ground, and passed through cots, blankets, oranges and food packets to the strikers, who ate with china and silver from the lunch counter. Similar sitdowns occured in 5 F. & W. Grand stores; in one, strikers staged an impromptu St. Patrick's Day celebration and a mock marriage to pass the time. Having no chairs to sit down on, 150 salesgirls and 25 stock boys in Pittsburgh staged a "folded arms strike" in 4 C.G. Murphy 5-and-10 stores for shorter hours and a raise, also complaining that "we have to pay for our uniforms and washing them and have to sweep the floor." When 12 stores in Providence, R.I. locked out the employees to prevent an impending sitdown, the unions called a general strike of retail trades.

Nor was the sitdown restricted to private employees. In Amsterdam, N.Y., municipal ash and garbage men sat down on their trucks in the city Dept. of Public Works garage when their demands for a wage increase were refused; when the mayor hired a private trucking firm, the strikers persuaded its men not to work as strikebreakers. A similar strike occured in Bridgeport, Conn., when 60 trash collectors sat down demanding immediate reinstatement of a fellow-employee and the firing of the foreman who had fired him. In New York, 70 maintenance workers, half whites, half blacks, barricaded themselves in the kitchen and laundry of the Hospital for Joint Diseases; services were continued for patients, but not for doctors, nurses and visitors.

A similar series of sitdowns occurred in the Brooklyn Jewish Hospital. Forty gravediggers and helpers sat down in the tool house of a North Arlington, N.J. cemetery and prevented burials to demand a raise for the helpers. Seventeen blind workers sat down to demand a minimum wage at a workshop run by the New York Guild for the Jewish Blind, and were supported by a sympathy sitdown of 83 blind workers at a workshop of the New York Association for the Blind. Draftsmen and engineers in Brooklyn sat down in the office of the Park Dept. against a wage cut. WPA workers in California sat down in the employment office as flying squadrons spread a strike through the Bay Area.

An important aspect of the sitdown was the extent to which it was used to challenge management decisions. We have already seen various examples of this, such as the Chicago freight subway workers' challenge to the decision to move more freight on the surface. On March 11, workers at the Champion Shoe Company sat down when they found the company had secretly transferred 50 machines to a new plant elsewhere. 250 workers, more than half of them women, occupied a Philadelphia hosiery mill which management intended to close and prepared to block efforts to move the remaining machinery. 115 workers at the Yahr Lange Drug Company in Milwaukee who had resisted efforts to unionize them sat down in protest against a company policy of firing workers as soon as their age and length of service justified a raise. Their sole demand was removal of Fred Yahr as general manager of the company. "The girls sat around and played bridge and smoked, and the men gathered in knots awaiting the results. The telephone was not answered and customers were not served. Salesmen on the road were notified of the strike by wire and responded that they were sitting down in their cars until it was settled." After a long conference with the workers, management announced that Mr. Yahr had resigned; the strikers had in effect 'fired the boss.'

Far from being limited to employer-employee relationships, sitdowns were used to combat a wide range of social grievances. In Detroit, for example, 35 women barricaded themselves in a welfare office demanding that the supervisor be removed and that a committee meet with the new supervisor to determine qualifications of families for relief. Thirteen young men sat down in an employment agency where they had paid a fee for jobs that had then not materialized. In New York, representatives of 15 families who lost their homes and belongings in a tenement fire sat down at the Emergency Relief Bureau demanding complete medical care for those injured in the fire and sufficient money for rehabilitation, instead of the token sums the Bureau had offered. A few days later 45 people sat in at another relief office, demanding aid for 2 families and a general 40% increase for all families on home relief. In Columbus, Ohio, 30 unemployed men and women sat down in the Governor's office demanding $50 million for poor relief. And in St. Paul, Minn., 200 people staged a sitdown in the Senate chamber demanding action on a $17 million relief plan. In the Bronx, two dozen women sat down in an effort to prevent the eviction of two neighbors by 25 policemen.

Prisoners in the state prison in Joliet, Ill., sat down to protest working in the prison yard Saturday afternoon, usually a time of rest, as did prisoners in Philadelphia against a cut in prison wages. Children sat down in a Pittsburgh movie theatre when the manager told them to leave before the feature film, as did children in Mexia, Texas when a theatre's program was cut. At Mineville, N.Y., 150 high school students struck because the contracts of the Principal and two teachers had not been renewed. Women students at the Asheville Normal and Teachers College in North Carolina sat down to protest parietal rules. In Bloomington, Ill., wives went on a sitdown strike, refusing to prepare meals, wash dishes, or answer door bells until they received more compensation from their husbands. In Michigan, 30 members of a National Guard company which had served in Flint during the GM sitdown, staged a sitdown of their own in March because they had not been paid.

The sitdown idea spread so rapidly because it dramatized a simple, powerful fact: that no social institution can run without the cooperation of those whose activity makes it up. Once the example of the sitdowns was before people's eyes, they could apply it to their own situation. On the shop-floor it could be used to gain power over the actual running of production. In large industries it could be used for massive power struggles like the GM strike. In small shops it could force quick concessions. Those affected by public institutions

—schools, jails, welfare departments and the like—could use similar tactics to disrupt their functioning and force concessions; these conflicts showed that ordinary people's lack of power over their daily lives led them to revolt not only in the workplace but in the rest of society as well. The power and spread of sitdowns electrified the country: in March, 1937 alone there were 170 industrial sitdowns reported with 167,210 participants—no doubt a great many more went unrecorded.

The sitdowns provided ordinary workers an enormous power which depended on nobody but their fellow workers. As Louis Adamic wrote of the non-union sitdowns in Akron,

"The fact that the sitdown gives the worker in mass-production industries a vital sense of importance cannot be overemphasized. Two sitdowns which completely tied up plants employing close to ten thousand men were started by half a dozen men each. Imagine the feeling of power those men experienced! And the thousands of workers who sat down in their support shared that feeling in varying degrees, depending on their individual power of imagination. One husky gum-miner said to me, "Now we don't feel like taking the sass off any snot-nose college-boy foreman." Another man said, "Now we know our labor is more important than the money of the stockholders, than the gambling in Wall Street, than the doings of the managers and foremen." One man's grievance, if the majority of his fellow workers in his department agreed that it was a just grievance, could tie up the whole plant. He became a strike leader; the other members of the working force in his department became members of the strike committee. *They* assumed full responsibility in the matter: formed their own patrols, they kept the machines from being pointlessly destroyed, and they met with management and dictated their terms. *They* turned their individual self-control and restraint into group self-discipline. . . . *They* settled the dispute, not some outsider."

This potential of ordinary workers organizing their own action posed an implicit threat to every form of hierarchy, authority, and domination. For if workers could direct a social enterprise as complex as, say, the Flint sitdown, why could they not reopen production under their own direction? Certain experts like engineers and chemists would at certain times be needed, but the foremen and the rest of management would be completely unnecessary. The workers would simply have to provide for their common needs and send out delegates to coordinate with their suppliers, with workers in the same industry, and with those who used their products. The sitdown movement was widely perceived as a threat to management power; as GM President Sloan wrote, the "real issue" of the GM sitdown was "Will a labor organization run the plants of General Motors . . . or will the management continue to do so?"

2

Mark D. Naison

THE SOUTHERN TENANT FARMERS' UNION AND THE CIO

CIO contracts institutionalized accommodation to the capitalist system. The typical CIO contract contained: (1) the promise not to strike, except under specific conditions, or at the termination of the contract; (2) a bureaucratic and hierarchic grievance procedure consisting of many steps during which control over the grievance is systematically removed from the shop floor and from the workers' control; (3) a system of management prerogatives wherein the union agrees to cede to the employer the power to hire and fire, and to make all other significant decisions about the operation of the industry; and (4) a checkoff of union dues as an automatic deduction from the workers' pay checks. (This summary comes from Stanley Aronowitz, "Which Side Are You On? Trade Unions In America," Liberation, *December 1971, p. 23.) Groups of working people who by choice or necessity were driven to espouse other goals, such as a change in the system of private ownership, could find little assistance from the CIO. Mark Naison tells the story of such a group in the following article.*

The history of the Southern Tenants Farmers Union, an interracial organization of sharecropper and tenant farmers which rose to national prominence in the Depression, illuminates with striking clarity both the potentialities and the limitations of the radical organizing drives in the '30's. Brought together in 1934 by Socialist Party workers in the Mississippi Delta, this union demonstrated the unique opportunities for radical organization which the depression had opened in the rural south, a section where class conflict had long been suppressed by racial divisions. Beginning as a critic of New Deal agricultural programs, the union grew into a mass movement which aimed at the reconstruction of southern agriculture along socialist lines and the elimination of the political and educational disabilities

SOURCE. Mark D. Naison, "The Southern Tenant Farmers' Union and the CIO," *Radical America*, September–October 1968, pp. 36–56.

which made poor white and black passive observers of their own exploitation.

To many American radicals, the STFU symbolized the revival of the old populist dream of a black-white alliance which would convert the southern working class into a powerful force for radical change. But as the STFU reached out for aid from other radical groups to magnify its power, the dream turned into a nightmare. An alliance with the labor movement, which the union leaders hoped would provide a new energy and a new independence, imposed a bureaucratic burden upon the union's affairs which drained it of its revolutionary spirit. The most powerful mass organizations on a national sphere, the Communist Party and the Congress of Industrial Organizations, possessed a world view which made them unable to appreciate the union's contribution. Onto a movement which had developed a socialist consciousness with enormous popular appeal, they imposed an organizational strategy which valued sound business practices above political appeal and financial stability above revolutionary militance. In the two years it fell under their influence, the STFU saw its ranks depleted by factional conflict, personality struggles, and racial strife.

GROWTH OF A MOVEMENT

To the eight million sharecropper and tenant farmers on southern cotton plantations, the depression signalled both unparalleled suffering and a first hope of liberation. The drastic decline in cotton prices which the crisis initiated drove the croppers' already depressed incomes far below subsistence. Starvation, evictions, and foreclosures were a common fate. But the same events dealt a heavy blow to the repressive, paternalistic system of labor control which had dominated the plantation system since the end of reconstruction. As bankruptcy overtook the planters, as farms reverted to the banks, the cohesiveness of the rural social order began to break. The merchant owners and their satellites, preoccupied with their own financial troubles, had little time to supervise the black and white tenants within their purview. Thousands of laborers roamed the highways of the south, seeking shelter, seeking work. For the first time since the 1890's, food riots became a common part of the southern scene.

The New Deal, strongly dependent upon southern support for its election, stepped in dramatically to restore order to the demoralized regional economy. By giving planters parity checks to remove acreage from production, it precipitated a rapid jump in cotton prices which restored the shaken confidence of the landowning class. But the crisis of the tenant was only intensified. The acreage reduction provisions offered a powerful incentive to rid the plantation of its excess labor supply. In the first two years of the Agricultural Adjustment Act, thousands of tenants were evicted from their homes, reduced in status to casual laborers, or forced to survive on intermittent and grudgingly administered relief grants. One critic doubted if the Civil War had actually produced more suffering and pauperization in proportion to the population than the AAA had done in the few short years of its life. Such was the meaning of New Deal liberalism to the southern sharecropper.

In the midst of this chaotic reorganization of the plantation economy, a movement arose to challenge both the old system of subordination and the rationalizing schemes of the New Deal reformers. In the cotton belt of Arkansas, two young socialists named H. L. Mitchell and Clay East, acting upon the advice of Socialist Party leader Norman Thomas, decided to organize a union of sharecropper and tenant farmers who had been evicted or reduced in status during the opening year of the Agricultural Adjustment Act. Their political work among the sharecroppers had convinced them that the discontent cut wide and deep, and that black and white tenants might be willing to cooperate in the crisis. Socialist Party leaders, anxious to develop a mass base for their critique of the New Deal, promised unlimited aid and support. In the spring of 1934, Mitchell and East organized meetings throughout eastern Arkansas urging sharecroppers to unite and organize. Within a few months, they had developed a solid following of two to three thousand members and had launched a propaganda attack on the New Deal's cotton program that made government officials very uncomfortable.

The early activities of the union, following Socialist Party traditions, emphasized legal and educational work above mass action. On the advice of their Socialist patrons, the union leaders directed almost all of their organization's energy into a nationwide campaign to expose the brutality of the plantation system and the inequities of the New Deal's agricultural policies. Suits were launched in state and federal courts to test the legality of the cotton contract, speaking tours arranged to mobilize liberal and radical groups behind the union's effort, books and pamphlets written to dramatize the hardships of the sharecropper's life. Socialist in theory, the campaign tended to assume a tone that was paternalistic and reformist in character. Its exposure of injustice, divorced from organization, became an appeal to conscience. The end result of Norman Thomas' speeches, eloquent though they were, was the development of a "Sharecropper's Lobby" to prosecute the union's cause in Washington.

This incipient paternalism, however, was rapidly destroyed by the enthusiastic, almost violent response to the union's organizing campaigns. The earliest union meetings were organized quietly, often secretly, by the STFU's founders, who feared that a militant posture would bring down the repression of the planters and would divide the croppers by race. Legal, nonviolent methods were stressed. Croppers were advised to organize around existing federal programs, and to publicize their grievances through peaceful demonstrations. But at meeting after meeting, union leaders were surprised and stirred by the sight of long-humble croppers demanding the seizure of the plantations and the banishment of the owners who had so long oppressed them. Mitchell and East, southerners themselves and the children of farmers, saw the potential for a revolutionary mass movement that could sweep through the south. In the summer and fall of 1934, they brought their organizing into the open and began to prepare the croppers for militant local action.

In this new organizing drive, a unique spirit began to emerge, one which had not been seen in the South since the days of the Populists. At mass meetings called throughout eastern Arkansas, white and black organizers, sharing the same platforms, told audiences of thousands of tenants to put aside racial animosities and unite against the plantation owners. Fundamentalist ministers and preachers, the "natural" leaders of the tenant population, became the most dedicated union organizers. When planters moved to arrest black organizers, mobs of white sharecroppers sometimes arrived to liberate them from jail. By the beginning of 1935, the union had a membership of more than 10,000 in 80 local units.

Faced with a range of problems staggering in variety, threatened with reprisals at every point, the union emerged as a "total institution" that absorbed the entire life process of its membership and commanded a loyalty that was passionate and unrestrained. To make an impact on the degradation of the sharecropper's life, the union had to organize against schoolboards, relief agencies, courts, health programs, and police forces as well as the planter. With all of these agencies in the control of the same class and administered with the single objective of keeping the sharecropper docile and ignorant, the struggle for public services seemed as fundamental as the battle for control of the plantation system.

STRIKE!

During the summer of 1935, the union leaders felt confident enough to launch their first mass campaign, a cotton picker's strike in the fields of Eastern Arkansas. Spreading the word by handbills, by articles in the union newspapers, and by that system of underground communication that poor people everywhere seem to develop, the union led tens of thousands of sharecroppers out of their fields in an attempt to raise wages from 50c to $1.25 per hundred pounds of cotton and to win written contracts. As a demonstration of worker solidarity and a stimulus to organizations, the strike was remarkably effective—sharecroppers in a vast area of the Delta stayed away from work—but negotiations with the planters did not ensue. For most of the croppers, staying out on strike meant hiding in the swamp or barricading themselves in houses, and the only bargaining that took place was non-verbal and indirect. After a month-long war of nerves, marked by considerable bloodshed, most of the sharecroppers returned to work at considerably higher wages, but without written contracts.

Although hardly a paragon of planned and disciplined action, this strike provided the union with an enormous injection of energy on several different fronts. First, it gave a powerful stimulus to the union's organizing drive. The strike brought the union into direct contact with tens of thousands of unorganized sharecroppers, many of whom joined the union when the strike was over. In addition, the economic success of the union's campaign, unprecedented in recent southern history, brought about the organization of union locals in sections of the country that the strike did not even touch. Sharecroppers spontaneously organized chapters in Oklahoma, Missouri, Tennessee and Mississippi. By the end of 1935 the union claimed a membership of 25,000. On a political level, the strike had an equally important impact. The dramatic quality of the sharecropper's protest and the brutality of the terror which greeted it focused a harsh beam of light on the New Deal's agricultural programs. Reporters eagerly catalogued the shootings, the burnings and the whippings which followed the course of the union's campaign, provoking a cathartic display of concern by liberals for the "plight of the sharecropper." The pressures became intense enough to extract at least a symbolic response from the New Deal: when the strike had ended, Roosevelt announced that he was initiating a comprehensive review of the problem of tenancy and appointed a federal commission to study it.

During the next year, the union continued to grow in size, in militancy, and in political impact. Ten thousand new members were added, another cotton pickers' strike organized, a more sophisticated political program developed. As the union grew in size, it clarified its position as a "movement of emancipation." Union literature railed against the poll tax, the discriminatory administration of federal programs, the denial of unemployment relief; suits, petitions, strikes and boycotts were employed to make the tenants' power felt. But as the New Deal responded with reforms to this attack on the southern social system, the union leaders began to perceive some of the limitations of their organization's power. Roosevelt's tenancy program was a beautiful example of symbolically gratifying palliatives. Increasing the tenants' share of parity payments from 15% to 25% and providing that their distribution be direct was an open recognition of the union's attacks on the AAA but had little meaning so long as planters controlled the administration of the program on a federal, state and county level. The appropriation of fifty million dollars per year to place impoverished tenants on subsistence farms was a nice gesture to the cropper's quest for self-determination but was only a quixotic diversion in a sector of the economy where large-scale units alone could be profitable. The plantation economy was mechanizing and reducing its need for labor; small scale gains in income and power won by programs of this kind would be wiped away like dust by the broad sweep of technological change. Roosevelt's "War on Rural Poverty" reaffirmed the union's need to make functional control of the plantation system and its political supports an *immediate goal* of the union's campaign—not just as a philosophic or religious ideal, but as a precondition of any final and permanent improvement in the sharecropper's status.

However, the STFU leaders clearly observed that the continuation of the union's growth along current lines would not achieve that goal. No matter how large the union grew, no matter how organized its constituency became, it would continue to be an interest group worthy only of temporary concession so long as its power remained regional. For the success of its program, the union needed to become part of a national radical movement capable of defeating the New Deal coalition and smashing the power of the planter in the national arena. The Socialist Party and the religious groups who had supported the union up to now could not supply such a force. For an alliance to transform American politics, the STFU began to turn to a newly vitalized wing of the labor movement—the CIO.

THUNDER ON THE LEFT

For most Depression-era radicals, the growth of the CIO was an inspirational event that evoked great dreams of political success. Born of a power struggle in a collaborationist labor movement, led by a Republican and a disciple of Samuel Gompers, the movement became, in two short years, the self-conscious advocate of the unorganized and unemployed worker and a sometimes bitter critic of the policies of the New Deal. Fighting lockouts, Pinkerton's agents and federal troops, the CIO organized four million workers into industrial unions and seemed to radicalize everyone connected with it. By 1937 John L. Lewis, a man who had begun his effort with the hope of "winning the American worker from the isms and philosophies of foreign lands," had begun to espouse a program which seemed anticapitalist. Proclaiming that "it was the responsibility of the state to provide every able bodied worker with employment if the corporations which control American industry fail to provide it" Lewis called for the organization of 25 million workers in a nationwide industrial union and the formation of a farmer-labor alliance to radicalize the Democrats or develop a third political party. This program, limited though it was, seemed to offer a hope of uniting the American working class into a conscious political force.

The STFU, with more optimism than the facts would justify, saw itself playing an important role in the "CIO Crusade." If Lewis seriously intended to create a third party which could break through the New Deal stalemate on questions of unemployment and job security, the union leaders reasoned, the allegiance of southern workers to their conservative political leadership would have to be broken by intensive organization. The STFU began to see itself as an "advance guard for the labor movement in the south" supported by its more affluent and powerful brethren in return for the political appeal it would bring to their organizing drives. It was with such hopes in mind that the union leaders began to press Lewis for direct affiliation with the CIO, a relationship which they expected would provide much needed funds to expand and solidify the union organization.

However, although the political rhetoric of the CIO seemed to suggest an important place for the union, its organizational decisions reflected a different dynamic. The evident failure of capitalism to rationalize itself had impressed Lewis (who, if an opportunist, was an intelligent one) but his natural strategic response was to unionize *everybody* in centralized industrial units rather than to transform capitalism politically from above. When the STFU leaders met Lewis, they were surprised at the kind of questions he asked: What kind of dues could the union pay? How long would it take before it could become self-supporting? The political appeal of the union and the quality of its program seemed less important to Lewis than its potential financial stability. While praising the union's work, he carefully avoided committing the CIO to support it.

Lewis' evasion reflected a quality of the CIO movement which the union leaders, in their enthusiasm, had totally failed to see: its dependence upon collective bargaining as both an economic and political technique. The CIO built its organizing drive around the recognition of vast industrial unions as the sole bargaining agents of workers in American industries; the great majority of its strikes were fought around issues of union recognition rather than wages or working conditions. These highly centralized units did not only aim at improving the conditions of life for workers—they also sought to maintain the stability of industries by keeping wage levels uniform in different sectors and by assuring a disciplined response by the work force to adjustments which industries had to make to maintain a competitive position. The political ideals which the CIO articulated—a commitment to full employment, the defense of the workers' right to organize, the encouragement of political action by organized labor—were important motivating principles, but they were not what the CIO organized people around. In every instance in which the CIO had extended funds for organization, its goal was to win signed contracts and to institutionalize bargaining on an industry wide level, a basis upon which the CIO could 1) extend its control of wage levels and productive conditions in the American economy and 2) extract a steady income for new organizing.

The STFU leadership, mistakenly viewing the political rhetoric of the CIO as an indication of a carefully worked out third party program, did not see the contradictions that affiliation would bring. There was no way the standard CIO organizing dynamic could operate in an industry as marginal as cotton agriculture, where an investment in organization would not necessarily yield a return in dues. With the cotton plantation mechanizing, and with fluctuations in the international market making for vast variations in plantation income, collective bargaining or any kind of institutionalized relationship between labor and management was impossible to achieve. Any stable improvement in the income of the sharecropper could only come about through political changes that would produce a total reorganization of the plantation system. The STFU could only give a "return" to the CIO if the latter engineered a mass political reorientation which evoked, as one of its goals, a socialist transformation of cotton agriculture.

But unhappily, radicals within the CIO did not themselves characteristically take an advanced position publicly, and this was at least partially because of the influence of the Communist Party, the most powerful and disciplined radical grouping in the movement. During the Popular Front period, and in its work in the CIO, the CP functioned with a split personality, each side of which was excessively stilted and false. In their public roles, Communists took the position of brutal pragmatists, comfortable with the most narrow and pro-capitalist definition of organizing if it succeeded in building unions. In their private roles, on the other hand, party members struggled to attain the maximum orthodoxy in what they conceived to be Marxist theory, an enterprise which, if nothing else, could maintain the notion that its participants were revolutionaries. This duality, exceedingly sharp in many CIO communists, worked against the development of a popular socialist ideology in the great industrial unions. In the case of the southern tenant farmers' union, for whom the struggle for socialism was a matter of survival, it worked toward the destruction of a movement.

A DISASTROUS AFFILIATION

In March of 1937, when the CIO finally entered the field of agricultural organization, it was the CP rather than the STFU which took the initiative, and it did so in a manner which would be acceptable to the most conservative business unionist. Rather than the CIO granting direct affiliation to the STFU or forming a national farm workers' federation, CP strategists proposed an international union to organize farm workers and cannery workers simultaneously, arguing that the presence of the latter would give the organization a better chance of becoming self-supporting. Lewis approved the plan and appointed Donald Henderson, a prominent communist theoretician and the head of the National Rural Workers' Committee, as the international's first president. The STFU, invited to participate in the new organization (called the United Cannery, Agricultural Processing and Allied Workers of America, UCAPAWA for short), were told that this was the only way that they could be assured of a connection with the CIO.

To the STFU leaders, frustrated by the (to them) inexplicable reluctance of the CIO to support their organization and its program, the formation of the UCAPAWA was a nightmare whose reality they could never quite accept. Donald Henderson, whose thinking the structure of the International reflected, was a bitter and open critic of the methods and style by which the STFU operated, who had openly declared his desire to see the union broken up. In Henderson's viewpoint, the STFU's greatest achievement—its development of an independent socialist consciousness based on agrarian and religious symbolism—was a dangerous political deviation. Like many communists of his time, Henderson believed that a true revolutionary consciousness could only stem from an industrial proletariat, and that movements which drew their base from groups other than a strict working class had to be subjected to rigid ideological and organizational control. His 1935 article in *Communist*, the "Rural Masses and the Work of Our Party" had warned of the need to tie agrarian movements to a proletarian base in order to prevent "political vacillations and organizational collapse," and the structure of the International seemed designed to meet precisely that objective. The STFU leaders knew that if they linked up with the International, their organization would be under constant pressure to adjust its program and tactics to CP directives. But in spite of these doubts, the STFU prepared to affiliate. It really had no choice. By joining the International, and working to persuade the CIO of the importance of the union's work, the STFU could at least keep alive the possibility of a political reorientation which could give meaning to its local struggles.

DECLINE AND FALL

The relationship with the International, chosen in the interest of long-term strategy, proved to be even more repressive than the STFU leaders imagined. The centralized framework of the UCAPAWA, modeled on that of CIO unions in the basic industries, left the STFU leadership with very little control of organizing policies. From the moment the union affiliated (September, 1937) its organization was subjected to a discipline which provoked tensions and conflicts it had struggled mightily to repress.

The first serious tensions emerged over the question of dues and accounting procedures—an ideologically neutral question one would think. The International sent every local of the STFU a charter, an accounting book and a list of requirements for participation in the International. Members were to pay dues of 25c per month plus a 5c per capita tax to CIO headquarters. Local secretaries were to fill out balance sheets in quadruplicate, keep one, send one to district headquarters (STFU office in Memphis), one to International headquarters (in California) and one to CIO headquarters (in Washington). These procedures were the basic organization cement of the CIO movement, and Henderson applied them without expecting a protest. But the union's organizers rebelled as a unit against those requirements. The southern sharecropper, deprived of education, burdened by debt, was in no position to pay the dues or do the paperwork which the CIO demanded of an industrial worker. After seeing the charter materials, Mitchell wrote Henderson he was convinced that the STFU did not have ten local secretaries who could handle them. One organizer's suggestion was that they be kept for the next 50 years, during which time the croppers might be sufficiently educated to handle them.

Henderson's response to the union's complaint was that both the dues and the accounting procedures had to be rigorously applied. When the union leaders went to Lewis to protest this decision, they were told that compliance was a precondition of their participation in the CIO. Helpless, the union leaders instructed their organizers to restructure the local units in line with international directives. At the same time, they revived their campaign to win a separate affiliation from the CIO.

The attempt to apply the international's guidelines, as the union leaders feared, began to undermine the basis of solidarity which the movement had developed. On a local level the STFU held and expanded its membership by two basic techniques: organized action to increase the sharecropper's standard of living and protection in times of crisis; and the cultivation, through rituals, mass gatherings and demonstrations, of an almost religious belief in the justice of the union's cause and the ultimate success of its program. To force the union members to pay high dues would hinder its efforts in the first dimension, for it would siphon off a major portion of the economic gains that the union was able to win, but to bureaucratize the union's structure would be more deadly yet, for it would draw energy away from the emotional bonds which held the union members together and which were, in the long run, the basis of the union's strength.

By the summer of 1938, nine months after the affiliation had occurred, the STFU was in serious difficulty. A recession of considerable magnitude had complicated the dues' collecting drive by dramatically reducing the effectiveness of the union's economic program. For the first time in its five-year history, the STFU was experienced as a burden by the sharecropper which drew upon, rather than added to, his tiny cash income. In addition the remoteness of the union's leadership from activities in the field, imposed by long and fruitless negotiations with the CIO and the international, brought suspicions of misconduct to a dangerous level. Almost half the union locals went inactive, waiting for the old personalized style of leadership to revive, and serious racial tensions began to develop. In one section of Arkansas, E. B. McKinney, a Garveyite minister who was one of the union's organizers, had become so incensed by the declining effectiveness of the union's program and the increasing distance of the union's (mostly white) executive board that he began to advocate the formation of an all-black union. McKinney's proposal did little more than get members demoralized, but it warned union leaders that their movement would be destroyed unless they restored the program and the spirit which had been its original basis. It was clear to them the STFU was in no position to rationalize itself along industrial union lines. In August of 1938, the union halted its campaign to collect dues and membership reports for the UCAPAWA office.

Henderson, a former Columbia instructor who had never organized in the South, was infuriated by this action. He found it inexplicable that a mass movement could be mobilized around ideology, and he interpreted the union's difficulties as a sign of incompetent leadership. After going to the CIO directors for confirmation, he informed the union leader that a separate affiliation for the STFU was unthinkable, and that its relationship with the CIO was contingent upon its conformity to the rules of the International. At the same time, he mobilized the CP apparatus for a takeover of the union from within.

During the succeeding three months, violent factional conflicts entered the STFU's ranks, paralyzing the union's effort to revive its local program. A popular union organizer, the Rev. Claude Williams, allowed a paper describing alleged CP plans to take over the union to fall into the hands of J. R. Butler, the STFU's president. When Williams was suspended from the organization by the STFU executive board, he appealed to chapters to express support to Henderson, further confusing the demoralized membership. Then in December the International provoked additional tensions by cutting union representation on the UCAPAWA Executive Board to half of its previous level, a "punishment" for its failure to collect dues and membership reports. The STFU retaliated by filing a protest with the CIO and by issuing press releases denouncing Henderson.

The final break came in the early months of 1939, during a severe and unexpected economic crisis. Planters in the "bootheel" region of Missouri, spurred by "reforms" in the AAA which increased tenants' share of parity payments, shifted their labor system from sharecropping to wage labor, evicting 2000 tenants in the process. When union organizers spontaneously led the evicted families into a "camp in" on the highway between St. Louis and Memphis, a bitter struggle emerged for the loyalty of the demonstrators. UCAPAWA officials organized a separate relief drive from that of the STFU, and began to openly seek support for its "strict trade union" position. Owen Whitfield, the leader of the Missouri group, bounced like a shuttlecock between St. Louis and Memphis, alternately wooed by union and CP officials. In February, the STFU leaders lost their patience. They wrote letters to the CIO executive board declaring that the International had sustained a systematic campaign to destroy its effectiveness and warned that the union would be forced to leave the CIO unless it cleaned up the situation in the International. Soon afterward, Henderson announced that he was calling a special convention to reorganize the STFU and expel its leadership.

The CIO directors at this point entered the dispute and the position they took indicated their preoccupation with the bureaucratic side of union organization and their distance from the problems which the sharecropper faced. Although they disapproved of Henderson's plan to call for a dual convention, they would not stop him unless the union leaders agreed to abide by the UCAPAWA constitution and meet outstanding dues and obligations. The union leaders' complaints that their movement could not survive within such a framework were deemed irrelevant; Henderson's action all fell within the bounds of standard trade-union practice and had been cleared in advance by CIO headquarters. After ten days of negotiation, it became clear that the CIO's approach to organizing was all too similar to that of Henderson, and that neither would allow the union to operate on suitable terms. On March 11, Mitchell announced that the union was breaking its ties with the CIO.

During the next few months, Mitchell chose to challenge Henderson's drive to reorganize the union. Rounding up whatever loyal members he could find, Mitchell crashed the dual convention, took it over, and led his supporters out. Henderson was left with a handful of croppers, most of them followers of Whitfield and McKinney. With no basis for an interracial movement, he was never to make a serious effort to reorganize in cotton.

But the STFU had been almost equally devastated by the dispute. In a survey of the field, Mitchell found only forty active locals out of a total of 200 which the union had at the peak of its strength. The faction fight had been so confusing to the people that they had simply shut down and quit for the time being, disgusted with all unions. The racial solidarity upon which the union had based its program, moreover, had been badly shattered by the fight. The best black organizers had left the movement, disillusioned with its declining level of performance, and the whites had gone inactive. But finally, and most important, the almost religious sense of mission from which the union had drawn its strength had been utterly destroyed by the crisis. From the union's earliest days, its members had been sustained by the hope that there were forces within America which could shatter the old plantation system and win a decent life for the sharecropper on its ruins. Now, no such hope could be maintained. The most radical mass forces for change in the society, the CIO and the Communist Party, had stood apart from the union's strivings, had smothered it with forms, had crushed it with obligations. Not even on the distant horizon were there forces of sufficient strength to transform the cotton economy into a free and ordered system of production. From 1939, the STFU confined its work to education and lobbying, serving as a liaison between sharecroppers and federal tenancy programs it had regarded as hopelessly inadequate two years before.

THE MEANING FOR THE LEFT

The destruction of the Southern Tenant Farmers Union epitomized the basic limitation of the most dynamic organizing drive staged by radicals in the thirties—the campaign of the CIO. With few exceptions, radicals within the CIO were willing to live with a definition of union organizing that made it impossible either to organize workers who were outside of an industrial system, or to concentrate on political organization that challenged capitalist institutions. In particular, CIO Communists, who should have known better, were so concerned with developing a working class base that they supported a strategy of unionization which had been consciously designed to rationalize a capitalist economy. And when they came in contact with a movement which could not apply such a strategy, whose economic problems were so severe that not even a temporary solution could be found within capitalism, they allowed and even encouraged its destruction because its supporters were not classic proletarians.

The consequences of these failures have been very serious and very lasting. First of all, they worked against the development of a broadly based radical party and the growth of a popular socialist consciousness. The obsession of many radicals with activities which created powerful financially stable organizations led them to neglect the very real opportunities to disseminate a cooperative, anti-capitalist ideology among the American laboring population. As the growth of the STFU indicates, workers in the most conservative, traditionalistic sections of the society were often receptive to a radical outlook if it was phrased in terms relevant to their experience and combined with effective organization.

But equally important, the strategic orientation of CIO radicals reinforced the isolation of the black population from the rest of the American working class, helping to set the stage for ghettoization and the social crisis of our time. The narrow definition of industrial unionism embodied in the CIO implicitly excluded most of the black working force, who operated within marginal sectors of the economy which could not be rationalized within capitalism. The colonized sharecropper on the southern plantation, living under conditions of dependence radically different from those of a factory worker, could not be organized in a centralized bureaucratic union. When old left strategists *chose* to avoid a campaign to reorganize the American economy, when they *chose* to neglect the program that the union had advocated, they were postponing the organization of rural black people to some vague and later date. The mistrust of white radicals by insurgents in the ghetto is one painful and indirect consequence of the failure of the union's program.

3

C. *Wright Mills*
THE MAIN DRIFT

By the end of World War II the militancy of the CIO in its organizing drive had faded. Even before the purges and expulsions of Left individuals and unions in 1948–1950, it had become clear that the function of CIO unions was as much to discipline the membership so that business could make long-range plans with confidence, as it was to represent the membership in making demands on business. In the following portion of his first major book C. Wright Mills (1916–1962) makes this point clearly. He also stresses the extent to which the new industrial unions of the 1930s owed their existence to the benevolence of the federal government. Labor, he argues, had allowed itself to be co-opted into a tacit partnership with big business and big government. Mills' hopes for the labor movement at the time he wrote The New Men of Power *are suggested by the quotation with which he began the book, "from an interview with an unknown worker, Sutcliffe, Nevada, June, 1947."*

When that boatload of wobblies come
Up to Everett, the sheriff says
Don't you come no further
Who the hell's yer leader anyhow?
Who's yer leader?
And them wobblies yelled right back—
We ain't got no leaders
We're all leaders
And they kept right on comin'.

A dozen years later, when Mills wrote his "Letter to the New Left," his attitude had changed. He stated in that influential pamphlet: "what I do not quite understand about some new-left writers is why they cling so mightily to 'the working class' of the advanced capitalist societies as the historic agency, or even as the most important agency, in the face of the really impressive historical evidence that now stands against that expectation."

During November, 1946, the mass public was polled for its opinion on whether "all corporations should or should not be required to put a union representative on their board of directors?" For most people the question contained a completely new idea, which makes it all the more startling that 42 per cent said they were in favor of including a union man.

The idea is no mere fancy of some poll-taker in search of his monthly quota of questions. It is in line with the very best liberal rhetoric, slightly extended; it is not outside the possibility of the co-operative relations earnestly desired by many labor leaders.

Co-operative relations between business and labor are rooted in the desire for peace and stability on the part of businessmen, labor leaders, and political officials. Such desires, with their monopolistic consequences, were back of the citywide labor-business cartel. Now, on a much larger scale, with consequences that go beyond pure and simple monopoly, a tacit sort of plan to stabilize the political economy of the U.S. is back of many current demands of the spokesmen of the three powerful bureaucracies in the U.S. political economy.

This conspiracy does not include the extremists in any of the camps. It is primarily a plan among the liberal spokesmen, although it is no doubt aided and abetted by the sophisticated conservatives.

Stabilization requires further bureaucratization of business enterprise and labor union. Given present industrial arrangements, it also involves amalgamating the union bureaucracy with the corporation's. This may occur either in the technical *place of work*, in the *economic enterprises* making up a given industry, or among the industries forming the *political economy* as a whole. So far there are American instances only of the first two kinds, except for one brief experiment with the third.

PEACEFUL SHOPS AND STABLE ENTERPRISES

Business-labor co-operation within the place of work means the partial integration of company and union bureaucracies. By seeking to collaborate in making and administering company rules, the union is a megaphone for the voice of the worker, just as the company hierarchy is a loudspeaker for the voice of management. If the union is efficient, the worker's gripes will receive attention from the shop steward and, if necessary, go on up the union and company hierarchies to the president of the union and his lawyers and the president of the company and his lawyers. This is the power aspect of the arrangement and its mechanics from the worker's point of view.

But for something gained, something must be given. The integration of union with plant means that the union takes over much of the company's personnel work, becoming the disciplining agent of the rank and file within the rules set up by the joint committee.

The union bureaucracy stands between the company bureaucracy and the rank and file of the workers, operating as a shock absorber for both. The more responsible the union is, the more this is so. Responsibility is held for the contract signed with the company; to uphold this contract the union must often exert pressure upon the workers. Discipline must be brought to bear if unauthorized leaders call unauthorized strikes. The rank-and-file leaders of the union, the shop stewards, operating as whips within the plant, become rank-and-file bureaucrats of the labor leadership. As foremen are responsible to the company hierarchy, so shop stewards are primarily answerable to the labor union hierarchy, rather than to the rank and file who elect them.

On December 11, 1945, the Automobile Workers released a proposed agreement with the Ford Motor Company whereby the company and the union agreed that ". . . any employer or employees found guilty of instigating, fomenting, or giving leadership to an unauthorized stoppage of work shall be subject to discharge." In such cases the union would act as judge and prosecutor. Workers who follow unregulated militants, acting without due authority, are subject to penalties. To have no strikes is the responsibility of both company and union. They are disciplining agents for each other, and both discipline the malcontented elements among the unionized employees.

In November, 1946, a local of the United Steelworkers, another member of the new industrial aristocracy of unionism, signed a contract containing a "mutual responsibility clause" by which "the local union, any of its members, or the company" might be financially liable for the reasonable costs of "strikes, work stoppages, or lockouts of any nature or condition" that might occur. The international cannot be held responsible, nor can the local if it or a majority of its members do not participate in the strike. Presumably this means that the individual adherent to unauthorized strikes is to be individually punished.

"Such an agreement, even so watered down," says a national businessman's organ, is "typical of what management wants in new labor agreements." The union's motive for accepting such terms was a desire to continue "union security provisions." This was acceptable to the company officials who reasoned that such provisions "would be necessary if the union should be called upon to enforce its responsibility to management by disciplining contract-breakers." In addition, the union was willing to go along because an AFL union "was maintaining friendly relations with management and obviously was awaiting an opportunity to edge out the CIO and take over the whole jurisdiction." Since the great organizing drives of the Thirties, employers have gotten into the habit of distinguishing between "good responsible unions" and "bad irresponsible unions." The competition between AFL and CIO thus furthers responsible co-operation.

These examples of the bureaucratic integration of labor unions with business enterprises involve large industrial unions which deal with big corporations. The integration is often more far-reaching where a big union deals with an industry composed of many scattered small-scale business enterprises. In such cases, the union is the most stable element in the entire industry and takes the primary role as stabilizing agent. Here the co-operation assumes a more obvious relevance for the economics of the industry as a whole.

An agreement signed by the International Ladies Garment Workers Union in 1941 provided for "obligatory standards of efficiency in plant management and empowered the union to hale before the impartial chairman any manufacturer who failed to live up to these standards." "The businessmen of the industry," writes the official historian of the union, "retain the rights of management": the union "accepts the premises of free enterprise," but "imposes upon the management the obligation of efficiency." Because "there can be no security in an insecure industry," the union took upon itself the job of rationalizing the industry as a whole and insisting upon "efficient management and merchandising by the employer." In the entire industry, this union is the richest and largest single organization in "a jumble of jobbers, manufacturers, sub-manufacturers, contractors, and sub-contractors." It can afford, therefore, to take a statesman-like view. Each one of the contractors and jobbers and sub-manufacturers continues to get his profits under the planning and rationalization imposed by the union. It is not surprising that employers come to the "management engineering" department established by this union to ask and receive aid on time and motion studies, plant layouts, and other information designed to increase production.

Golden and Ruttenberg, men with experience in CIO steel, discuss labor-management co-operation in a manner reminiscent of any of several spokesmen for the garment industry talking of an "efficient" labor-business cartel. "Union-management co-operation tends to make management more efficient and unions more cost-conscious, thereby improving the competitive position of a business enterprise, and increasing the earnings of both workers and owners," write these steel unionists; and they quote with approval the happy managers of unionized plants and Ordway Tead's classic statement of worker reasons for business-labor co-operation: "There is a real sense in which the affiliated workers of an industry have more at stake in helping an industry than the salaried managers or the scattering of absentee stockholders."

The union most obviously acts in the economic interests of the worker in bargaining for increased wages, directly and indirectly. The union is a jobber of labor power, selling it as dearly as the market will bear. And the market increasingly narrows down to a dozen or so bargaining tables. Now, co-operation implies a definite and mutual objective between the co-operators. But the company wants its labor power to be as cheap as possible, whereas the union, in so far as it operates as a union is supposed to operate, wants wages as high as possible. If one enterprise gives higher wages than other competing enterprises, to maintain its level of profit it will have to charge higher prices, thus endangering its competitive relations with the other enterprises.

There is a solution: wages may be set for an entire industry, so that no one business enterprise will have cheaper labor costs than any other. Here on the industry level, true co-operation rather than compromise is possible: all the corporations forming the industry, along with the industrywise union, can pass on to the consumers (in the end, mainly the workers in other industries) the higher costs involved, and thus maintain high profits and high wages. Within the industry there is no real conflict between business and labor.

In their search for security and in the realization of their basic economic character and strategy, labor unions further the tendency to rationalize the job sphere by setting up job hierarchies and rules of conduct within the establishment. They further the rationalization of the social organization of work, and they extend the standardization and monopoly aspects of the economy. They would, as we have said, rationalize production without socializing it.

There are, of course, counter-tendencies. While one set of unions utilizes all technological developments, making semi-skilled and unskilled workers more important than skilled workingmen, other unions, such as the Musicians, look to the security of present members and fight for craft-like formations within the great industry.

Older craft unionists fought hard for job control through the closed shop to aid organization. Now the closed shop makes for peace and stability; it therefore fascinates many businessmen as well as many labor leaders. The electrical contractors, for example, fear legislation which would abolish the closed shop in their industry. The union, policing its contracts by this means, stabilizes its tenure; "cutthroat competition leading to chaos" might result from open shop conditions. Often businessmen see the closed shop as an asset in those areas of free private enterprise where there is free competition.

The big industrial monopolists show a similar concern to the degree that they understand the extent to which the new aristocracy of labor would go with its attempts to establish a form of profit sharing. In 1938, while business was still bad, the U.S. Steel Corporation suggested to Philip Murray that the Steel Workers Organizing Committee accept a wage cut. The union leader refused, but went on to demonstrate the possibilities of a more modern kind of union-management co-operation: "They advised against price cuts and put pressure on Washington in June, 1938, to delay a monopoly investigation of the steel industry, the TNEC hearings on steel, at a time when increased competition might have caused price and wage cuts. Pointing to the 'terror-stricken condition of the steel industry brought about by a system of cutthroat competition,' the chairman of the SWOC said in October, 1938: 'If the steel corporations cannot put their house in order, it is the avowed purpose of the organized steel workers in this nation to promote a constructive legislative program that will adequately protect the interests of the industry and its workers.'" That cutthroat competition had reduced the steel industry to terror was news to economists who had for decades been using the steel industry as the classic example of rigid monopoly pricing. It is clear that the labor leaders had lined up with the vested interests of the industry against the general business community, not to mention the public. "What would Judge Gary have said," Dwight Macdonald has asked, "if he had been told that fifteen years after his death, not only would his steel corporation be unionized, but that this union would come out as the protecting champion of the great monopoly price structure he had devoted his life to creating?"

Demands for stability in the plant and enterprises of an industry point to a third level of business-labor co-operation: the political economy as a whole. The more the implications of the concrete demands for peace and security are thought through, the more they point toward nationwide co-operation, under state control. Business-labor cartels can exist in a scattering of industries without governmental sanction, but as unions and trade associations grow bigger and make more co-operative deals, the state steps in and regulates the total structure of business-labor co-operation. Over the last two decades, the liberal state in America has felt the drive to stability and has been greatly moved by it.

THE LIBERAL STATE

One of the trends characterizing U.S. society and accelerated by the New Deal is the increasing integration of real and, more particularly, potential democratic forces into the apparatus of the political state. This is part of the steady long-term shift in the locus of power from representative bodies, such as Congress, to administrative agencies, such as labor boards.

Often in this situation, politics becomes a battle between various pressure organizations represented by lawyers and technicians, not understood or participated in by the masses of people. As they bargain for economic power and maneuver for better positions, the leaders of these organizations must discipline their members. Their attempt to "bore from within" the state apparatus is accompanied by the desire to maintain their organizations intact, even to the point of ritualistically losing sight of their ends in their frenzy to maintain their means. The associations, including labor unions, lose their independence of action; thus they ensnare one another.

The New Deal was an attempt to subsidize the defaults of the capitalist system. Part of this attempt consisted in the effort to rationalize business and labor as systems of power in order to permit a continued flow of profits, investments, and employment.

Under the NIRA,[1] the businessmen of each industry were allowed to agree among themselves, and with the employees, on the terms of business. They could set prices of products and wages of workers. Such a scheme differed from the old business-labor cartel idea in its nationwide scope and in that the Federal government was policing "fairness," relaxing the anti-trust laws accordingly.

Most of what was written on labor in the Thirties says a great deal about section 7–A and the less well-known section 7–B of the NIRA. It is true that these sections gave the unions an official go-ahead to

[1]National Industrial Recovery Act of 1933; in May, 1935, the Supreme Court declared the NIRA unconstitutional.

organize labor and to represent it in the code making. But to study only this aspect of the NIRA is to be guilty of a superficial, pro-labor bias in the interpretation of the meaning of the act. This act must be seen in terms of its meaning for business-labor co-operation on the level of industrial solidarity and within the political economy as a whole. What it amounted to was an attempt to governmentalize business-labor cartels, nationwide, industry by industry.

In its objective function, it was similar to the Italian idea of the corporate state: to unify the employer and the employee class within each industrial combine. It tried to give sovereignty to the monopoly unions and sovereignty to the trade associations, each in its proper sphere, and co-sovereignty to the trade associations and labor associations in their common spheres of action.

NIRA failed, first because not even the amount of political power delegated by Congress to Roosevelt was sufficient to enforce the co-operation; and at that time the unions were neither big enough nor wise enough in the ways of security-seeking to uphold the arrangement voluntarily. Secondly, the practical conservatives were strongly against NIRA; the small businessmen feared they would be squeezed out by the agreements between the monopolies of labor and of capital. They were of too much political importance to Roosevelt, a sophisticated conservative, to be ignored. Finally, by the time NIRA was invalidated, the economy was somewhat improved, so that those who had been frightened relaxed, feeling they might get out of trouble in some other, more old-fashioned way.

To be successful in industrywide bargaining, a union must be monopolistic. In its negotiating and policing work, it cannot allow one of its sectors, or some other union, to set a different pay scale and conditions for a specific local area. Nor can the corporative system be allowed to give its employees freedom to choose their unions. There must be a monopolistic union co-operating with a monopolistic trade association.

The Wagner Act[2] embodied in law a principle that is repugnant to the idea of monopolistic unions: the right of employees to choose their union representatives by majority vote, and the right to review or change that decision. The Wagner Act compelled all industries to observe the principle of choice, first legislated in the Railway Labor Act of 1926[3] But the Wagner Act came into being under the spell, as it

[2]The National Labor Relations Act of July, 1935. It was upheld by the Supreme Court in 1938.

[3]Its electoral machinery and other features were somewhat revised in 1934 and 1936.

were, of the corporate state idea behind the NIRA and the experience of the boards operating under the NIRA. In the sequence of political fact, the Wagner Act was adopted to replace NIRA when it ended.

Unequal bargaining power between employee and employer, it was believed, leads to depressions "by preventing the stabilization of competitive wage rates and working conditions." The Wagner Act claimed to equalize this power. We want to make sure, its makers said, that (1) workers have the right to organize and to bargain collectively; (2) employers have no right to interfere with the formation of unions or to hamper their organizing; (3) the appropriate bargaining unit is decided for the workers' organization; (4) an election is held, if necessary, by which a majority of the workers in a unit may choose their union representatives; and (5) the union they choose is certified as the "exclusive bargaining agent" for that unit.

Elections under NLRB auspices determined which union was to be given the monopoly and excluded minority unions. The Wagner Act changed the basis of the monopoly by making it possible for the employees, by a shift in majority opinion, to destroy or to change the monopoly agent. It institutionalized the basis of monopoly for the union and, within the liberal state framework, guaranteed its democratization.

The power of the union is thus in part dependent upon the continuation of the governmental framework and in part upon the majority will of the employees. Union power is no longer directly dependent upon the strength it has accumulated and put into a direct arrangement with the employer. Every labor leader knew that the Taft-Hartley amendment of the law, enacted in the summer of 1947, might do much to break the power of the unions, particularly the power of those union leaders who had been leaning more on the national administration and its policies than on the massed force of the unionized workers.

One next step in this sequence of law is clear. The industrywide monopolies may be forced to shed their somewhat private character. They may become objects of regulation by government bodies who will outlaw strikes and compel arbitration of various kinds. They will next become, in practical effect if not formal law, organs of the state which protects their power, even as they have been during the late war. We cannot yet tell how fast the administration of the Taft-Hartley law will move in this direction. But the dialectic of business and labor and government has reached a stage where the state, in the interests of domestic stability and international security, increasingly appropriates the aims of the employer and expropriates or abolishes the functions of the unions.

This is the threat of increased labor-business co-operation within the system of private enterprise. This is the blind alley into which the liberal is led by the rhetoric of co-operation. This is the trap set by the sophisticated conservative as he speaks of the virtues of the great co-operation.

4

Mathew Ward
UAW

At the local level, the growing conservatism of the CIO expressed itself in poorly attended union meetings and a general alienation of the rank and file. Racism, at least rhetorically overcome during the CIO organizing drive, reappeared in the new industrial unions once they were established. Mathew Ward is a radical black auto worker who moved to Detroit from the South during World War II. His vivid description of the death of the dream of the 1930s is the more poignant because the UAW incarnated that dream more fully than any other CIO union. Unlike the Knights of Labor and the IWW, the CIO remained strong, but at the price of what had distinguished it from the AFL. It was a reflection of reality when in the mid-1950s the two organizations reunited into the AFL-CIO.

Today was the fifth time this year that the Council meeting had to be called off because they didn't get a quorum of fifty-five people. This is the General Council of our local union, U.A.W., a union of seventeen thousand members with nine hundred members in the Council. I've been on the Council four consecutive years. We have adjourned more meetings this year than in all the previous years put together. Two months ago the union leaders blamed the poor attendance on the bus strike. Fifty percent of the members have cars and this is the second meeting to be adjourned since the end of the bus strike. Every chief steward is a member of the Council. The steward on my line hasn't attended a meeting in two years.

There was a big change in the union from 1943, when I first went in, to the present day. We used to hold our meetings in the auditorium of Cass Tech, a big high school. We had to hurry to get there. There were as many workers standing outside trying to get in as were inside at the meeting. There was a free and democratic set-up. Any member could

SOURCE. Mathew Ward, "UAW," *Indignant Heart*, News and Letters, 1900 East Jefferson, Detroit, Mich., 1952, pp. 149–166.

bring his grievance to the membership as a whole. Now, if any worker, white or Negro, tries to bring up a grievance at a membership meeting, the union officers tell him,

"There are four of us at the union hall all the time. Come down and discuss it with us."

If we go down to see the union officers, as they tell us to, they either put us off or give us the business.

In the early days there was rarely a meeting that didn't mention something about our Negro brothers and sisters. There was a discussion around this at every meeting. Many Negro women were working in the plants then. Many of today's union leaders would discuss shop problems and issues that face our Negro brothers with the membership as a whole taking part. We used to go to listen to the other guys. We would always come away with something from these meetings. Now, there is no such thing as our union leader bringing a problem facing our Negro brothers and sisters before the members as a whole to be discussed.

I'm not saying this change was made the same day or the same year Reuther got control of the U.A.W. The powerful machine was not organized the same day or year. But since Reuther came in, if there is an issue raised by Negroes, as Negroes, we are told by the union leaders that this is the most damaging thing we can do to ourselves. They say don't raise the question of Negroes. The first two years a Negro woman, Alice Phillips, was on the Reuther staff her picture appeared in the Negro press every month at least, but it has not appeared this year.

During the U.A.W. convention held in Cleveland, Ohio, a Negro delegate told me that many Negroes were assigned to leading white hotels. In some cases, a white worker put in for the room. But when his roommate, a Negro worker, would come in, the hotel clerks would stop him. They would ask the Negroes to leave. The U.A.W. had a housing committee and they would send a Negro international representative to talk to the Negroes about a place to stay. The international rep would take them to his room.

He would say, "We're going to straighten this thing out. Have a drink?"

He would keep pushing the whiskey at them until they were drunk. When they were drunk, the rep would say that they had found rooms for them in a Negro hotel.

He'd say, "You see, we're good to you. We always do our best. If you will just stay at this place tonight, then tomorrow we'll really fight this thing out."

The next day the Negroes would ask for a meeting with the housing committee. The committee would be tied up all day. The day after they would be told the same thing. The committee was always busy. This would go on until the end of the convention when it didn't matter any longer. Every time a Negro brought up an issue along the lines of discrimination he would be sent to the Negro international rep. The rep would calm him with whiskey. All the reps had eight to ten quarts of liquor in their room at every convention. They also had women for the men. All of this is at the expense of the dues paid by the workers. Some delegates did not go to more than one session during the whole convention.

In Dodge, during a strike, union functionaries gave the Negro workers the run around about where to go for picket duties. At lunch time they sent Negroes upstairs to eat and left the downstairs for the white unionists.

A white worker asked a union official: "What if the Negroes make trouble at having to eat upstairs?"

The official pulled a black jack out of his pocket and said, "If they give any trouble I got something to handle them with."

A friend of mine worked in the kitchen. She told me that when the Negroes came to be served she was told, "Watch those pork chops with the niggers when they come in. Just give them one chop. Let them come back if they want any more. You can give two chops to the white guys."

George Addes, ex-secretary-treasurer of the U.A.W. opened a beer garden over on Gratiot. The Negro unionists say that Negroes can't go in to be served.

I was told by one of the ex-officers of our local that at the local's anniversary party the union hired Negroes to serve. They had the most Uncle Tom kind of Negro they could get. It was just like the South. The whites danced and talked to themselves. There was no mixed dancing.

Three years ago the lunch wagon owned by an outside chain company, brought food into the plants to sell to the workers at lunch time. They raised the price of their food after a few weeks. The workers felt this was too much to pay and put up a holler so the union decided to boycott all the lunch wagons. The stewards were to see to it that no one bought anything. The first day no one came near the wagon. The second day five Negroes went to the wagon and began getting food.

The white chief steward yelled and said, "Put down that damn stuff."

The Negroes looked around, very angry, and continued to pick up food.

The steward rushed to me and said, "What I say about your people is true, they won't cooperate. Go over and see if you can stop them."

I went over and before I could speak one said, "Mathew, we want to cooperate but yesterday we went outside and the restaurant where we can eat was packed. There was a long line waiting and half of us didn't get anything to eat. We were so hungry in the afternoon we had to check out early. We just couldn't make the day without eating. All the whites ate because they can go in any restaurant. We can't bring lunch because we don't have wives to fix them."

All the restaurants around the plant are jim crowed, there are only three places where Negroes can eat, and there are about three thousand Negroes working on my shift. I went to the white chief steward and told him the story.

I said, "If you can get some white workers tomorrow, I will get some Negro workers and we can go out and break these restaurants discriminating around the plant. We will see that the restaurants serve all of our union members. I will stand guard every day after that and guarantee that no one will buy off of this wagon."

This stunned him. He said he couldn't do it. He would have to take it up with our union officers and that would take some time. The Negro fellows continued to eat from the wagon and pretty soon all the workers came back to eat there too. The lunch wagon kept selling at a high price which hurt both Negro and white workers.

The Negro weekly newspapers in Detroit, carried an article on the 1949 U.A.W. convention held in Milwaukee, Wisconsin. The articles said that a Negro delegate from St. Louis, Missouri, got the floor and called Reuther's attention to the discrimination that was being carried out in his plant, Local 25. He pointed out an agreement between the union and the company that Negroes would receive less wages for doing the same work as whites. Reuther replied that this agreement was negotiated by the former left wing leadership.

The Negro delegate said, "But after four years of right-wing leadership this still exists and you did not answer my question."

A week or two after the article appeared, a friend of mine was visiting here from St. Louis. He works in the same plant as the man who spoke to Reuther. He told me that it is a General Motors plant. Reuther has been the top negotiator for General Motors for years. He also felt very sure that this was the home local of Livingstone, one of the U.A.W. vice presidents. He told me the company would hire a Negro as quickly as a white; there were no complaints about discrimination in hiring. When the company wanted to speed up, they put pressure on the whites first and said,

"If you don't want to do it, we can get Negroes to do it for fifteen cents less an hour."

He felt sure this kept hostility between Negroes and whites. This hurt the white workers as much as the Negroes.

Sure, Reuther is always mentioning the Negroes in his big speeches. I heard him speak at an N.A.A.C.P. meeting this year, attacking America about the way Negroes are treated here.

He said, "In America we can talk about our atomic bomb that can split this earth asunder—we can talk about the Iron Curtain here of Stalin, but we will never be the America we could be until we drop the iron curtain here, and let fifteen million Negroes have their full freedom as any other American citizen." After Reuther finished his talk, a Negro international rep asked me what I thought of the talk.

"Good," I said, "He always gives a good talk, but he has not as yet raised the Curtain on the International Executive Board high enough to appoint one Negro on it."

Reuther's line in the union is that there is no Negro problem. The bureaucrats say if you bring it up on the floor as a Negro problem it will hurt you. The Polish and Jewish and Italian don't do it, so why should Negroes?

When I was first elected to the Council it had been set up to discuss the problems of the workers in production. But it has turned into a machine of the union leaders. Whatever comes up on the floor, if the leaders want it passed—that's it. Any time one of the rank and file workers gets up and says anything particular about our work in the shop or asks about a specific incident in his department, he gets squashed down. Workers say there is no use going to meetings. They say what they want to bring up won't hit the floor. If a question does get on the floor, the Reuther bureaucracy calls the previous question. That means stop the debate and vote on the discussion. One worker may speak sharp and ten or fifteen hands go up. The labor bureaucrat knows his stooges and he recognizes one of them. Sometimes workers jump all over the hall trying to talk. The president gets up and gives his line, the chairman says, "We have to proceed along democratic lines. We are not going to let you have special privileges. Now we will vote on it," and the issue is killed.

When the bureaucrats want to put over an issue they have a way of taking their cars to pick up supporters. They haul out everyone they know, even some who haven't been in the plant or the union for three years. It is always on a political issue, city officials or something to do with the state elections. Two years ago the workers came out in a group to try to force discussion. They were so whipped and crushed down that now they say, "The hell with the union."

I point out the difference between the union and the union leadership to the men on my line. I say what the union means to me and to us. When I first joined the union in 1943, the words brother and sister—I didn't grasp their full meaning. But after getting active in the union and understanding what the workers did and went through in organizing the UAW-CIO, I could see that this was the first real emancipation for the white worker and the second emancipation for the Negroes. Then brother and sister meant something to me. Since then I felt that our relations as union members should exist as close as possible, next to the immediate family relations.

When we talk on the line, after a meeting, the men say, "Yes, what you say about the union, that's all true. But this is the union, the way it is today and not what we want, so what the hell. The hell with the union."

But a question can come out about the company, or somebody trying to break the union and you'll have all the workers out the next day. If it is the usual meeting the workers won't attend.

When Ford Local 600, UAW-CIO, held its tenth anniversary celebration last year and announced John L. Lewis as their principal speaker, I felt that I could not miss it. I had always wanted to see and hear John L. Lewis, ever since I saw those pictures of the sit-down strikes while I was living in the South. At the celebration there were some eighty thousand workers from all over the city packed into an open field joining the union hall. I saw several busses loaded with workers from the coal fields. When Lewis appeared, the applause was so great, it felt to me the earth was trembling. When he started to speak, I felt I had known him personally for years. No one who had ever seen his pictures in the paper could mistake him. He was identically the same, not resembling anyone. He had strange features, it seemed to me his look was strange. He had a very deep heavy voice which roared through the audience. The more I tried to gather up in my mind some features of someone I had seen before, the stranger he seemed. Then I remembered one time I had seen a cartoon in the paper; it showed Winston Churchill with the features of a bull-dog. I said to myself, "Yes, John L. Lewis has the features of a lion." His voice is like that of a lion, his face and his head, all of his looks seemed to go with his fight in helping to build the CIO.

Lewis said, "I am here with you to celebrate the tenth anniversary of your local union. I have heard there is a saying among many of you that I am also here to celebrate as the founder and organizer of the UAW-CIO. I do not agree with those who say that I am the founder and organizer. The UAW-CIO was founded and organized by many of you who are here today, and many like you who are not here. But if you want to bestow some honor upon me, I will accept that I did as much to help organize the UAW-CIO as anyone else.

"Don't pay any attention to those labor leaders and intellectuals running around the place with a new briefcase and one piece of paper in it, getting up telling you what to do. Many of them don't know as much what to do as you do yourselves. They should be in the plant with you."

Somewhere in his talk he asked, "Who is responsible for the UAW-CIO?"

Someone in the audience yelled out, "You."

He said, "No, it was you, all organizing yourselves together, understanding the situation that was involved, that brought General Motors to sit down and bargain collectively."

He said, "This huge gathering here today is power, it is force, the working force of production that America and the world exist upon. It is the force and power that can bring any corporation to recognize you when you are organized together."

This was what I was thinking. This working force that everything hinges on; this was the answer. Lewis stated it. How much he meant it, I don't know. I was glad to be a part of this force that Lewis was speaking of and I knew there was no other place for me to go. Before Lewis finished speaking, I made my way through the crowd into the hall. I felt I wanted to touch him. He came down the aisle, pausing every step, shaking workers' hands. I reached out mine. He shook it, smiled and said, "Good luck." He walked outside and got in a large convertible and shook hands with workers for five or ten minutes. Motorcycle cops all around the car opened their sirens and the car pulled off.

The way that Lewis spoke; that's not how the bureaucrats act. I had a worker tell me today, swearing, that the union represents nothing but the company.

"Nobody can tell me these guys aren't paid by the company. The only guys who have fun in the shop are those who shoot crap all day or the guys who write the numbers."

Numbers are collected openly in my shop. A guy works numbers on my line. On Thursday he goes to the bank and draws out two thousand dollars. When the workers come on Friday to pay for the numbers they played during the week, he cashes their checks. There are always ten or fifteen workers standing around. The big shots walk up and down. They never say anything. Some workers think the numbers men pay off the union and the union makes it right with the company. Once in awhile the company will fire a small guy, but it's just like the racket outside, they never fire a leading numbers man. Numbers playing goes on all over the shop in every department and in every plant in the city. In a predominantly Negro department there is one fellow, who, the Negroes think, must be doing it for the company. He has a job but he doesn't do any work. The numbers man on my line brings a pistol to work on Friday. Many of us wonder why he doesn't get fired. He hangs his coat up with the gun showing but the company never says a word to him. If a worker hasn't any money left after paying, he stays and borrows from the same guy, paying him twenty-five cents on the dollar interest. He walks around all week and lends workers money. This is no different than what I saw in the South.

A Negro drove up to the union hall today with one of the biggest Chryslers made. He was so dressed up that we thought he was one of the international representatives. We were standing around talking and we all said, "Porkchopper."

He came out with the vice president of the local and they stood talking at the car. The vice president kept his hand on the Negro's shoulder and he was smiling all over his face. One of the men with us was so worried, not knowing this man, that he went to ask. After the guy drove off, the vice president said that he was a line steward in the plant.

He told us this and everyone said, "Oh, he's a numbers guy or else a loan guy."

Nobody would have taken him for a worker. He was dressed up and wearing a diamond ring and the car was a special Chrysler. The vice president was never so warm to any Negro before.

It makes me sick. There is a guy on my line taking numbers. I asked him one day how he had the heart to take the workers' money. I know one man whose wife came and begged the manager to make her husband stop playing. They had five children and he never brought home any money. When I asked the numbers fellow he said he was making money, had just bought a new car and was building a house soon. He didn't give a damn for workers or their problems. One Negro I know worked with me during the war. He started writing numbers and in four years he made twenty-eight thousand dollars cash.

Many workers won't come in to work on Friday. They get their check in the front office and when they see the numbers guy on Monday they say they are broke. Some wildcats are pulled on a Friday. These numbers men practically go insane if a strike is pulled before lunch on Friday. Sometimes a man will ask the foreman if he can go home at noon to avoid the numbers man. The foreman says, no, but the guy will leave anyway. The man will sometimes get fired for going home when the foreman said no.

Two years ago, with the model changeover, they tried to speed up production on the job. The bargaining committee said we wouldn't have to run one piece more than before. They said it was the same job. We had been running one hundred jobs an hour. The time study man turned in a report that we should do one hundred thirty-five jobs an hour and the company tried to beat us into speeding up. With stationary jobs, there is an agreement that a worker gets six minutes out of the hour, if he does not make production. If he makes production ahead of the hour, then he gets whatever time is left for himself. The workers were so mad about the speed up, that they gave up their fifteen minutes and took the six that were due them every hour. They said they'd be damned if they'd make one thirty-five an hour. The bargaining committee told us that as long as we worked fifty-four minutes we didn't have to make production. They were thinking that in a week or so the workers would give in so they would get fifteen minutes rest like the other workers.

After two weeks they still couldn't make the men do one hundred thirty-five jobs. They were still doing one hundred. The company called the bargaining committee into the office and the committee agreed that the workers should do one hundred twenty-five. The company always sets the figure higher than they expect so that they can eventually get what they want. The union tried to get the workers to agree to one twenty-five. They wouldn't do it for three days. The bargaining committee said they had to do it, that the time study watch showed one thirty-five and that "figures don't lie." They told us if we didn't do it we'd be in the street.

The workers hollered and yelled and said, "What kind of an agreement is this? We were told on the job changeover that we would do as we had before, and now you tell us that figures don't lie."

The committee said, "You have to do it."

The workers had to give in. In this speed up the union worked hand in glove with the company.

When Reuther came out against wildcat strikes it just meant the company would clamp down. All of us knew it. The union leaders said the wildcat was caused by the Commies, and at the same time, they said the workers were lazy and didn't want to work. One worker, Samuels, an old guy who had been in the ship for twenty-five years was looking out the window one morning. He saw some workers going out and cursed them; he said they didn't want to work. I told him he was talking like the company and the union. I tried to tell him what strikes meant. This was something I knew he didn't accept. His line was that we voted for these union leaders and we should follow them. Older workers are usually more conservative.

In the speed up from one hundred to one twenty-five the company put a special foreman over this old guy. They figured if they broke him the others would follow. The company was putting pressure on him and the workers were putting pressure on him. One day he said he was forced to go to the men's room. He quit working eight minutes before the hour instead of six. The foreman rushed into the office and gave him a warning slip. Samuels got so mad he started talking about what we should do to the company.

He said, "We need a strike."

I carried a group over to him and told him, "You remember what I said the other day? You remember what you said about wildcats?"

He said he had been wrong. "You told me it was always the fault of the company. God damn it, it's true. I thought the days were wiped out when they could put a man to stand over you."

The bargaining committee said the company could have a foreman anywhere they wanted as long as he didn't drive a worker. The old guy didn't have proof that the foreman was driving him. But he was driving.

We have benches to sit on to eat lunch. The foreman finally got so mad because we wouldn't do one hundred twenty-five jobs, that he broke up one of the benches. We got the chief steward in a position where he said if the bargaining committee didn't support him he'd pull off his button and go back to work on the line; it was too much to let the company get away with. He asked me if I would accept the job of chief steward. Before this time he had been afraid I might get his job because of the workers who liked me. I told him I didn't want the job and that it would be a mistake for him to take off his button. It was a fight the company was pulling off and he should see that all the workers supported him and not call the bargaining committee at all. I promised to help him and he felt good. He got us a new bench. He would have been pretty well wrecked if he had stood for breaking up our bench. It would have been open to the workers that he hadn't supported them.

One morning I heard that the workers in another department were being sent home because of a shortage of material. I went to Samuels, the old guy, and told him that we all got so mad at what the company did to him, that we were wildcatting in the afternoon. He was so happy, he said he would be the first to walk out. To this day he thinks the workers left because of him. Now he's the first one to get the workers to walk out and always defends them. He's the most militant worker we have in the shop today.

If one worker gets in a sharp argument with a foreman, every worker who can get away from his job will come to find out what's up. Fifty will be around in no time at all. The crowd will be so thick you won't be able to see the two who were arguing. The union and the company try to keep a disagreement within its own department. A bargaining committee man will never tell the truth about a dispute. He'll give the workers some story. None of us ever believe him. They keep a grievance quiet because they know workers will support workers.

The company fired twenty-five men on the night shift and the union was stalling about getting them back. We didn't know for two days, that the night shift had gone out twice. On a Saturday the union held a department meeting of the night and day shifts. The workers got so mad they cursed the local officer. They told him if nothing was done by Monday morning they would put up a picket line of their own on Tuesday to keep the day shift out. This shook the union leaders because they knew it would spread around. Every worker would know the men were having trouble. The union had the bargaining committeemen go into every department of the plant and tell the chief stewards to instruct the workers that they were to ignore the picket line. The chief steward came to me first and told me to tell the thirty guys on my line. The bargaining committee man stood off to the side, listening. I asked the steward to repeat what he had said.

Then I told him: "Do you know who you are talking to? I won't tell a worker on my line a damn thing. You know who I am. These workers know who I am. I stand on principles. I'm surprised at you telling me to go through a picket line. What's going on in this union? We used to fight and kill scabs. Now you're telling me to tell these workers to scab. You're trying to make me a scab. That's something I'll never be."

The committee man stepped up and said the strike was not authorized by the union.

I told him, "That's why we are having a strike. The company knows that the union will try to whip us down on anything they want to put over on us. They make us walk out. I'm positive, and I'm sure every worker will say, that the company has forced these workers to call the strike. I'm sure the company knows we're not supposed to strike until we get an okay from the union. They'll drive the workers to do anything they want them to do. If the workers don't strike, then by the time the union gives its okay the men will be forced to do what the company wanted. If a worker does the work for one day then the company will put out that they should do it all the time because they are able to do it."

I pointed out the strike of the plant guards. The union made us support the guards, and they're nothing but cops for the company. They're not even members of our union. The union gave us the line that some day the guards might join our union. None of us wants these cops in our union. I told him that the union tried to poison us saying that the workers don't want to work. I said if a worker didn't want to work he wouldn't have to come to the plant in the first place.

But the company knows we're not supposed to strike, and it knows the position of the union. They know that's the way to defeat the workers with the only weapon they have, the strike.

"You can tell the committee man that I work every day but if a picket line of my brothers is up, then I won't be in the shop."

The chief steward said he hadn't thought about it like that. He said, "It's the truth. I won't tell any of the workers in my department what to do. If they come in on their own, if they don't come in, that's up to them. If there's a line I won't be in to work either."

The union got the same resentment throughout the shop. At three o'clock every committee man and chief steward was in front of the gate handing out leaflets. The leaflets told the workers not to support the strike. It was a very well printed leaflet.

A worker said, "I'm sure the company is working hand in hand with the union. It's impossible that the union could run out seventeen thousand leaflets between two-thirty and three o'clock."

One worker said, "We should have shotguns and shoot every committee man first. Those bastards are trying to push us through the line."

The workers feel they'll never be able to beat the union bureaucracy in an election.

"They'll stuff the ballot boxes, and if they get beat there'd be blood around the ballot box."

The next morning there was no picket line. The union got eighteen men back that afternoon and promised to have the rest back the next day. But the union had a sound truck out, in case the picket line was up. They weren't sure, and if there was a line they'd yell for the workers to go through.

A worker friend walking in with me said, "A stool pigeon and a scab used to hide and cover his face. Now, the union is the biggest stool pigeon and scab and is trying to get the workers to be scabs."

At another plant the union had the flying squadron ready to take the scabs through the picket line.

One white worker said, that if a member of the flying squadron hit him he'd walk with a shot gun the rest of his life to kill those sons of bitches. He said that the flying squadron was paid from our money, and set up to help us fight the police. But now they talk about beating us back into the plant for the company.

All this is why they can't get the workers to a Council meeting. Last month we finally got a quorum for a General Council meeting. I reached the hall while the president was reporting on the wildcat strikes. Twenty-three workers had been fired. The union promised the strikers that they would get the men their jobs if they wouldn't wildcat. They got all back to work except nine. So the workers went out again. On the second night, the workers sat down in the plant for two hours.

The president of the local was speaking more viciously than I had ever seen him. He was talking about stopping the wildcats. He said the men would be brought up on charges and expelled. They had been listening to cheap left wing politicians. They were cheap and yellow and without guts enough to come out in the open and speak against the local officers. They would be behind the union's back and get the workers to wildcat. They always managed to evade getting fired themselves. He also said that the workers in one plant were the biggest liars he'd ever heard. They'd said the union hadn't done anything about the fired men, but only seventeen of them came to the meeting to discuss with the union.

The floor was opened for discussion. A Negro was the first to speak. He said he was opposed to accepting the president's report. The general attitude of the president was vicious, low type politics. He said the president said left wing politicians caused the wildcat, but he wasn't left wing. He didn't care a damn about politics in the union. This was what the union always used when the workers faced them with any problem, this was used to evade the issue. When the president called the workers liars he had plenty to say in answer. At the last election the president of the local spent one hundred dollars or more of union money for stickers and advertisements saying that he opposed the dues increase. The Ford workers were fighting the dues increase too at the convention. He had suggested that our local unite with the Ford workers. He spoke to the recording secretary of the union about it and the secretary said they weren't opposed to the dues increase. "We are for it."

The fellow asked the president, "If that phony work with stickers and advertisements isn't being a liar, then what is?"

He went head on in a fight with the president. He did one of the best jobs I've witnessed.

A Trotskyist spoke. He said he had been away organizing. He said he was disturbed. This was the third Council meeting this year and workers didn't turn out. Why, when the present administration controlled seventy-five percent of the members on the Council didn't they attend meetings? He was disturbed about executive board meetings too. They couldn't get a quorum of seventeen members out of a board of one hundred. This was a board with ninety-five percent control by Reuther. He said the meetings should be advertised well and the workers should be told there would be free discussion in meetings. He was disappointed with this in the union.

An old timer spoke next. He said he didn't know what was wrong with the union. The members should get an intellectual with clear understanding to help us in our union. That's what we needed.

A bargaining committee man spoke next. He said, "I do everything I can for the workers. I can't seem to satisfy them. I wish someone would tell me what is wrong with the workers. We get three raises and insurance benefits for the workers. But when they were on strike they cursed the committee men. During the wildcat strike, a worker pulled a knife, put it against me and said if I ever came back in the department he'd kill me. I surely wish someone could tell me what is wrong with the workers?"

I got the floor. This is what I said:

"I noticed quite a few ovations when they said the workers didn't attend meetings and that the workers were not following the officers of the local and that they should and that that was what the trouble is. We're missing the boat and missing it far. I don't see it as you say, that you got the insurance benefit for the workers. The workers got it by putting on the pressure. When the present administration came in the first proposition Reuther made was that we could live peacefully with management. From that alone, management understood as well as anyone else that if we were not going to strike, but would live peacefully, then they could speed up the line and beat the workers at the point of production to make more profits than they did before they gave us ten cents and the benefits. The proof is that every year the president of the International gets up and tells that the corporation is doubling its profits and that we need to get more of what we produce. How can this be when the company has the right to control production by speed up?

"I don't agree with the old time union leaders of the local trying to say that a worker must be born in one department of the plant before he understands anything about the union, that we need an intellectual. That's saying we're dumb. The bargaining man thinks because he's a bargaining committee man he's teaching the workers and getting a few things for them. This is it and they should go with him. Workers don't have to be in the union twenty-five years before they know what's what. The average worker comes into the plant, and according to the contract, the foreman is supposed to spend three days showing him his operation. The average worker has the foreman with him for only three hours. It's not that long before he can do his operation. In three days he is able to do the operation as well as anyone who has been in the plant twenty-five or thirty years. Many workers who have been in for thirty years, if sent over to the new worker could be shown by him. And as easy as a worker can learn an operation he can learn and knows unionism just that well in less than three months.

"One thing I notice that we are doing now in all of these issues, the workers are faced with the idea that it is cheap left wing politicians making them do everything. That says the worker is dumb. The company is oppressing him and he isn't supposed to have sense enough to fight back. The union hasn't mentioned one time the role the company plays in relation to a worker at the point of production. But Harry Bennett has to write a book *We Never Called Him Henry* to let these union leaders know that this is the role the company plays. He only mentioned Ford, but all workers know that this is the role that all leading industries play.

"The brother that mentioned an intellectual. You should understand this—that the worker knows and understands better than the teacher, the President, or the intellectual, the role he has to play in relation to the company. He knows better than any plan that could be thought out for him. I think if we take the side of the worker and if the union leader becomes a part of the struggle he's carrying on, then we'll see and not be so confused. I heard a hundred workers if I heard one, make the statement that our president was at one time a good union man. He led many wildcat strikes. But, they ask, what has happened to him, today? I tell them, 'That's the sixty-four dollar question. But you won't get sixty-four dollars if you find the answer. You'll probably get thrown out of the union'."

The discussion was closed and the president came back with his rebuttal. He said very little about the other speakers. He started in on me.

He said, "That's what I meant. These politicians know how to operate. They don't go far enough, they don't cross the line so that they can be brought up on charges. That brother just did one of the damndest chop jobs on us that was ever done in the union but he didn't go far enough to where he'd have to prove what he says and could be tried."

This tickled me. The president thought every worker around him is so dumb that he had to tell them what I said.

The president went on. "Many workers, he said, tell him we were good fellows six or seven years ago. What's happened to us now? The brother tells the workers that if they find the answer to the sixty-four dollar question they'll get thrown out of the union. He's accusing us openly, and frankly, before this Council meeting of being company stooges. But he won't go across the line. He just comes up to it and stops and leaves it hanging. I want everybody to know what he is saying. He knows if he says that we are stooges he'll have to prove it before a trial committee and will probably get kicked out of the union."

After the meeting the president came to me and said he wanted to have a talk about my accusation. I said that I hadn't made an accusation.

I said, "You made the accusation that you are company stooges. I didn't say that, but if you want to say it before all these workers you can say it and I'll accept what you say."

Part Three
STIRRINGS

1

Harvey Swados
THE MYTH OF THE HAPPY WORKER

Appearance, in the 1950s, suggested that American workers were affluent and content. Only a few prescient observers disagreed. In "The Myth of the Happy Worker" Harvey Swados (1920–1972) describes the gripes and the fantasies of his fellow workers in an automobile assembly plant. Swados is also the author of the novel Standing Fast.

"From where we sit in the company," says one of the best personnel men in the country, "we have to look at only the aspects of work that cut across all sorts of jobs—administration and human relations. Now these are aspects of work, abstractions, but it's easy for personnel people to get so hipped on their importance that they look on the specific tasks of making things and selling them as secondary . . ."
William H. Whyte, Jr., The Organization Man

The personnel man who made this remark to Mr. Whyte differed from his brothers only in that he had a moment of insight. Actually, "the specific tasks of making things" are now not only regarded by his white-collar fellows as "secondary," but as irrelevant to the vaguer but more "challenging" tasks of the man at the desk. This is true not just of the personnel man, who places workers, replaces them, displaces them—in brief, manipulates them. The union leader also, who represents workers and sometimes manipulates them, seems increasingly to regard what his workers do as merely subsidiary to the job he himself is doing in the larger community. This job may be building the Red Cross or the Community Chest, or it may sometimes be—as the Senate hearings suggest—participating in such communal endeavors as gambling, prostitution, and improving the breed. In any case, the impression is left that the problems of the workers in the background (or underground) have been stabilized, if not permanently solved.

SOURCE. *The Nation*, August 17, 1957.

With the personnel man and the union leader, both of whom presumably see the worker from day to day, growing so far away from him, it is hardly to be wondered at that the middle class in general, and articulate middle-class intellectuals in particular, see the worker vaguely, as through a cloud. One gets the impression that when they do consider him, they operate from one of two unspoken assumptions: (1) The worker has died out like the passenger pigeon, or is dying out, or becoming accultured, like the Navajo. (2) If he *is* still around, he is just like the rest of us—fat, satisfied, smug, a little restless, but hardly distinguishable from his fellow TV-viewers of the middle class.

Lest it be thought that (1) is somewhat exaggerated, I hasten to quote from a recently published article apparently dedicated to the laudable task of urging slothful middle-class intellectuals to wake up and live: "The old-style sweatshop crippled mainly the working people. Now there are no workers left in America; we are almost all middle-class as to income and expectations." I do not believe the writer meant to state—although he comes perilously close to it—that nobody works any more. If I understand him correctly, he is referring to the fact that the worker's rise in real income over the last decade, plus the diffusion of middle-class tastes and values throughout a large part of the underlying population, have made it increasingly difficult to tell blue-collar from white-collar worker without a program. In short, if the worker earns like the middle class, votes like the middle class, dresses like the middle class, dreams like the middle class, then he ceases to exist as a worker.

But there is one thing that the worker doesn't do like the middle class: he works like a worker. The steel-mill puddler does not yet sort memos, the coal miner does not yet sit in conferences, the cotton mill-hand does not yet sip martinis from his lunchbox. The worker's attitude toward his work is generally compounded of hatred, shame, and resignation.

Before I spell out what I think this means, I should like first to examine some of the implications of the widely held belief that "we are almost all middle-class as to income and expectations." I am neither economist, sociologist, nor politician, and I hold in my hand no doctored statistics to be haggled over. I have had occasion to work in factories at various times during the Thirties, Forties, and Fifties. The following observations are simply impressions based on my last period of factory servitude, in 1956.

The average automobile worker gets a little better than two dollars an hour. As such he is one of the best-paid factory workers in the country. After twenty years of militant struggle led by the union that I believe to be one of the finest and most democratic labor organizations in the United States, he is earning less than the starting salaries offered to inexperienced and often semiliterate college graduates without dependents. After compulsory deductions for taxes, social security, old-age insurance and union dues, and optional deductions for hospitalization and assorted charities, his pay check for forty hours of work is going to be closer to seventy than to eighty dollars a week. Does this make him middle-class as to income? Does it rate with the weekly take of a dentist, an accountant, a salesman, a draftsman, a journalist? Surely it would be more to the point to ask how a family man can get by in the Fifties on that kind of income. I know how he does it, and I should think the answers would be a little disconcerting to those who wax glib on the satisfactory status of the "formerly" underprivileged.

For one thing, he works a lot longer than forty hours a week—when he can. Since no automobile company is as yet in a position to guarantee its workers anything like fifty weeks of steady forty-hour pay checks, the auto worker knows he has to make it while he can. During peak production periods he therefore puts in nine, ten, eleven and often twelve hours a day on the assembly line for weeks on end. And that's not all. If he has dependents, as like as not he also holds down a "spare-time" job. I have worked on the line with men who doubled as mechanics, repairmen, salesmen, contractors, builders, farmers, cabdrivers, lumberyard workers, countermen. I would guess that there are many more of these than show up in the official statistics: often a man will work for less if he can be paid under the counter with tax-free dollars.

Nor is that all. The factory worker with dependents cannot carry the debt load he now shoulders—the middle-class debt load, if you like, of nagging payments on car, washer, dryer, TV, clothing, house itself—without family help. Even if he puts in fifty, sixty, or seventy hours a week at one or two jobs, he has to count on his wife's pay check, or his son's, his daughter's, his brother-in-law's; or on his mother's social security, or his father's veteran's pension. The working-class family today is not typically held together by the male wage-earner, but by multiple wage-earners often of several generations who club together to get the things they want and need—or are pressured into believing they must have. It is at best a precarious arrangement; as for its toll on the physical organism and the psyche, that is a question perhaps worthy of further investigation by those who currently pronounce themselves bored with Utopia Unlimited in the Fat Fifties.

But what of the worker's middle-class expectations? I had been under the impression that this was the rock on which socialist agitation had foundered for generations: it proved useless to tell the proletarian that he had a world to win when he was reasonably certain that with a few breaks he could have his own gas station. If these expectations have changed at all in recent years, they would seem to have narrowed rather than expanded, leaving a psychological increment of resignation rather than of unbounded optimism (except among the very young—and even among them the optimism focuses more often on better-paying opportunities elsewhere in the labor market than on illusory hopes of swift status advancement). The worker's expectations are for better pay, more humane working conditions, more job security. As long as he feels that he is going to achieve them through an extension of existing conditions, for that long he is going to continue to be a middle-class conservative in temper. But only for that long.

I suspect that what middle-class writers mean by the worker's middle-class expectations are his cravings for commodities—his determination to have not only fin-tailed cars and single-unit washer-dryers, but butterfly chairs in the rumpus room, African masks on the wall, and power boats in the garage. Before the middle-class intellectuals condemn these expectations too harshly, let them consider, first, who has been utilizing every known technique of suasion and propaganda to convert luxuries into necessities, and second, at what cost these new necessities are acquired by the American working-class family.

Now I should like to return to the second image of the American worker: satisfied, doped by TV, essentially middle-class in outlook. This is an image bred not of communication with workers (except as mediated by hired interviewers sent "into the field" like anthropologists or entomologists), but of contempt for people, based perhaps on self-contempt and on a feeling among intellectuals that the worker has let them down. In order to see this clearly, we have to place it against the intellectual's changing attitudes toward the worker since the Thirties.

At the time of the organization of the CIO, the middle-class intellectual saw the proletarian as society's figure of virtue—heroic, magnanimous, bearing in his loins the seeds of a better future; he would have found ludicrous the suggestion that a sit-down striker might harbor anti-Semitic feelings. After Pearl Harbor, the glamorization of the worker was taken over as a function of government. Then, however, he was no longer the builder of the future good society; instead he was second only to the fighting man as the vital winner of the war. Many intellectuals, as government employees, found themselves helping to create this new portrait of the worker as patriot.

But in the decade following the war intellectuals have discovered that workers are no longer either building socialism or forging the tools of victory. All they are doing is making the things that other people buy. That, and participating in the great commodity scramble. The disillusionment, it would seem, is almost too terrible to bear. Word has gotten around among the highbrows that the worker is not heroic or idealistic; public-opinion polls prove that he wants barbecue pits more than foreign aid and air-conditioning more than desegregation, that he doesn't particularly want to go on strike, that he is reluctant to form a Labor Party, that he votes for Stevenson and often even for Eisenhower and Nixon—that he is, in short, animated by the same aspirations as drive the middle-class onward and upward in suburbia.

There is of course a certain admixture of self-delusion in the middle-class attitude that workers are now the same as everybody else. For me it was expressed most precisely last year in the dismay and sympathy with which middle-class friends greeted the news that I had gone back to work in a factory. If workers are now full-fledged members of the middle class, why the dismay? What difference whether one sits in an office or stands in a shop? The answer is so obvious that one feels shame at laboring the point. But I have news for my friends among the intellectuals. The answer is obvious to workers, too.

They know that there is a difference between working with your back and working with your behind (I do not make the distinction between handwork and brainwork, since we are all learning that white-collar work is becoming less and less brainwork). They know that they work harder than the middle class for less money. Nor is it simply a question of status, that magic word so dear to the hearts of the sociologues, the new anatomizers of the American corpus. It is not simply status-hunger that makes a man hate work which pays *less* than other work he knows about, if *more* than any other work he has been trained for (the only reason my fellow workers stayed on the assembly line, they told me again and again). It is not simply status-hunger that makes a man hate work that is mindless, endless, stupefying, sweaty, filthy, noisy, exhausting, insecure in its prospects, and practically without hope of advancement.

The plain truth is that factory work is degrading. It is degrading to any man who ever dreams of doing something worth while with his life; and it is about time we faced the fact. The more a man is exposed to middle-class values, the more sophisticated he becomes and the more production-line work is degrading to him. The immigrant who slaved in the poorly lighted, foul, vermin-ridden sweatshop found his work less degrading that the native-born high school graduate who reads "Judge Parker," "Rex Morgan, M.D.," and "Judd Saxon, Business Executive," in the funnies, and works in a fluorescent factory with ticker-tape production-control machines. For the immigrant laborer, even the one who did not dream of socialism, his long hours were going to buy him freedom. For the factory worker of the Fifties, his long hours are going to buy him commodities . . . and maybe reduce a few of his debts.

Almost without exception, the men with whom I worked on the assembly line last year felt like trapped animals. Depending on their age and personal circumstances, they were either resigned to their fate, furiously angry at *themselves* for what they were doing, or desperately hunting other work that would pay as well and in addition offer some variety, some prospect of change and betterment. They were sick of being pushed around by harried foremen (themselves more pitied than hated), sick of working like blinkered donkeys, sick of being dependent for their livelihood on a maniacal production-merchandising setup, sick of working in a place where there was no spot to relax during the twelve-minute rest period. (Someday—let us hope—we will marvel that production was still so worshiped in the Fifties that new factories could be built with every splendid facility for the storage and movement of essential parts, but with no place for a resting worker to sit down for a moment but on a fireplug, the edge of a packing case, or the sputum- and oil-stained stairway of a toilet.)

The older men stay put and wait for their vacations. But since the assembly line demands young blood (you will have a hard time getting hired if you are over thirty-five), the factory in which I worked was aswarm with new faces every day; labor turnover was so fantastic and absenteeism so rampant, with the young men knocking off a day or two every week to hunt up other jobs, that the company was forced to overhire in order to have sufficient workers on hand at the starting siren.

To those who will object—fortified by their readings in C. Wright Mills and A. C. Spectorsky—that the white-collar commuter, too, dislikes his work, accepts it only because it buys his family commodities, and is constantly on the prowl for other work, I can only reply that for me at any rate this is proof not of the disappearance of the working class but of the proletarianization of the middle class. Perhaps it is not taking place quite in the way that Marx envisaged it, but the alienation of the white-collar man (like that of the laborer) from both his tools and whatever he produces, the slavery that chains the exurbanite to the commuting timetable (as the worker is still chained to the time clock), the anxiety that sends the white-collar man home with his briefcase for an evening's work (as it degrades the workingman into pleading for long hours of overtime), the displacement of the white-collar slum from the wrong side of the tracks to the suburbs (just as the working-class slum is moved from old-law tenements to skyscraper barracks)—all these mean to me that the white-collar man is entering (though his arms may be loaded with commodities) the gray world of the working man.

Three quotations from men with whom I worked may help to bring my view into focus:

Before starting work: "Come on, suckers, they say the Foundation wants to give away *more* than half a billion this year. Let's do and die for the old Foundation."

During rest period: "Ever stop to think how we crawl here bumper to bumper, and crawl home bumper to bumper, and we've got to turn out more every minute to keep our jobs, when there isn't even any room for them on the highways?"

At quitting time (this from older foremen, whose job is not only to keep things moving, but by extension to serve as company spokesmen): "You're smart to get out of here. . . . I curse the day I ever started, now I'm stuck: any man with brains that stays here ought to have his head examined. This is no place for an intelligent human being."

Such is the attitude toward the work. And toward the product? On the one hand it is admired and desired as a symbol of freedom, almost a substitute for freedom, not because the worker participated in making it, but because our whole culture is dedicated to the proposition that the automobile is both necessary and beautiful. On the other hand it is hated and despised—so much that if your new car smells bad it may be due to a banana peel crammed down its gullet and sealed up thereafter, so much so that if your dealer can't locate the rattle in your new car you might ask him to open the welds on one of those tail fins and vacuum out the nuts and bolts thrown in by workers sabotaging their own product.

Sooner or later, if we want a decent society—by which I do not mean a society glutted with commodities or one maintained in precarious equilibrium by overbuying and forced premature obsolescence—we are going to have to come face to face with the problem of work. Apparently the Russians have committed themselves to the replenishment of their labor force through automatic recruitment of those intellectually incapable of keeping up with severe scholastic requirements in the public educational system. Apparently we, too, are heading in the same direction: although our economy is not directed, and although college education is as yet far from free, we seem to be operating in this capitalist economy on the totalitarian assumption that we can funnel the underprivileged, undereducated, or just plain underequipped, into the factory, where we can proceed to forget about them once we have posted the minimum fair labor standards on the factory wall.

If this is what we want, let's be honest enough to say so. If we conclude that there is nothing noble about repetitive work, but that it is nevertheless good enough for the lower orders, let's say that, too, so we will at least know where we stand. But if we cling to the belief that other men are our brothers, not just Egyptians, or Israelis, or Hungarians, but *all* men, including millions of Americans who grind their lives away on an insane treadmill, then we will have to start thinking about how their work and their lives can be made meaningful. That is what I assume the Hungarians, both workers and intellectuals, have been thinking about. Since no one has been ordering us what to think, since no one has been forbidding our intellectuals to fraternize with our workers, shouldn't it be a little easier for us to admit, first, that our problems exist, then to state them, and then to see if we can resolve them?

2

Sidney Peck
THE POLITICAL CONSCIOUSNESS OF RANK-AND-FILE LABOR LEADERS

In this selection Sidney M. Peck (1926–) argues, on the basis of interviews in Milwaukee in 1955–1958, that local shop stewards were far more class conscious than their overt support of established political parties implied.

In his classic work, *A Theory of the Labor Movement*, the late Professor Selig Perlman argued that the "Tom, Dick and Harry" of the American labor movement is job-conscious rather than class-conscious in outlook. Basing itself upon the practical-minded ideology which sought limited objectives of wage and job control, the American labor movement, says Perlman, was able to evolve stable forms of trade union organization. Thus, Perlman is led to defend Gompers' pragmatic collective bargaining approach to the "leaders or bosses of the two old parties" as the realistic attitude of organized labor toward American politics. More recently, in 1951, he echoes the same thoughts, and he repeats them in slightly revised form six years later. And what is the evidence for Perlman's fixed ideas about American labor which have spanned a period of thirty years? Brushing aside the impact of the New Deal decade, he points to the quite obvious facts that American workers are still committed to capitalism and have not formed a labor party. Perlman writes:

"Broadly speaking, the American labor movement has so far shown little indication of breaking away from Gomperian moorings, if these are taken in the sense of the basic social order it favors and of the method it employs in its political action."

Let us take organized labor's allegedly "job-conscious" approach to politics and see how it is interpreted by the rank-and-file.

It is our thesis that the politics of organized American workers is

SOURCE. *Studies on the Left*, Volume 2, Number 1, pp. 43–51.

informed by class as well as job concerns. We do not deny the existence of a job-minded outlook among working people but we do assert that union folk think and act politically in terms of a class frame of reference. We suggest that workers feel themselves part of a solidary class sharing common problems and interests. We contend that this consciousness of class identity is expressed both in political activity and in political ideology.

First of all, as the politicians might say, let's look at the record. In their 1952 and 1956 election surveys of the political attitudes of UAW members, Arthur Kornhauser and Harold Sheppard demonstrate quite conclusively that the majority of auto workers in the Detroit area expressed support for and approval of labor endorsement and involvement in politics. Detroit auto workers not only *acted in agreement* with union recommendations but also expressed the desire that labor should have greater influence in the political sphere. A similar conclusion may be drawn from the recent political record in Milwaukee.

The 1956 Milwaukee mayoralty election and the 1957 special election to fill the senatorial vacancy of the late Republican Joseph McCarthy serve to highlight the existence of a significant labor vote. In the April, 1956 mayoralty contest, which the *Milwaukee Sentinel* viewed in sharp, pointed, lead editorials as a struggle between "Americanism and socialism," the Milwaukee electorate chose "socialism over Americanism" by a margin of more than 250,000 votes. Operating through Labor's Political League, the Milwaukee labor movement played a decisive role in (and is credited with) the re-election of socialist mayor, Frank Zeidler. Shall we conclude, therefore, that working folk in the "machinery-capital" of the world actively express a commitment to "Zeidler-Marxian" socialism? Obviously not! What the election results do demonstrate, however, is *the existence of a "labor vote" which can be effectively organized and mobilized during a crucial electoral period.*

This conclusion is also clearly evident in the tensely fought 1957 senatorial campaign which resulted in a surprising victory for the Democratic candidate, William Proxmire. While a number of factors contributed to the Proxmire victory, the smooth-working electoral machinery of the Milwaukee trade unions, underwritten by voluntary labor funds, proved to be of immeasurable support in securing a large Milwaukee Democratic plurality. Industrial workers voted solidly in favor of their labor-endorsed candidate. In short, what took place on the 1956 and 1957 Milwaukee electoral scene was direct confirmation of the Detroit survey findings.

Little wonder then that the "organized labor vote" expressed itself so decisively in the 1958 Wisconsin congressional and state elections. Confronted with "right-to-work" bills, charges of union corruption and racketeering, mounting unemployment, discriminatory welfare legislation and inadequate health coverage, organized working people eagerly looked to the ballot as the political cure-all. In the city of Milwaukee, the Democratic candidates for Governor and Senator polled a two-to-one electoral victory.

In sum, when the issues are sharply defined, when there appears to be some semblance of political choice, labor votes *en masse*. The 1958 election results offer conclusive proof that union people look to the political scene for the defense and advancement of their perceived class interests. As Braverman suggests,

"The fact is that there has been a great transformation in labor's political role, though it is not possible to analyze it by a comparison restricted to the resolutions of Gompers' day and ours. In the first place there has been a big change in the bloc—not unanimously, but in sufficient numbers to show a rudimentary consciousness of common class interest."

It is quite essential to understand the elements of this "rudimentary consciousness" if we are to appreciate the current political orientations of the rank-and-file. There is empirical evidence to substantiate our belief that the "labor vote" is the concrete manifestation of class-conscious attitudes which under-pin the political thinking of industrial unionists. Thus, in the middle of August, 1958, we had a sound basis for predicting the political response of Milwaukee labor in the fall elections. What took many by surprise—in the totality and direction of the vote—was expected so far as our research was concerned. That is because our data highlighted the profound ties of class solidarity which politically bind industrial unionists. Our material is drawn from a 1955–1958 study of industrial union stewards in the Milwaukee labor area.

At this point a legitimate question can be raised as to whether industrial workers share a body of opinion with their union stewards. This is a complicated issue, the resolution of which depends primarily on an understanding of the elements of strain inherent in the steward role. . . .

The shop steward is the rank-and-file union representative in the department or division of the industrial plant. Legally speaking, he is not regarded as part of union officialdom. Usually he is elected by the workers he represents, although stewards are often appointed or designated by the local union president. In all plants, regardless of productive focus, the main function of the steward revolves about the grievance procedure. The steward intervenes on the first level between the workers and the employer. He is the spokesman for the union in the department and represents the demands of the workers particularly as they relate to contract violations by management agents.

Thus, the steward constitutes the closest union link to the rank-and-file worker. He is often referred to as the "key man in the union movement." Yet, as the grass roots leader of the people in the plant, *the steward can never forget that he, too, is a worker. He can never escape his men. Their judgments are constantly upon him.* A steward can be tried on like a pair of shoes and if he pinches, or slides or squeaks, he will either be quickly discarded or go through a long breaking-in process. But eventually he comes to fit the department—its interest and character. So the steward, more than any other union leader, reflects the concerns of the people in the shop.

In short, the industrial union steward is a rank-and-file leader in shop society. Sensitive to the reactions of his fellow plant workers, he also stands out as a "significant other" who shapes and guides the conduct of departmental membership. In this respect, the steward not only internalizes the attitudes of rank-and-file workers, but he also functions as an opinion-maker in his own right. There is no other level of union leadership which commands such an intimate, personal relationship with the industrial worker. Hence, if there is anyone in the union structure who is aware of the feelings, concerns and aspirations of the industrial workers, it must surely be the union steward. And if there is any one person in union leadership who can influence the thinking of organized industrial laborers on a work-a-day basis, it is most certainly the steward. Consequently, an analysis of shop steward attitudes may prove to be extremely revealing in any assessment of working-class ideology.

In the Milwaukee study, two basic research techniques were employed. Participant-observation as a worker in diverse industrial settings are used to gain first-hand knowledge of factory culture and the shop steward role. In addition, a "group discussion" interview technique was used, which involved union stewards in 17 separate group sessions. Held during the spring and summer of 1958, these discussion groups were drawn from the most significant industrial union organizations in the Milwaukee community. A sound-recorded fictional report served to evoke unstructured, spontaneous discussion of several interrelated social themes. The material to follow is primarily based on tape-recorded discussion responses to the themes on political action, the two-party system and the development of a labor party.

The participation of organized labor in the political life of the country is no longer a heated question for rank-and-file elements to decide. Most stewards recognized the necessity for union political action. They argued that labor must be politically active in order to be alive. Contrary to C. Wright Mills' pessimistic comments about ordinary workers, which apparently give support to Perlman's position, stewards did not sharply dichotomize economics and politics as distinct and separate areas of social life. They saw the impact of legislative action on specific shop issues and maintained that "there has to be the connection between union and politics."

At the Region 9 AIW group session, a 44 year old woman timekeeper concluded:

"I think definitely unions have to participate. Because, for instance, in a state where there is the possibility of a 'right-to-work' law, then the very life of the union depends on political action. You can't get away from it. And when the two become so closely related and one dependent upon the other for life, you can't have the one without taking part in the other. The union must participate."

On the one hand, stewards viewed political action as the only means by which organized labor can overcome the political supremacy of "Big Business." On the other hand, political action was primarily considered a weapon of defense against anti-labor, pro-monopoly forces. At the UAW 248 session, a 50 year old maintenance machinist urged that until the American labor movement increased its activity in local and national politics, "we will never be able to stop the *money changers*, call them anything you want, from doing just what they are doing in this country now."

Or, listen to the remarks of the 49 year old Harvester 22631 press operator who said:

"You know the only way we'll ever beat Big Business is politically. We'll never beat them economically. It's as simple as that. You're bucking what you call the stockholders. He doesn't care. He's somewhere in California, sitting on the beach of some kind, he's not interested in what's going on down here at the Milwaukee works. He's the guy that's back of the backbone, actually, of Big Business, the guy that's got the money in there controlling the stocks. Now, the common man, the guy that works for a living, who actually puts his ten fingers, and ten toes on the job, there are a hell of a lot more of us than those guys clipping coupons. And we can beat them politically. But economically, it's going to be the hardest job in the world."

In sum, stewards advocated the deep immersion of trade unionism into the stream of political action; perceived that the economic enemies of working people can only be defeated in the arena of politics; and looked to politics as the only way for labor to protect the shop interests of working folk.

In the light of this political commitment, we must reinterpret the old Gomperist slogan, "Reward your friends and punish your enemies." Stewards approach the issue of political endorsement from a class point of view. They are concerned about what the candidate "will do for the working-man." Their focus is not on the job, plant or union per se: rather, they believe candidates should be supported only if they are for the interests of *laboring people as a whole.* Thus a 42 year old IUE 1131 set-up man declared:

"That's what I think the whole thing is: how he votes for the workingman and the poorer class of people. If a guy is in there and he is for the big shot all the time, why he hasn't got much of a chance with the working class of people."

And a 28 year old UAW 75 assembler admitted:

"Well, in talking to the men in my department about voting, I tell them 'I don't care who you go out and vote for but make sure who you vote for is going to be for the workingman and not for the companies.' That's the idea I have."

This class outlook is central to an understanding of the steward's image of the two-party system.

In the most general sense, the majority of stewards considered the Republican Party the official political organ of Big Business, whereas the Democratic Party was viewed as the party of the working class. Stewards openly acknowledged their political allegiance to the Democratic Party because (rightly or wrongly) they believed it to be the party of their class. In the words of the 24 year old UAW 248 machinist, "Your Democratic Party in the United States is more or less your workers' party." At the District 1-Machinists discussion session, a 37 year old assembler summed up the group sentiment when he declared:

"I don't agree with the speaker on why we don't bring a third party in the United States. I think two parties is good enough. (laughter) The Democratic Party has always been the Labor Party . . . the unions should stick with the Democrats."

In sum, the *dominant view* among union stewards is four-pronged: the political home of the organized labor movement belongs in the Democratic Party; the difference in class basis and focus between the two parties is markedly apparent in the Wisconsin area; the labor movement has no other political alternative but to wage all-out support for the Democratic Party (which has consistently worked in the interests of the poorer class of people); and most industrial workers view the two-party system in this way.

However, a strong segment of steward opinion does not perceive the two major parties to be divided along class lines. This *minor but influential* point of view among stewards suggests the following theme:

"There is no real difference between the two parties, possibly, in name only. Therefore, neither party has a right to claim the mantle of liberalism toward the working class. Both parties are beholden to the propertied classes. In fact, the southern based anti-labor, conservative forces in the Democratic Party are to be considered as much an enemy of labor as the corporation-supported Republican administration."

Thus, a 34 year old UAW 438 delegate to the County Council remarked, "I'm a Democrat not by choice, but by necessity." And then he continued:

"Frankly speaking, the Democrats today are not the home for labor, they are the lesser of two evils. If anyone believes that a Democrat is to my mind of thinking, my way of thinking . . . he's crazy. If you don't think so, just go south of that Mason and Dixon line. Where you know what the economic structure and what the political structure . . . down there . . . you know what it can really be down there. So I don't buy their political party—because as far as I'm concerned they are a party of prostitution because they have to accept that kind of approach . . . [which is] contrary to all my union ideals."

The answer to the present political dilemma for these stewards is to hope for a more rational realignment of class interests within the framework of the two-party system. To state it briefly, these stewards were convinced that the two-party system as it is now constituted merely allows the working class to choose the lesser of two evils. They agreed that the country needs a fundamental political realignment so that the two-party system would, in fact, reflect basic class divisions in society. Until this change comes about, workers should have available political protest alternatives. Otherwise, they will not be stimulated to make the choice between the lesser of two evils. This outlook is significant not only because it is apparently held at some of the higher reaches of union leadership, but also because of the political consequences of the 1958 labor electoral victory.

Very few stewards openly advocated the need for an independent labor party. Of those who did, it is likely that many of these retain organizational connection with "splinter" political sects. Nevertheless, among these stewards were also some who independently stressed the desire for an alternative to the two-party system. These labor spokesmen emphasized the need for political alternatives in the form of a party "strictly representing labor," especially on the national level. They also claimed that such a party would come into being, though the "time is not ripe now," at the moment of working class disillusionment with the Democratic Party and of independent political initiative by top labor leadership. They asserted that after organized labor tries "the Democrats one more time and the Democrats don't produce . . . labor will find out she will have to do what labor has done [elsewhere]."

A 38 year old Region 9 AIW machinist called attention to the fact that he is a "card carrying Democrat." Nevertheless, he added:

"But I feel this, if the Democratic Party fails to do good for the rest of the land and do for the majority of the people, and the Republican Party fails, and it has up to now, that I think if they would put up a Farmer-Labor bloc and have a Farmer-Labor party. . . . And if the farmers ever got together with labor people, instead of going apart from them, then we could actually have a party which would actually rule the land. We could have a third party! In other words, if the Democrats can't do for us what we need, or the Republicans, and they haven't until now, maybe we will have to have a third party, regardless of the cost."

At the County Council group discussion, a 37 year old communications worker attacked labor leadership for its unqualified support of the Democratic Party. This PBX installer continued on to say that the political answer for working people "is the labor party," but he did not think that "we'll get it too soon." Then he explained the dilemma which faces advocates of a labor party and placed the primary responsibility on the shoulders of labor leadership:

"The simple reason is that the higher echelons of labor say that there is no agitation from the fields . . . from the working people. And the working people say, we're not going to stick our necks out with you plugging all these Democrats out there. . . . So there it's going to stand. And, perhaps things will have to get a lot worse until somebody grabs the bull by the horns and gives a little encouragement. I think that's all it would take . . . is a little encouragement on the behalf of certain people and certainly—my encouragement is next to nothing. I can think about it, and talk about it personally to different people . . . but as far as convincing anybody, I don't think I am capable. . . . I don't think they would take my word against . . . as . . . well . . . as to get the blessings, they get from the so-called higher ups in the labor movement."

The fact remains, however, that most stewards did not view the formation of an independent labor party as the road to political salvation. Arguments against a third party ranged from belief that the new party would begin to engulf the trade unions to fear that the development of a mass labor party in the U.S. might lead to political totalitarianism. At the Brewery 9 group discussion, a 47 year old brewhouse worker concretized the logic of this fear when he exclaimed:

"There shouldn't be a . . . union party only. Having Republicans and Democrats keeps the level so long as one don't go ahead and take advantage of the other. Say now, that the Democrats would be entirely union and that they had power. They would snow the capitalists, you know, and it would ruin the capitalist system. That would be the next thing, it would lead to dictatorship or communism."

It is quite evident that the "Tom, Dick and Harry" of the labor movement do not project identical feelings and attitudes. It is certainly a fallacy to believe that American unionists *are merely* informed by a "job-conscious" outlook. Throughout the discussion, industrial union stewards also evinced a class-conscious orientation. Their image of the political and economic structure of society is based upon the recognition of class divisions and differences. Union stewards see themselves not only as "job-minded" workers, but also as part of a total working class group. Therefore, they are sensitively attuned to social and economic issues which confront working people as a whole. They demonstrate, in Franklin H. Gidding's phrase, a "consciousness of kind" in their response to social questions of the day. We submit that this "consciousness of kind" goes beyond the concern for "job control" and extends to broadly defined class interests. Therefore, we seriously question the traditional image of American labor ideology as "job-conscious." We believe that the empirical evidence no longer justifies a rigid allegiance to Perlman's theoretical defense of Gomperism as the "true" ideology of American workers. We maintain that industrial unionists *think* in working class terms and *act* politically according to what *they perceive to be* in the interests of industrial laboring people. That is why we also suggest that their outlook on politics is principled rather than opportunistic.

As one major facet of working class mentality, we can refer to these class-based political attitudes of rank-and-file union leaders. No matter whether union stewards are committed to the Democratic Party, whether they seek a "rational" realignment of the two-party structure, or whether they urge the formation of an independent labor party, the political *rationale* is strikingly similar. The core thought expresses a profound identification with perceived class interests. It is a matter of some importance to note that the attitudes which these stewards expressed in the spring and summer of 1958 were dramatically acted upon in the ensuing fall elections.

An awareness of this class-orientation is particularly important if we are to properly assess the prevailing political mood of industrial workers. It is apparent that the labor-supported Democratic electoral victory in the 1958 congressional elections has not produced the desired results. Congressional failure to enact liberal domestic legislation and congressional passage of an allegedly anti-labor bill by overwhelming two-party consent are bitter pills to swallow. Judging from the recent AFL–CIO and UAW conventions, rank-and-file delegates were disillusioned, embittered and openly cynical about the role of the Democratic Party as a "party for the working people." A striking illustration of this indignant mood may be found in the remarks of Cleveland delegate Granakis (Local Union 1250), who rose in opposition to the UAW administration line. He said, in part:

"Personally,I find no difference at all between the Democratic and the Republican Party. They are both out to give the worker the deal all right, but not the kind we want. They both stink. I think that we should say to both parties, 'You don't own us. You don't pigeonhole us. We are independent and we are looking for people in our own ranks who can represent us properly, honestly, with the type of integrity that we feel a guy should have.' And that's for me."

Workers in the shop do not believe in an opportunistic "collective bargaining" approach to political action. They are moved to support a party which clearly and unequivocally works for the interest of laboring people. They believe that, in specific local situations, the Democratic Party does constitute the organizational means to achieve their political tasks. However, they evince strong disgust against the same party on the national scene for what they consider a betrayal of labor support. Thus, political "apathy" among industrial unionists, when it results from the lack of a meaningful political choice, may be the *considered class response* of workers who believe they are being misled. It apparently signifies that many class-conscious workers refuse to remain a party to "collective bargaining" in politics. Although an act of political withdrawal may not be wise, it can hardly be reduced to mere apathy or lack of class concern.

3

Cesar Chavez
THE ORGANIZER'S TALE

What Swados and Peck found to be true of unionized workers was even truer of the unorganized majority of American working people, many of them doubly exploited because of race and sex. A symbol of this forgotten majority was an organizer of the Latin farm workers of the American West, Cesar Chavez (1928–).

It really started for me 16 years ago in San Jose, California, when I was working on an apricot farm. We figured he was just another social worker doing a study of farm conditions, and I kept refusing to meet with him. But he was persistent. Finally, I got together some of the rough element in San Jose. We were going to have a little reception for him to teach the *gringo* a little bit of how we felt. There were about 30 of us in the house, young guys mostly. I was supposed to give them a signal—change my cigarette from my right hand to my left, and then we were going to give him a lot of hell. But he started talking and the more he talked, the more wide-eyed I became and the less inclined I was to give the signal. A couple of guys who were pretty drunk at the time still wanted to give the *gringo* the business, but we got rid of them. This fellow was making a lot of sense, and I wanted to hear what he had to say.

His name was Fred Ross, and he was an organizer for the Community Service Organization (CSO) which was working with Mexican-Americans in the cities. I became immediately really involved. Before long I was heading a voter registration drive. All the time I was observing the things Fred did, secretly, because I wanted to learn how to organize, to see how it was done. I was impressed with his patience and understanding of people. I thought this was a tool, one of the greatest things he had.

SOURCE. *Ramparts* Magazine, July 1966. Reprinted with permission.

It was pretty rough for me at first. I was changing and had to take a lot of ridicule from the kids my age, the rough characters I worked with in the fields. They would say, "Hey, big shot. Now that you're a *politico*, why are you working here for 65 cents an hour?" I might add that our neighborhood had the highest percentage of San Quentin graduates. It was a game among the *pachucos* in the sense that we defended ourselves from outsiders, although inside the neighborhood there was not a lot of fighting.

After six months of working every night in San Jose, Fred assigned me to take over the CSO chapter in Decoto. It was a tough spot to fill. I would suggest something, and people would say, "No, let's wait till Fred gets back," or "Fred wouldn't do it that way." This is pretty much a pattern with people, I discovered, whether I was put in Fred's position, or later, when someone else was put in my position. After the Decoto assignment I was sent to start a new chapter in Oakland. Before I left, Fred came to a place in San Jose called the Hole-in-the-Wall and we talked for half an hour over coffee. He was in a rush to leave, but I wanted to keep him talking; I was that scared of my assignment.

There were hard times in Oakland. First of all, it was a big city and I'd get lost every time I went anywhere. Then I arranged a series of house meetings. I would get to the meeting early and drive back and forth past the house, too nervous to go in and face the people. Finally I would force myself to go inside and sit in a corner. I was quite thin then, and young, and most of the people were middle-aged. Someone would say, "Where's the organizer?" And I would pipe up, "Here I am." Then they would say in Spanish—these were very poor people and we hardly spoke anything but Spanish—"Ha! This *kid*?" Most of them said they were interested, but the hardest part was to get them to start pushing themselves, on their own initiative.

The idea was to set up a meeting and then get each attending person to call his own house meeting, inviting new people—a sort of chain letter effect. After a house meeting I would lie awake going over the whole thing, playing the tape back, trying to see why people laughed at one point, or why they were for one thing and against another. I was also learning to read and write, those late evenings. I had left school in the 7th grade after attending 67 different schools, and my reading wasn't the best.

At our first organizing meeting we had 368 people: I'll never forget it because it was very important to me. You eat your heart out; the meeting is called for 7 o'clock and you start to worry about 4. You wait. Will they show up? Then the first one arrives. By 7 there are only

20 people, you have everything in order, you have to look calm. But little by little they filter in and at a certain point you know it will be a success.

After four months in Oakland, I was transferred. The chapter was beginning to move on its own, so Fred assigned me to organize the San Joaquin Valley. Over the months I developed what I used to call schemes or tricks—now I call them techniques—of making initial contacts. The main thing in convincing someone is to spend time with him. It doesn't matter if he can read, write or even speak well. What is important is that he is a man and second, that he has shown some initial interest. One good way to develop leadership is to take a man with you in your car. And it works a lot better if you're doing the driving; that way you are in charge. You drive, he sits there, and you talk. These little things were very important to me; I was caught in a big game by then, figuring out what makes people work. I found that if you work hard enough you can usually shake people into working too, those who are concerned. You work harder and they work harder still, up to a point and then they pass you. Then, of course, they're on their own.

I also learned to keep away from the established groups and so-called leaders, and to guard against philosophizing. Working with low-income people is very different from working with the professionals, who like to sit around talking about how to play politics. When you're trying to recruit a farmworker, you have to paint a little picture, and then you have to color the picture in. We found out that the harder a guy is to convince, the better leader or member he becomes. When you exert yourself to convince him, you have his confidence and he has good motivation. A lot of people who say OK right away wind up hanging around the office, taking up the workers' time.

During the McCarthy era in one Valley town, I was subjected to a lot of redbaiting. We had been recruiting people for citizenship classes at the high school when we got into a quarrel with the naturalization examiner. He was rejecting people on the grounds that they were just parroting what they learned in citizenship class. One day we had a meeting about it in Fresno, and I took along some of the leaders of our local chapter. Some redbaiting official gave us a hard time, and the people got scared and took his side. They did it because it seemed easy at the moment, even though they knew that sticking with me was the right thing to do. It was disgusting. When we left the building they walked by themselves ahead of me as if I had some kind of communicable disease. I had been working with these people for three months and I was very sad to see that. It taught me a great lesson.

That night I learned that the chapter officers were holding a meeting to review my letters and printed materials to see if I really was a Communist. So I drove out there and walked right in on their meeting. I said, "I hear you've been discussing me, and I thought it would be nice if I was here to defend myself. Not that it matters that much to you or even to me, because as far as I'm concerned you are a bunch of cowards." At that they began to apologize. "Let's forget it," they said. "You're a nice guy." But I didn't want apologies. I wanted a full discussion. I told them I didn't give a damn, but that they had to learn to distinguish fact from what appeared to be a fact because of fear. I kept them there till two in the morning. Some of the women cried. I don't know if they investigated me any further, but I stayed on another few months and things worked out.

This was not an isolated case. Often when we'd leave people to themselves they would get frightened and draw back into their shells where they had been all the years. And I learned quickly that there is no real appreciation. Whatever you do, and no matter what reasons you may give to others, you do it because you want to see it done, or maybe because you want power. And there shouldn't be any appreciation, understandably. I know good organizers who were destroyed, washed out, because they expected people to appreciate what they'd done. Anyone who comes in with the idea that farmworkers are free of sin and that the growers are all bastards, either has never dealt with the situation or is an idealist of the first order. Things don't work that way.

For more than 10 years I worked for the CSO. As the organization grew, we found ourselves meeting in fancier and fancier motels and holding expensive conventions. Doctors, lawyers and politicians began joining. They would get elected to some office in the organization and then, for all practical purposes, leave. Intent on using the CSO for their own prestige purposes, these "leaders," many of them, lacked the urgency we had to have. When I became general director I began to press for a program to organize farmworkers into a union, an idea most of the leadership opposed. So I started a revolt within the CSO. I refused to sit at the head table at meetings, refused to wear a suit and tie, and finally I even refused to shave and cut my hair. It used to embarrass some of the professionals. At every meeting I got up and gave my standard speech: we shouldn't meet in fancy motels, we were getting away from the people, farmworkers had to be organized. But nothing happened. In March of '62 I resigned and came to Delano to begin organizing the Valley on my own.

By hand I drew a map of all the towns between Arvin and

Stockton—86 of them, including farming camps—and decided to hit them all to get a small nucleus of people working in each. For six months I traveled around, planting an idea. We had a simple questionnaire, a little card with space for name, address and how much the worker thought he ought to be paid. My wife, Helen, mimeographed them, and we took our kids for two or three day jaunts to these towns, distributing the cards door-to-door and to camps and groceries.

Some 80,000 cards were sent back from eight Valley counties. I got a lot of contacts that way, but I was shocked at the wages the people were asking. The growers were paying $1 and $1.15, and maybe 95 per cent of the people thought they shld be getting only $1.25. Sometimes people scribbled messages on the cards: "I hope to God we win" or "Do you think we can win?" or "I'd like to know more." So I separated the cards with the pencilled notes, got in my car and went to those people.

We didn't have any money at all in those days, none for gas and hardly any for food. So I went to people and started asking for food. It turned out to be about the best thing I could have done, although at first it's hard on your pride. Some of our best members came in that way. If people give you their food, they'll give you their hearts. Several months and many meetings later we had a working organization, and this time the leaders were the people.

None of the farmworkers had collective bargaining contracts, and I thought it would take ten years before we got that first contract. I wanted desperately to get some color into the movement, to give people something they could identify with, like a flag. I was reading some books about how various leaders discovered what colors contrasted and stood out the best. The Egyptians had found that a red field with a white circle and a black emblem in the center crashed into your eyes like nothing else. I wanted to use the Aztec eagle in the center, as on the Mexican flag. So I told my cousin Manuel, "Draw an Aztec eagle." Manuel had a little trouble with it, so we modified the eagle to make it easier for people to draw.

The first big meeting of what we decided to call the National Farm Workers Association was held in September 1962, at Fresno, with 287 people. We had our huge red flag on the wall, with paper tacked over it. When the time came, Manuel pulled a cord ripping the paper off the flag and all of a sudden it hit the people. Some of them wondered if it was a Communist flag, and I said it probably looked more like a neo-Nazi emblem than anything else. But they wanted an explanation, so Manuel got up and said, "When that damn eagle flies—that's when the farmworkers' problems are going to be solved."

One of the first things I decided was that outside money wasn't going to organize people, at least not in the beginning. I even turned down a grant from a private group—$50,000 to go directly to organize farmworkers—for just this reason. Even when there are no strings attached, you are still compromised because you feel you have to produce immediate results. This is bad, because it takes a long time to build a movement, and your organization suffers if you get too far ahead of the people it belongs to. We set the dues at $42 a year per family, really a meaningful dues, but of the 212 we got to pay, only 12 remained by June of '63. We were discouraged at that, but not enough to make us quit.

Money was always a problem. Once we were facing a $180 gas bill on a credit card I'd got a long time ago and was about to lose. And we *had* to keep that credit card. One day my wife and I were picking cotton, pulling bolls, to make a little money to live on. Helen said to me, "Do you put all this in the bag, or just the cotton?" I thought she was kidding and told her to throw the whole boll in so that she had nothing but a sack of bolls at the weighing. The man said, "Whose sack is this?" I said, well, my wife's, and he told us we were fired. "Look at all that crap you brought in," he said. Helen and I started laughing. We were going anyway. We took the $4 we had earned and spent it at a grocery store where they were giving away a $100 prize. Each time you shopped they'd give you one of the letters of M-O-N-E-Y or a flag: you had to have M-O-N-E-Y plus the flag to win. Helen had already collected the letters and just needed the flag. Anyway, they gave her the ticket. She screamed, "A flag? I don't believe it," ran in and got the $100. She said, "Now we're going to eat steak." But I said no, we're going to pay the gas bill. I don't know if she cried, but I think she did.

It was rough in those early years. Helen was having babies and I was not there when she was at the hospital. But if you haven't got your wife behind you, you can't do many things. There's got to be peace at home. So I did, I think, a fairly good job of organizing her. When we were kids, she lived in Delano and I came to town as a migrant. Once on a date we had a bad experience about segregation at a movie theater, and I put up a fight. We were together then, and still are. I think I'm more of a pacifist than she is. Her father, Fabela, was a colonel with Pancho Villa in the Mexican Revolution. Sometimes she gets angry and tells me, "These scabs—you should deal with them sternly," and I kid her, "It must be too much of that Fabela blood in you."

The movement really caught on in '64. By August we had a thousand members. We'd had a beautiful 90-day drive in Corcoran, where they had the Battle of the Corcoran Farm Camp 30 years ago, and by November we had assets of $25,000 in our credit union, which helped to stabilize the membership. I had gone without pay the whole of 1963. The next year the members voted me a $40 a week salary, after Helen had to quit working in the fields to manage the credit union.

Our first strike was in May of '65, a small one but it prepared us for the big one. A farmworker from McFarland named Epifanio Camacho came to see me. He said he was sick and tired of how people working the roses were being treated, and he was willing to "go the limit." I assigned Manuel and Gilbert Padilla to hold meetings at Camacho's house. The people wanted union recognition, but the real issue, as in most cases when you begin, was wages. They were promised $9 a thousand, but they were actually getting $6.50 and $7 for grafting roses. Most of them signed cards giving us the right to bargain for them. We chose the biggest company, with about 85 employees, not counting the irrigators and supervisors, and we held a series of meetings to prepare the strike and call the vote. There would be no picket line; everyone pledged on their honor not to break the strike.

Early on the first morning of the strike, we sent out 10 cars to check the people's homes. We found lights in five or six homes and knocked on the doors. The men were getting up and we'd say, "Where are you going?" They would dodge, "Oh, uh . . . I was just getting up, you know." We'd say, "Well, you're not going to work, are you?" And they'd say no. Dolores Huerta, who was driving the green panel truck, saw a light in one house where four rose-workers lived. They told her they were going to work, even after she reminded them of their pledge. So she moved the truck so it blocked their driveway, turned off the key, put it in her purse and sat there alone.

That morning the company foreman was madder than hell and refused to talk to us. None of the grafters had shown up for work. At 10:30 we started to go to the company office, but it occurred to us that maybe a woman would have a better chance. So Dolores knocked on the office door, saying, "I'm Dolores Huerta from the National Farm Workers Association." "Get out!" the man said, "you Communist. Get out!" I guess they were expecting us, because as Dolores stood arguing with him the cops came and told her to leave. She left.

For two days the fields were idle. On Wednesday they recruited a group of Filipinos from out of town who knew nothing of the strike, maybe 35 of them. They drove through escorted by three sheriff's patrol cars, one in front, one in the middle and one at the rear with a dog. We didn't have a picket line, but we parked across the street and just watched them go through, not saying a word. All but seven stopped working after half an hour, and the rest had quit by mid-afternoon.

The company made an offer the evening of the fourth day, a package deal that amounted to a 120 per cent wage increase, but no contract. We wanted to hold out for a contract and more benefits, but a majority of the roseworkers wanted to accept the offer and go back. We are a democratic union so we had to support what they wanted to do. They had a meeting and voted to settle. Then we had a problem with a few militants who wanted to hold out. We had to convince them to go back to work, as a united front, because otherwise they would be canned. So we worked—Tony Orendain and I, Dolores and Gilbert, Jim Drake and all the organizers—knocking on doors till two in the morning, telling people, "You have to go back or you'll lose your job." And they did. They worked.

Our second strike, and our last before the big one at Delano, was in the grapes at Martin's Ranch last summer. The people were getting a raw deal there, being pushed around pretty badly. Gilbert went out to the field, climbed on top of a car and took a strike vote. They voted unanimously to go out. Right away they started bringing in strike-breakers, so we launched a tough attack on the labor contractors, distributed leaflets portraying them as really low characters. We attacked one—Luis Campos—so badly that he just gave up the job, and he took 27 of his men out with him. All he asked was that we distribute another leaflet reinstating him in the community. And we did. What was unusual was that the grower would talk to us. The grower kept saying, "I can't pay. I just haven't got the money." I guess he must have found the money somewhere, because we were asking $1.40 and we got it.

We had just finished the Martin strike when the Agricultural Workers Organizing Committee (AFL-CIO) started a strike against the grape growers, DiGiorgio, Schenley liquors and small growers, asking $1.40 an hour and 25 cents a box. There was a lot of pressure from our members for us to join the strike, but we had some misgivings. We didn't feel ready for a big strike like this one, one that was sure to last a long time. Having no money—just $87 in the strike fund—meant we'd have to depend on God knows who.

Eight days after the strike started—it takes time to get 1,200 people together from all over the Valley—we held a meeting in Delano and voted to go out. I asked the membership to release us from the pledge not to accept outside money, because we'd need it now, a lot of it. The help came. It started because of the close, and I would say even beautiful relationship that we've had with the Migrant Ministry for some years. They were the first to come to our rescue, financially and in every other way, and they spread the word to other benefactors.

We had planned, before, to start a labor school in November. It never happened, but we have the best labor school we could ever have, in the strike. The strike is only a temporary condition, however. We have over 3,000 members spread out over a wide area, and we have to service them when they have problems. We get letters from New Mexico, Colorado, Texas, California, from farmworkers saying, "We're getting together and we need an organizer." It kills you when you haven't got the personnel and resources. You feel badly about not sending an organizer because you look back and remember all the difficulty you had in getting two or three people together, and here *they're* together. Of course, we're training organizers, many of them younger than I was when I started in CSO. They can work 20 hours a day, sleep four and be ready to hit it again; when you get to be 39 it's a different story.

The people who took part in the strike and the march have something more than their material interest going for them. If it were only material, they wouldn't have stayed on the strike long enough to win. It is difficult to explain. But it flows out in the ordinary things they say. For instance, some of the younger guys are saying, "Where do you think's going to be the next strike?" I say, "Well, we have to win in Delano." They say, "We'll win, but where do we go next?" I say, "Maybe most of us will be working in the fields." They say, "No, I don't want to go and work in the fields. I want to organize. There are a lot of people that need our help." So I say, "You're going to be pretty poor then, because when you strike you don't have much money." They say they don't care about that.

And others are saying, "I have friends who are working in Texas. If we could only help them." It is bigger, certainly, than just a strike And if this spirit grows within the farm labor movement, one day we can use the force that we have to help correct a lot of things that are wrong in this society. But that is for the future. Before you can run, you have to learn to walk.

There are vivid memories from my childhood—what we had to go through because of low wages and the conditions, basically because there was no union. I suppose if I wanted to be fair I could say that I'm trying to settle a personal score. I could dramatize it by saying that I want to bring social justice to farmworkers. But the truth is that I went through a lot of hell, and a lot of people did. If we can even the score a little for the workers then we are doing something. Besides, I don't know any other work I like to do better than this. I really don't, you know.

4

Stanley Weir

RANK-AND-FILE LABOR REBELLIONS BREAK INTO THE OPEN: THE END OF AN ERA

Among workers as among students, discontent lay just beneath the surface. When economic circumstances changed because of the escalation of the Vietnam war and the revival of competition between the United States and other capitalist economies, rank-and-file movements emerged. These are described by Stanley Weir in an article first published in 1967, before most student radicals had begun to think again about working people as a force for change. Weir, himself for twenty years a rank-and-file organizer of sailors, auto workers, and longshoremen, is now a professor of labor relations.

I

The rank-and-file union revolts that have been developing in the industrial workplaces since the early 1950s are now plainly visible. Like many of their compatriots, American workers are faced with paces, methods and conditions of work that are increasingly intolerable. Their union leaders are not sensitive to these conditions. In thousands of industrial establishments across the nation, workers have developed informal underground unions. The basic units of organization are groups composed of several workers, each of whose members work in the same plant-area and are thus able to communicate with one another and form a social entity. Led by natural on-the-job leaders, they conduct daily guerrilla skirmishes with their employers and often against their official union representatives as well. These groups are the power base for the insurgencies from below that in the last three years have ended or threatened official careers of long standing.

During the same period, farm laborers, teachers, professionals, white collar, service and civil service workers, who were not reached by labor's revolt of the 1930s, have demonstrated an adamant desire to organize themselves into unions. For the first time in over three decades the United States faces a period in which the struggles of the unionized section of the population will have a direct and visible effect on the future of the entire population. Because the press coverage of the revolts has been superficial and because they have been ignored by the liberal and a majority of radical publications, it is necessary that the major revolts be examined in some detail.

WIDESPREAD REVOLT BEGINS IN AUTO

The General Motors Corporation employs as many workers as all other auto manufacturers combined. In 1955, United Automobile Workers' president, Walter Reuther, signed a contract with GM which did not check the speedup or speed the settlement of local shop grievances. Over 70 percent of GM workers went on strike immediately after Reuther announced the terms of his agreement. A larger percentage "wildcatted" after the signing of the 1958 contract because Reuther had again refused to do anything to combat the speedup. For the same reason, the auto workers walked off their jobs again in 1961. The strike closed every GM and a number of large Ford plants.

The UAW ranks' ability to conduct a nation-wide wildcat strike is made possible by a democratic practice that has been maintained by GM workers since the thirties. Every GM local sends elected delegates to Detroit to sit in council during national contract negotiations. They instruct their negotiators and confer with them as the bargaining progresses. Ideally the council and negotiators arrive at an agreement on the package that the latter have been able to obtain from the employer and both the rank-and-file delegates and leaders recommend ratification by the ranks at the local union level. In 1961, when the council unanimously recommended rejection and strike, Reuther notified the press that the strike was official, that he was leading it and that it would continue until all grievances concerning working conditions had been settled in separate local supplemental agreements rather than in the national contract. He thus maintained control. The ranks were outmaneuvered and angered.

Just prior to the negotiation of the 1964 contract, a development took place in the UAW that is unique in American labor history. Several large Detroit locals initiated a bumper sticker campaign. In all cities across the country where UAW plants are located the bumpers of auto workers' cars pushed the slogan: "Humanize Working Conditions." Lacking the support of their official leaders, they were attempting to inform the public of the nature of the struggle they were about to conduct and that its primary goal would be to improve the condition of factory life rather than their wages.

Their attempt to bypass Reuther failed. Contrary to established practice, he opened negotiations with Chrysler, the smallest of the Big Three auto makers. He imposed the pattern of this contract on the Ford workers and announced that the Chrysler-Ford agreements would be the pattern for the GM contract. The dialogue of the GM workers with their president was brief. They struck every GM plant for five weeks and were joined by thousands of Ford workers. They returned to work under a national contract no better than those signed with Ford and Chrysler. Their strike won the settlement of a backlog of local grievances; created pride in the knowledge that it was primarily and publicly directed against Reuther's maneuver; and made possible the further development of rank-and-file leaders. They demonstrated that they would not give ground in their efforts to make their national contract a weapon against the speedup and to rid themselves of a grievance procedure that allows the settlement of individual grievances to take up to two years.

Aware that the ranks would be continuing their fight and seeking revenge at the UAW's September 1966 convention in Long Beach, California, Reuther sought issues that could be used to divert their wrath. In early 1965 the ballot count in the election between incumbent International Union of Electrical Workers (IUE) President James B. Carey and his challenger Paul Jennings was in doubt. Reuther issued a statement to the press announcing his offer to merge the IUE with the UAW. The merger might have salvaged Carey's reputation and employment in the labor movement. It could also have been used as a major agenda item necessitating extended discussion at the UAW convention, but Carey rigidly turned down the offer claiming that he had learned of Reuther's offer only hours before it was made public.

The Long Beach UAW convention in May of last year was the first labor convention experience for over 60 percent of the delegates. Many of the faces that had become familiar to Reuther during previous conventions were absent. None of the delegates got a chance to discuss what was the main issue of the ranks who elected them—the demands they want to make and win in the negotiations for the 1967 contract; that point on the agenda was postponed to a special conference in April 1967. Reuther won more than a breathing spell at Long Beach. In the months preceding the convention the rebellion in the UAW's 250,000 man Skilled Trades Department had reached crisis proportions. Their wages had fallen behind those of craft union members doing comparable work in other industries. They threatened to disaffiliate and join the rival International Society of Skilled Trades (independent). The convention amended the UAW constitution to give the Skilled Trades Department, containing less than 20 percent of the UAW's members, veto power over all national contracts. It is likely that they will get a substantial wage increase in the 1967 contract. They do not work under the same conditions as the semi-skilled who buck the assembly lines and who are the majority and now second class citizenry of the UAW. Reuther has obtained an aristocratic power base and laid the foundation for another and more violent rupture in the UAW.

For more than a decade it has been absolutely clear that the UAW ranks demand top priority be given to the fight to improve working conditions. Their efforts to make Reuther lead this fight have been herculean. At this late date it is almost paradoxical that he remains rigid in his refusal to make that fight. And so he must try to go into the April conference equipped with a diversionary tactic of gigantic proportions—based on more than a transparent maneuver that will only further enrage his ranks. His recent resignation as first vice president of the AFL-CIO and his open split with that body's president, George Meany, has, among other things, armed him with such a diversion. The question of total withdrawal from the AFL-CIO is the first point on the agenda of the April conference which is now scheduled to last only three days.

Leaflets circulated by UAW members in Detroit auto plants last January and prior to the split, ridiculed Reuther's inability to stand up to Meany. They were picked up by the national press and significantly hurt Reuther's prestige. Evidence mounts to indicate that Reuther was finally driven to sever his distasteful relationship with Meany for two principal reasons: (1) the demands of the UAW's revolt and internal struggle, and (2) the widespread revolts throughout the labor movement, particularly in the unions that form Reuther's domain in the AFL-CIO (Industrial Union Department). The latter may include a third principal factor. The revolts are numerous enough to have given Reuther the vision that the revolts in the 1930s gave to John L. Lewis—the formation of a powerful new labor confederation through the organizational centralization of the unions that are in rebellion—a confederation that could now include white collar, professional, service and farm workers.

The wildcat strike of UAW-GM Local 527 in Mansfield, Ohio, in February, revealed the depth of the liberal stance Reuther has taken in his fight with Meany. The total walkout at Mansfield occurred because two workers were fired for refusing to make dies and tools ready for shipment to another plant in Pontiac, Michigan. GM has long followed a policy of transferring work out of plants where workers have established better working conditions, or are conducting a struggle to improve them, to other plants with less militant work forces. The Mansfield workers had long observed this practice in silence. To be forced to participate in the transferral and their own defeat was the final indignity.

Mansfield is a key GM parts feeder plant and their strike idled 133,000 men in over 20 shops. Instead of utilizing this power to win his men's demands, Reuther declared the strike illegal. Moreover, he threatened to put the local into trusteeship and suspend local democracy. In an all-day session on February 22, his leadership pressured Local 727 leaders into asking their men to return to work without winning a solution of their grievances. The local leaders were told that the strike was poorly timed because it came on the eve of the UAW's big push for annual salaries and profit-sharing in 1967 bargaining. These two demands are to be given preference over all others. It is probable that the Mansfield strike has prematurely revealed the argument that Reuther will use in the April Conference against rank-and-file demands that the big push be to eliminate the speedup and inoperable grievance machinery.

The above probability is reinforced by the February 8 UAW Administrative Letter issued to elaborate upon Reuther's position on his split with Meany. It contains a long and detailed "Outline of UAW Program for the American Labor Movement." Under its section on collective bargaining it stresses the "development of a sound economic wage policy." No mention or hint is made of the need to improve working conditions which to this moment is the cause of the major crisis for Reuther's leadership.

Under "Aims and Purposes of a Democratic Labor Movement" the February 8 letter stresses collective bargaining and "appropriate progressive legislation" as the methods to be used to advance the interests of union members and their families. But Reuther's current policies insure that direct action, including wildcat strike and minor acts of sabotage in the plants, will daily continue to interrupt production. His program's concessions to the revolt can only encourage the fight against conservative union leadership and does not include goals that will enable him to lead and contain it. His failure to champion an improvement of working conditions will create a consequent dimming of enthusiasm and support for Reuther's new program for American labor, both within the UAW ranks and the ranks of unions whose support he hopes to win. His actions will tend also to undercut the possibility of success for the many good policies the program contains.

LONGSHOREMEN AND STEELWORKERS

In 1964 the ranks of the International Longshoremen's Association (east and Gulf coasts) conducted a strike-revolt against both their employers and union officials that was identical to and almost simultaneous with that accomplished by the UAW rank and file. The stevedoring companies and ILA officials had negotiated what appeared to be an excellent contract. It contained, by past standards, a significant wage increase. It guaranteed every union member a minimum of 1,600 hours of work per year and minor economic fringe benefits. The dockers struck immediately upon the announcement of the terms. Their president, Thomas W. Gleason, hurriedly toured all locals at the request of George Meany on a mission called "Operation Fact." Gleason claimed his ranks wildcatted because they didn't understand the contract. They understood only too well. In return for the recommended settlement the number of men in each work gang was to be cut from 20 to 17. The employers originally demanded a gang size reduction to 14 men, a size more nearly in line with manning scales negotiated by International Longshoremen's and Warehousemen's Union President Harry Bridges for west coast longshoremen. The ILA ranks did not give in to this or the many other undercutting pressures. President Johnson declared a national emergency and invoked the 80-day "cooling off" period under the provisions of the Taft-Hartley Act.

Wildcat strikes resumed on December 21, one day after the "cooling off" period ended and continued through January. All ports were on strike at the same time for over 18 days, and longer in southern and Gulf ports where separate and inferior contracts were offered. Longshoremen in New York and northern east coast ports returned to work, having lost on the main issue of gang size, but their defeat in this battle was not accompanied by a deep demoralization. Their union has long been unofficially divided into separately-led baronies. For the first time in the history of the ILA the entire membership initiated and conducted an all-union strike.

The United Steelworkers' Union revolt deserves special attention because it demonstrates how long it takes in some instances for a revolt to develop. In 1946 the steelworkers conducted a 26-day strike;

in 1949, 45 days of strike; in 1952, 59 days; in 1956, 36 days. All of these strikes were conducted with only reluctant or forced support from the international leadership.

In 1957, an obscure rank-and-file leader named Donald Rarick ran against USW President David McDonald. Rarick, a conservative who has since become a reactionary, based his entire program on opposition to a dues increase and increase in the salaries of officials. As the campaign for the presidency developed, the rank-and-file could see that Rarick was not a militant unionist. Militants couldn't vote for Rarick with enthusiasm. His candidacy was used in the main to record opposition to McDonald. He beat McDonald in the Pennsylvania region by a slight margin, but lost nationally. The vote ran 223,000 for Rarick, 404,000 for McDonald. I.W. Abel, running for Secretary-Treasurer, got 420,000 and his opposition got 181,000. In effect, Rarick disappeared after the election, but the vote he received alarmed the leaders of the large unions.

Four years later, McDonald ran unopposed and received only 221,000 votes. It was obvious that McDonald had been able to win a large vote against Rarick because he was able to utilize the treasury and resources of the International. To beat McDonald a candidate had to be recruited from inside the International who also had access to its facilities.

As early as the Special Steelworkers Conference of 1952, the regional and local union leaders of the USW had warned McDonald that he would have to do something about the deterioration of working conditions in the plants. They further warned that the resulting rank-and-file anger was threatening their position and they might have no other alternative than to transmit this pressure to him.

Twelve years later many of these same secondary and tertiary leaders realized that they could not survive under McDonald's leadership. They picked I. W. Abel, a man who had not worked in a mill for 25 years, to challenge McDonald. After a long dispute over the ballot count, Abel was declared the winner. Under his leadership a significant democratizátion of the negotiation process has begun. Delegates to the 1966 USW convention terminated the union's participation in the joint employer-union Human Relations Committee whose function was to study plant working conditions and to determine how they could be changed in order to cut the costs of production and speed the automation process. The union's 165 man Wage Policy Committee which had the power to ratify contracts was also completely stripped of its power. A new and somewhat liberalized method for allowing the ranks a voice in negotiations was instituted. The policy of last minute "shotgun" bargaining a few days prior to contract expiration was substituted for McDonald's practice of beginning negotiations a year in advance of deadline.

ELECTRICAL WORKERS AND THEIR SECONDARY LEADERS UNITE

James B. Carey, President of the International Union of Electrical Workers was removed from office in a struggle similar to that which deposed David McDonald. By 1953, he had been out of contact with his membership for many years. He had failed to lead them in a fight for improved working conditions against the General Electric and Westinghouse corporations. He had been less successful than Reuther or even McDonald in obtaining wage increases to ease his ranks' anger. However, he felt the pressure of coming rebellion and sought to oppose rather than appease it. He proposed a constitutional change for his union that would have had the employers collect union dues and send them directly to the union's Washington, D.C., headquarters, which would in turn dispense to the locals their stipulated share.

The secondary leaders recognized the danger to themselves and in 1964, with the backing of the ranks, organized an opposition to Carey. In Paul Jennings of the Sperry local in New York they found a candidate with a good union reputation. Jennings beat Carey, but a majority of the ballot counters were Carey supporters and they declared Carey the winner. Jennings forces challenged the count and Carey supporters readied a second set of ballots to show the challengers. They would have given Carey the victory. Because of the ease with which Carey made enemies, even among men like George Meany, the supporters of Jennings were able to obtain aid in a world unfamiliar to the union's ranks. The U.S. Department of Labor impounded the original ballots before a ballot switch could be made.

The struggle for rank-and-file autonomy in the IUE did not end with Jennings' 1964 part-coup victory. In a very short time Jennings did more to improve wages than his predecessor, but he too neglected the fight for working conditions. Under his leadership the IUE engineered a united effort of eleven unions in the 1966 negotiations and subsequent strike against GE. A showdown was long overdue. GE had a 1965 volume of \$6.2 billions, up one billion over 1964. It spent \$330 million for capital expansion and still netted \$355 million after taxes. Profits after taxes for the 1960–1965 period were up 52 percent. They had grown accustomed to docile union negotiators. The IUE-led united front broke GE's Boulwarist approach to bargaining, i.e., GE's practice of making their first settlement offer their last settlement offer under Board President Boulwaris' chairmanship. It also broke President Johnson's 3.2 percent wage guideline and obtained a 5 percent wage increase. However, after the contract was signed, major locals of all unions in the front, including thousands of workers of the IUE, UAW, International Brotherhood of Electrical Workers and the independent United Electrical Workers, stayed out on strike. Jennings and the leaders of the other unions had failed to negotiate an improvement of grievance machinery and working conditions. A Taft-Hartley injunction was necessary to end the strike of those involved in defense production.

Carey and McDonald were not the only leaders of large industrial unions to be felled since 1964. In that year O. A. "Jack" Knight, President of the Oil, Gas and Atomic Workers, retired three years early in the face of a developing rank-and-file revolt. During the Miami convention of the United Rubber Workers' Union in September 1966, the widespread unrest and revolts in the local unions that had preceded the convention forced incumbent President George Burdon to withdraw his candidacy for renomination. In an emotional speech he conceded the "serious mistakes" made during his administration. The major criticisms leveled against him were: loss of touch with the ranks, lack of personal participation in negotiations and an attempt to have the union pay his wife's personal traveling expenses. Veteran vice president Peter Bommarito was swept into office by acclamation. He immediately pledged to take a tougher position against the employers.

COAL MINERS AND THE LEWIS LEGACY

The 1963–1966 and still-continuing revolt in the United Mine Workers' Union did not unseat its president, W. A. "Tony" Boyle, the hand-picked successor of John L. Lewis. However, the insurgent nominees for all top offices at the 1963 UMW convention, standing firm in spite of the violence committed against them, provided the first formal opposition to top UMW incumbents since the 1920s. Steve "Cadillac" Kochis (Boyle's challenger from Bobtown, Pennsylvania) and his supporters lost as they predicted. They knew they had decisive strength in the Ohio-Pennsylvania-West Virginia region, but they also knew the dangers of the very loose UMW balloting system. They knew that the Boyle forces would build up a commanding block of votes in far-away districts that they found impossible to monitor.

Boyle inherited the revolt. Immediately after World War II, John L. Lewis turned from his policy of leading militant strikes for demands closest to the desires of his membership to an all-out program to speed the mechanization of the richest mines. The shift was hailed in the press for its technological progressiveness, but the human cost was staggering. Between 1947 and 1964 the UMW lost over 380,000 members. Lewis retained as members only those who worked in mines that could afford to automate; the rest were cut loose.

The abandoned did not all lose their jobs. More than 100,000 remained in the small mines or after a period of unemployment found work in mines that had been shut down because their veins were near exhaustion. The Lewis shift enabled them to re-open by hiring displaced miners at low pay. In West Virginia, Pennsylvania and Ohio there are now a large number of mines that have a headroom that is often no more than 36 inches. The miners who work them literally spend their lives on their hands and knees. By 1965, the production of coal in the poorer, non-automated and non-union mines accounted for 30 percent of total U.S. coal production. Their owners are again making fortunes. They employ embittered and impoverished former UMW members who have top experience and skill, at $14 a day, little more than half the union rate, and do not have to pay pension or fringe benefits. Thus, a small scale mechanization of the small mines has been made possible.

The increase in the strength of the competitive position of the non-union mines has in turn forced the large mine operators to impose a speedup on their employees. Pressure is applied, resulting in a deterioration of protective working and safety conditions. Fatalities are as high as they were during World War II when 700,000 men were working coal underground.

During the summer of 1965 in the Ireland Mine near Moundsville, West Virginia, five local union leaders refused to work under unsafe conditions and were fired. An unauthorized strike ensued which in one week spread over the West Virginia, Ohio and Pennsylvania region. Roving bands of pickets easily shut down mine after mine, including United States Steel's large captive Robena mine. The UMW International leadership including the grievance processors they appoint at the local levels lost all control. The halfhearted legal efforts of the U.S. Department of Labor, that had the year before attempted to increase the democratic rights of the local and regional UMW organizations, had failed. The local leaders, the only authority the rebel ranks would follow in a disciplined and responsible manner, were labeled "instigators of anarchy."

The main reason for this large unauthorized strike was the jam of unsettled grievances in mine after mine; in addition, the rank-and-file miners were angered that their top officials had negotiated a wage increase in the previous contract at the expense of improving working conditions. The main demands of the rebels became the right to elect their own local business agents and a democratized union structure from bottom to top. They felt that only by obtaining these rights could they find ways of helping themselves and their friends, relatives and former union brothers in the small mines. They returned to work only after being promised a greater voice in the negotiation of the next contract. In what was a major departure from past practice in the UMW, Boyle sent out a call for the Contract Policy Committee to meet *before* the opening of formal negotiations with the operators in 1966.

The contract obtained a 3 percent wage increase for the 100,000 soft coal miners who are left in the UMW. Their economic fringe benefits were slightly improved, but they are still far behind the workers in auto and steel. They won the right of first preference to any job openings in other mines in their district if laid off. During the negotiations they had to conduct a series of wildcat strikes to obtain these gains and their only satisfaction lay in the knowledge that the contract was an improvement over the one negotiated two years earlier. The revolt and the conditions that generate it persist. "Non-union" union men work for poverty level wages under nineteenth century conditions. In this period between contracts, sporadic acts of all forms of sabotage are on the increase.

BRIDGES, AUTOMATION AND B MEN

In 1960 International Longshoremen's and Warehousemen's Union President Harry Bridges negotiated the first six year "Mechanization and Modernization" contract with the Pacific Maritime Association. Like the contract that John L. Lewis negotiated for the automation of Big Coal, Bridges' contract allowed the unrestricted introduction of containerization of cargo, the use of vans, and automated cargo handling machinery. At the same time, it eliminated thousands of jobs. Primarily because of increased maritime activity due to war shipments, widespread unemployment up to now has been avoided.

Just as in coal, however, the human costs have been staggering. In the first year of the contract, the accident rate in what has become the nation's most dangerous industry went up 20 percent.[1] In the same

[1]*Longshore Bulletin*, ILWU Local 10, February 8, 1962.

year the longshore accident rate on the east coast declined one-half percent. To obtain this contract Bridges gave in to the employers' request that they be allowed to "buy" the elimination of the major working and safety conditions improvements won in the militant struggles of the 1930s. The long established manning scales and the 2,100 pound sling load limit were eliminated. These provisions were not only eliminated for labor performed on containerized cargo, but on the still very sizeable amount of cargo manhandled piece by piece and sack by sack.

Even more than Lewis, Bridges won the respect of employers everywhere, admiration in many liberal circles, and from the press—the title of "labor statesman." The contract established one gain for only one section of the longshoremen: during the six-year life of the contract those who entered the industry before 1948, had achieved union membership prior to 1960, had reached the age of 65 and who additionally had 25 years of service, could retire with a $7,900 bonus in addition to their unimproved pension. They could retire earlier if disabled and receive a smaller bonus on a pro-rated basis. Or, if they had 25 years in the industry at age 62 they could collect the $7,900 in monthly installments until they reached 65 when the regular pension payments began.

Although the fund that pays the bonuses is created by the tonnage worked by all longshoremen, the recipients are older union members who work little more than half that tonnage. The balance is moved by B men and casuals working under the jurisdiction of the union and the younger men who became union members (A men) after 1960, none of whom are allowed to share in the fund.

The B men are a permanent and regular section of the work force who get the pick of the dirtiest and heaviest jobs that are left over after the A, or union, men have taken their pick. After the B men, casuals hired on a daily basis get their turn at the remainders. The casuals get none of the regular fringe benefits and are not compensated for that loss.

The B man system was created simultaneously with negotiations for Bridges' automation contract. The production of B men is appreciably higher than that of the union men because they lack union representation on the job. They pay dues but have no vote. In Bridges' San Francisco base and home Local (No. 10) they can attend union meetings provided they sit in a segregated section of the meeting hall's balcony. These eager-to-be-organized non-union men do most of the work that is performed deep in the holds of the ships, the area of production that produced the militants who built the ILWU in the thirties.

Bridges fears these young men. In 1963, in collusion with the employers, he led the Kafkaesque purge that expelled 82 of them from the waterfront jobs they had held for 4 years. (Over 80 percent of the 82 are Negroes.) They were tried in secret. The charges against them were not revealed. Their number, but not their identities, was made known to ILWU members. Bridges' witch hunt methods and double standards make the bureaucratic procedures used to expel his union from the CIO, and the insidious tactics used by the government to prosecute both him and James Hoffa, bland by comparison. Hoffa and Bridges at least had the right to counsel, to produce witnesses, to know the charges and to formal trial prior to judgment or sentencing.

The atmosphere of intimidation resulting from the framing of the 82 has, until now, successfully silenced open opposition among B men and younger men. However, to Bridges' surprise, a revolt against his automation contract and leadership has recently developed among the older men. Unlike B men and casuals, most of them work on the ships' decks and the docks rather than down in the hold where the major burden of the current speedup is being carried. It appeared for a time that the prospect of their receiving a bonus upon retirement and lighter daily labors would conservatize them; but 42 percent of all ILWU longshoremen (union or A men) on the coast voted against the second six-year "Mechanization and Modernization" Agreement negotiated in July 1966. The speedup had reached these men as well. The contract won a majority in the large San Francisco local where retired members (pensioners) are allowed to vote, but lost in the other three large Pacific coast ports of Los Angeles, Portland and Seattle. Had the B men been allowed to vote, there is little doubt that it would have been overwhelmingly defeated.

The dissension that has developed between Bridges and other top ILWU leaders since last July has become so deep that news of it has appeared in the San Francisco press. Rumors persist that the fall out is over the question of how to handle the growing revolt in the ranks. Whether Bridges continues to pursue the automation policies on which he has staked his entire reputation or abandons it to pursue a re-winning and improvement of the working conditions desired by his ranks, the effect will be to stimulate a continuance of the revolt. He is now plagued by lawsuits, including one filed by the expelled B men and another filed in federal court several years ago by ILWU Local 13 in the name of all members in the large port of Los Angeles. James B. Carey and David McDonald learned, and now Bridges is learning, that the pursuit of policies that alienate the ranks can also isolate a top leader from his co-officials and hasten his fall from power.

MORE TROUBLE IN MARITIME

The accelerated advancement of cargo-handling technology during the last decade has in the last two years created an opposition to the leadership of Joseph Curran, president of the National Maritime Union. There has been a sharp decrease in the time that ships remain in American ports and the seamen are allowed ever shorter time with their families. The seamen's anger has been increased by the small monetary compensation for the special sacrifices of family and social life demanded by their industry. Curran has not responded to these problems, but instead has attempted to improve his position with the large New York membership by announcing plans for the construction of rent-free housing built with the union's pension fund. The announcement—an example of a positive and conservatizing reform initiated from above to quiet dissatisfaction—did not quell the revolt.

An aspirant to office in the NMU must already have served a term as a paid official. James M. Morrissey was one of the few oppositionists who could meet this requirement. The press has done nothing to inform the public of the fight made by Morrissey and his supporters. To this date the only source of printed information about it comes from Issue No. 23 of editor H. W. Benson's respected journal, *Union Democracy in Action*, published in New York. In an election [of questionable] honesty . . . , the incumbent officialdom conceded that Morrissey got 34 percent of the total vote and 14 percent of the New York vote in his struggle to unseat Curran.

Morrissey got close to what is the full treatment risked by rank-and-file opposition leaders in unions, whose democratic practices are limited. Last September three unidentified assailants beat him with metal pipes outside his union hall. No arrests have been made. His skull was shattered in several places and the bone over one eye was crushed. He still lives as does the opposition he leads. Curran is still [involved] in his fight to retain the job that pays him $83,000 annually.

By the autumn of 1966 it was possible to observe that, with the exception of the United Packinghouse Workers (UPW), every major union that contributed to the creation of the CIO in the 1930s had experienced a major revolt. Conditions in the coal, auto, rubber, steel, electric and maritime industries in the sixties are now renovating the unions whose formation they stimulated in the thirties. It should also be observed that most of the unions being renovated belong to and are a majority in the AFL–CIO Industrial Union Department, headed by Walter Reuther. The reasons for the UPW's exemption from the revolt process thus far are apparent: to the credit of its president, Ralph Helstein, the first day of its 1966 convention was thrown open to the delegates to voice their gripes about conditions in both their union and industry.

THE AIRLINE MECHANICS STRIKE

Most of the major industrial union revolts broke into the open prior to last summer. The press reported each as an individual phenomenon, if it reported them at all, and the full significance was missed. It took the five week July–August strike of the airline mechanics who are affiliated with the International Association of Machinists (IAM), to make the general American public conscious of what *Life* magazine's August 26, 1966 strike-end issue called the "New Union Militancy," and the November issue of *Fortune* documented as a period of "dramatic shift from the familiar faces to the facelessness of the rank and file." This strike of less than 30,000 men did what the much larger strike-revolts failed to do. By stopping 60 percent of the nation's air passenger travel they directly touched the lives of the nation's middle class.

Without advance signalling from liberal social analysts, who are usually among the first to call attention to signs of labor unrest, the daily press gave recognition to labor's new era—and no wonder. The mechanics made it impossible for reporters to ignore the observation. But the press stressed wages as the issue. Robert T. Quick, President and General Chairman of IAM District 141, gave an indication of the real issue in one of his strike press releases: "We're working under chain gang conditions for cotton picking wages."

The public had not witnessed a stance like that taken by the mechanics since the 1930s. They rejected the first contract proposed by their new president P. L. Siemiller. They rejected a second contract worked out under the direct intervention of the Johnson administration. Siemiller stated he was sure his ranks could live with this contract, but the strike continued without pause. They went further: not only did they make plain their opposition to Johnson's intrusion in their affairs, they rejected labor's allegiance to the Democratic party. The four largest mechanics locals on the Pacific coast—Los Angeles, San Francisco, Portland and Seattle—sent telegrams to George Meany, Walter Reuther, James Hoffa and Harry Bridges asking that "immediate action be taken to form a third political party that will serve the best interests of labor."

The mechanics returned to work, having broken more than the 3.7 percent wage guideline of the nation's chief executive. More than damaging his prestige, they increased their own. It is certain that back on the job they will be treated with more respect by their immediate supervisors and that it will be easier for them to unofficially institute improvements of their "chain gang" working conditions.

REVOLT AGAINST HOFFA RULE

The revolts have not all been national or union-wide in scope, but this does not diminish their potential or importance. In the latter months of 1965 James Hoffa's Teamster leadership became unable to restrain the rebellion of the Philadelphia Teamsters. Local 107, City Freight Drivers, have a long tradition of opposition to their international. The leader of their local in 1963–1964 was Ray Cohen, a Hoffa supporter. The ranks were dissatisfied with the representation he supplied. Two caucuses existed in the local: "The Real Rank-and-File Caucus" (pro-Hoffa) and "The Voice Caucus," so called because of its publication.

The opposition to Cohen became so great that Cohen became a liability to the international. Hoffa made his first appearance in Philadelphia, after becoming International Brotherhood of Teamsters president, to announce Cohen's demotion. The elimination of Cohen evidently created no basic changes in the local. In June, 1965, at Roadway Express Incorporated's freight loading dock, a young worker, 18 years old and a son of a night over-the-road teamster's shop steward, was helping to load a big box into a trailer. He refused to work under conditions he considered unsafe. The foreman said: "If you don't do it, I'll fire you." The young freight handler answered: "Screw you. Fire away." He was fired. Four other men were ordered to do the same job, they said the same and were also fired. The five men left the job together and went to the union hall. They told their story to the ranks standing around the hall and to the local leaders. A meeting was held. The Voice Caucus took the lead away from its opponent caucus and made a motion for a general strike of all Philadelphia Teamsters; it carried and the strike was on: from five men to a strike of every driver and handler in the city and outlying region in less than 24 hours. Now to insure that the strike was totally general, the Teamsters patroled the streets, stopped trucks and made out-of-town drivers get off their trucks. As a main location for the latter activity, they chose the area in front of Sears and Roebuck's department store. There is an immense lawn and the highway widens out allowing room to parallel park trucks and trailers in large numbers. After several days of this activity, the police attacked the local drivers. The out-of-town drivers joined the strikers against the police. A pitched battle ensued. Within five minutes, the boulevard in front of Sears and Roebuck was impassable due to overturned trailers. This guerrilla-type warfare continued in many areas of the city for several days. Finally by injunction and because *both* factions of the leadership backed down, the strikers were forced back to work. Although none of their strike gains have been contractualized, they are working under better conditions because they are able to express their strike-won strength on-the-job.

At present, both caucuses—Real Rank-and-File and the Voice—are in disrepute among the ranks because both backed down in the face of local authorities. Hoffa has threatened to take the local under trusteeship. The rank-and-file, to demonstrate that it is not defeated, had a meeting and passed a resolution which stated that such an attempt would be met by another strike.

THE PAINTERS AND DOW WILSON

The 1965 Building Trades strike in northern California's giant home-building industry was particularly important because it involved skilled workers with relatively high wage scales. Plumbers, laborers, sheet metal workers and painters struck against the wishes of their international union leaders. All but the painters settled within a few days. Ten thousand painters stayed out for 37 days.

San Francisco Painters' Local No. 4 is the largest local in the International Brotherhood of Painters. It was led by Dow Wilson and Morris Evenson. Its strike demands, including coffee time, were some of the most radical ever made by painters. Painting labor processes, due to the rapid advances in paint chemistry, are more rationalized than those of any other trade in the building industry. Time studies and resulting speedups are the rule. Paint foremen, rushing to make new tracts ready for the developers' sales forces, stand over painters with blank wage checkbooks protruding from their pockets. If a man falls behind he can be summarily fired and paid off in full. Tension of all kinds is high. Unsatisfied, the employers have for some time been pressuring the union to allow them to institute the use of new methods of paint application—the elimination of brushes for rollers, pressure rollers and spray guns.

During the strike the leaders of the international union publicly sided with the employers' automation demands. Local No. 4 and its leadership stood firm. Leaders in several other northern California locals backed down and their ranks rebelled. Less than half way through the strike Dow Wilson, in effect, became the leader of the entire strike and a majority of San Francisco Bay area locals. The painters won their strike, their coffee time, a big wage increase and temporarily checked the advance of technological unemployment.

Wilson knew that the international leaders would be vindictive and that they would try to get at the ranks through him. The strike filled out his reputation as a model union leader, unique in these times. He was an independent political radical who was unhampered by dreams of wealth. He saw himself as a servant of the ranks, had exposed collusion and corruption in the painting of government housing that was cheating the taxpayers of millions of dollars, and had used his prestige to bring Negro workers into the industry. He was a threat to the international union and employers. Wilson realized he would have to carry his ranks' fight for union democracy to the international convention.

In the early morning hours of April 6, 1966, Dow Wilson was assassinated in front of the San Francisco Labor Temple—gangster style, by a shot gun blast in the face. A month later Lloyd Green, president of the nearby Hayward local and a colleague of Wilson's, was killed in an identical manner. The leaders and ranks of Local No. 4 accompanied by Wilson's widow and children demonstrated on the main streets of San Francisco and in front of the homes of city and federal authorities. Arrests were made shortly thereafter.

An official of a painting employers' association confessed a major role in authoring the assassinations and driving the murder car. His trial made it clear that his power in labor relations came from money he stole from the painters' pension fund and by threatening recalcitrants with a visit from his friend Abe "the Trigger" Chapman, whose name was formerly identified with Murder Incorporated. He also indicated a top regional union official who is a supporter of the international union's policies. The official's guilt has not been proven; legal proceedings continue.

In a matter of weeks after the burial of the assassinated leaders, the international officials of the painters union made their first unsuccessful attempt to take several Bay Area locals into trusteeship and suspend local autonomy. The courts have refused to grant an injunction against further attempts of the International to take control, but the rank-and-file painters and their remaining leaders, headed by the courageous Morris Evenson, continue to show a willingness to protect their independence in every way.

DISAFFILIATION AS A REVOLT TOOL

The revolt of California, Oregon and Washington pulp and paper workers in 1964 received little publicity. However, it caught the attention of labor leaders nationally. In compliance with National Labor Relations Board requirements, workers in locals that were affiliated with two aging and eastern based AFL–CIO internationals (International Brotherhood of Pulp Sulphite and Paper Mill Workers and the United Papermakers and Paperworkers) broke away to form the independent Association of Western Pulp and Paper Workers (AWPPW). The old unions lost face and $500,000 a year in dues monies.

The AWPPW members whose work in 49 mills accounts for 90 percent of pulp and paper production on the Pacific coast, set up headquarters in Portland, Oregon. They announced the birth of their union through the publication of a monthly newspaper, *The Rebel.* They elected a president who is typical of the new union's staff; before taking office he was a mill electrician.

Since its initial organization, the AWPPW has had strong support from regional and local unions in areas where they set up locals, but life has been hard for this new union. Its newness and small membership has made it impossible to build the large treasury needed to operate a union today. It is not just the high cost of routine operation, collective bargaining against large corporations and legal costs that have created problems. The AWPPW is continually harassed by the two bureaucratized unions from which it split, both of which have the support of George Meany and the conservative AFL–CIO hierarchy. As their isolation increases and the official support they receive from other unions shrinks, owing to pressure from Meany, their energies are expended in a fight for existence rather than growth.

Throughout the United States there are large numbers of workers in local and regional units whose position is similar to that of the Pacific coast pulp and paper workers, prior to their establishment of independence in 1964. Their working conditions and wages are artifically depressed because of what amounts to captive affiliations with conservatively-led international unions. Their tolerance of their captivity seems unlimited only because at present there is no progressive alternative available.

II

WHY WORKERS REVOLT

Almost without exception, the revolts were conducted primarily to improve the conditions of life on-the-job. This is absolutely contrary to what the public has been led to believe. Newspaper, television and radio reporting rarely relate the existence, let alone the details, of labor's non-economic demands. The following statement by the Director of Research in Technology and Industrial Relations at Yale University stands as a classic definition of strike causes in American industry:

"In 1936 and 1937, a wave of sit-down strikes swept through the rubber and automobile plants of the United States. The workers on strike wanted higher wages, union recognition, and an organized machinery for the handling of day-to-day grievances, but, above all, they were striking against what they called the "speedup" of work as governed by the assembly line. The causes of every major strike are complex and frequently so interwoven as to be inseparable. But somewhere among the causes (and frequently basic to the others, as in the sit-downs) are work methods and working conditions.

Two years before the first sit-down strike the country experienced a nation-wide walk-out of textile workers. Here, discrimination against union members, wages, and many other issues were involved, but the dynamic origin of the distrubance (not only in 1934, but through the remaining thirties and after) was the introduction of new work methods and machinery, all of which were generally lumped by the workers and denounced as the "stretch-out." If particular work methods or undesirable working conditions may sometimes cause a national walk-out, they are also the common origin of innumerable lesser conflicts in the world of industry. The net result of a minor conflict over a work method may be a day's slow-down or a grievance fought through the local's plant grievance machinery or, perhaps, hostilities expressed in low-quality work or by a high rate of absenteeism. . . . When neglected or misunderstood, these merely local disturbances can, with surprising rapidity, grow into a national emergency."[2]

Walker does not deny the importance of issues other than those

[2]Charles R. Walker, "Work Methods, Working Conditions, and Morals," *Industrial Conflict*, A. Kornhauser, R. Dubin and A. Ross, eds. (New York: McGraw-Hill, 1954).

involving working conditions, he simply says that they are secondary. Work methods and conditions are not the only issues in the current revolts. Wage increases have not kept up with price increases since the end of World War II. Americans have become accustomed to the pattern and have adjusted to it. Workers have maintained or increased their purchasing power by working long overtime hours, "moonlighting" (working two jobs) or putting their wives to work. This is not to say that the unusually big jump in the cost of living that occurred last year failed to increase anger, frustration and discontent. It did, but the American working class has not yet found an effective way to oppose price increases. Workers in the larger and stronger unions in particular have come to believe that wage increases are a defensive or holding action. Even when they have won substantial raises, price increases have wiped them out in a matter of months. They no longer believe that a collective bargaining contract whose major achievement is a wage increase represents a victory of more than temporary progress.

The above belief notwithstanding, it is always difficult and often impossible for workers to make the improvement of working conditions the formal as well as primary goal of contract negotiation.[3] It is absolutely impossible for the employed near-poor and poor to do so. For example, the conditions of work of the farm laborers in California's central valley are brutal and improvements are sorely needed, yet the United Farm Workers Organizing Committee headed by Caesar Chavez continues to give the wage demands top priority. His ranks would have it no other way. In a sense, the farm worker puts aside his own most immediate need because he has responsibilities to his wife and children. Then too, it should not be forgotten that workers who have incomes twice as large as the farm workers find it difficult to keep their wives in good spirits or their creditors patient during a strike whose major goal is anything other than a sizable wage increase.

Employers take the attitude that their authority over work methods and conditions is unchallengeable and sacrosanct. Most of all they fear any kind of employee control over the production process. No matter that the union sometimes forces them to grant sizeable wage boosts, they cover their increased costs and more by getting more work out of their employees. American employers have made it clear that they will make a principled stand against any demand that would give a union any authority over the methods, conditions and speed of production. Union officials fear fighting so determined an enemy, and

[3]An informative discussion of this point is contained in Alvin W. Gouldner, *Wildcat Strike* (Yellow Springs, Ohio: Antioch Press, 1954).

they fear the new union leaders that would be developed in such a fight. The fight for better conditions cannot be made every one, two or three years like the wage fights; it must be fought every day inside the plants. During such a fight the base and authority of the union would be moved from the union hall back inside the plant. Workers who are willing to fight their employer to obtain a better life on-the-job have to be prepared to fight their union leaders as well.

The struggle of American industrial workers to improve the conditions under which they perform their labors is not an effort simply to obtain a better physical work environment. The goals go far beyond clean air and surroundings. Work paces and safety take higher priority.

Of equal, if not greater importance, is the drive to obtain formal contractual control over the methods whereby they are forced to perform their productive duties and to control their relationship to the machines with which they live. Cheated of the opportunity to make decisions of any kind, they are unable to take responsibility for what they do. In many cases, they are not told the identity of the product part which they help produce, let alone its function. Yet, they may be forced to remain at that labor for years, denied the right to transfer to other jobs that would allow a break in the monotony and increased knowledge of both the end product and total technology involved in its manufacture. Alienated, adjuncts to the machine, they resent the respect the machinery commands from their employers. In a word, industrial workers are fighting for dignity. Without it there is no daily gratification in their lives.

It was precisely this struggle that in the early 1930s caused mass production workers to organize independent local unions on a plant for plant basis without outside help and which inspired John L. Lewis to create the CIO by centralizing the power of those locals in the mid 1930s. But the CIO was not to become a weapon that would win significant improvements of work conditions, methods and controls. Those goals had to be subordinated to more immediate ones. The first priority of the CIO had to be the winning of collective bargaining recognition and the negotiation of corporation or industry-wide contracts so that workers in one plant would not be forced to compete against those in others.

By 1941, the industrial unions had accomplished these immediate goals to a substantial degree. The time had arrived when the workers, through their new unions, could be free to return their attention to the problems of the work process. World War II cheated them from doing so.

The war provided employers with an opportunity to check the

momentum of the CIO. With the exception of John L. Lewis, the official labor leadership, especially those who were pro-Communist, pledged that for the "duration," their unions would not strike. The employers responded by trying to win back organized labor's recent gains. Alone, workers were forced to defend just the fundamental victories of the 1930s. The attempts to do so were often branded as "aid to the enemy."

The war, however, by its very totality, had a far more crippling effect on labor's ranks than those directly imposed on them by their employers, the government and their official leaders. Within a year after it had begun, the war atomized the rank-and-file's on-the-job union cadres. It took large numbers of experienced local union leaders and shop stewards from the workplaces. It decimated the personnel of labor's most fundamental organizational unit, the informal work groups created by the productive process. These groups, with their informal leaders, form a social unit able to discipline their members and restrict production. The CIO was born in these groups. They pyramided their power, plant-wide, and an independent local union was formed. The process was called "self organization." A typical example of the effect of World War II on the groups was as follows: A group of ten welders and grinders who worked in close contact with one another were employed in a plant that unionized in the late 1930s. Half of them became employed there in the late 1920s or early 1930s. Others came later, but all participated in a portion of the long fight that brought the union into the plant, and more importantly, to obtain the right to *openly* bargain with their immediate supervisor—the foreman. By 1943, five of them had gone into the armed forces and two had gone to the shipyards on the west coast. They were replaced by two housewives, a draft-exempt youth and four men beyond draft age from farms and marginal jobs. How could the three remaining members of the original group impart to the newcomers the history, tradition and knowledge of their group's struggles or the union lessons learned in years of fighting? They could not. Before it sustained war losses the group was able to conduct actions that would tame a foreman. They could participate in that process which keeps union leaders militant. If they saw a local president softening in his attitude toward management he would be told: "Look, remember when you worked with us and how it was, and how you complained louder than anybody else? And now you're talking out of both sides of your mouth and letting us live under these conditions." Neither did they spare their own members who showed signs of weakening. A failure to attend union meetings brought jibes, serious but with smiles, that reminded the absentees of what they had all been through together and the need to continue. No such pressures could be applied to their group's wartime replacements. To the new members, the union officials were unapproachable "big shots."

When the war was over, the reconversion to peacetime consumer production once again broke up the personnel of the work groups. Large numbers who had entered the armed forces or war industries did not return to their old jobs. The old groups could not re-establish themselves. In one plant after another, workers were divided into segments with three major identities: old timers, vets, and kids, so-called. For a time their attentions focused primarily on stockpiling home furnishings. Who could blame them? For the first time in American history a majority of workers were able to consume a large number of the products made. But the brightness of that goal diminished. The routine drudgery of workers' lives soon re-established its monotonous predictability. Besides, television sets and dishwashers at home did not bring gratification to life on-the-job. And the workers were getting to know one another again. They were learning who, among those near them, liked to bowl, sew, garden, repair cars and fish. The questions had been asked: "How many kids do you have?" and "Where do you want to go next vacation?" The social cohesion and the work eliminated the separate identities. Work groups again attained leaders. The selection, as always, was natural. No formal elections were held. The vote was by a nod, by the raising of a brow, or by a silent consensus that at first is not always conscious. Someone in a group emerges as courageous and articulate, stands up to a foreman, and the rest support him or her, with the result that it is once more a fighting unit involved in guerrilla warfare.

By the mid-1950s, American workers, particularly in the mass production, transportation and maritime industries, were ready once more to resume the struggle that had caused the revolts of the 1930s. They found, however, that the leadership created during the rise of the CIO was not responsive to their desires. There was an unwillingness among the official leaders to give up the control they had so easily attained during the war. The workers had no choice but to conduct a fight on two levels. Inside the workplaces, they fought their employers, and at the same time conducted a campaign to win the in-plant local union officials—the only section of the labor leadership with whom they have daily and direct contact—to their cause. Officials who identified with them were supported. Every possible pressure was brought to bear on those who would not. By 1964, the tactic had achieved enough success to separately pit large numbers of individually unified local unions against their regional leaders who, in turn, were forced to apply pressure on those top leaderships that were not responsive. Thus, the revolts broke into the open. They were created, grew, and became a fact visible to the public, first because of the need and secondly *because the rank-and-file of American unions had been able to build from their work groups the basic organizational vehicle for them.*

The revolts continue to grow in both depth and magnitude. Wildcat strikes show a steady increase. Each year the Federal Mediation and Conciliation Service enters nearly 8,000 disputes. Last year union rank-and-file members rejected 11.7 percent of the contracts negotiated with the Service's aid, an all time high that is still rising. In the first month of fiscal 1967 the rejections rose to 19.3 percent. There is continued increase in the number of elections in which long-time incumbents are being challenged from below.

The present struggle to improve work conditions, methods, and controls is far more desperate than that of the 1930s, and represents a far deeper potential crisis for the nation. The productivity of the entire labor force is far higher. Employers have retained the right to establish the speed at which assembly lines will travel and the methods by which work shall be performed. No major union, including the UAW, has made a concerted effort to restrict that right. Workers in most modern automobile assembly plants often turn out between 60 and 70 cars an hour. Neither the human anatomy nor mentality was designed to endure such strain or monotony.

A manifestation of this may be the reported increase in the use of drugs within the plants:

"Pep pill use by factory workers draws increasing concern as a hidden hazard. Plant medical directors and safety specialists fear scattered signs of drug use by production workers are symptomatic of an underground factory safety problem. A major farm equipment maker, a big food processor, detect increased use of pep pills in their plants. One worker's tool box turns up a hundred bennies (benzedrine capsules). One executive suspects 'there are several pushers in our plants.' 'The problem is most acute in California,' he adds, 'but we've found a little of this to be countrywide.'

Los Angeles narcotics authorities turn up a well-supplied pusher in an auto plant; they aid big aerospace companies seeking remedies to the problem. One California narcotics specialist figures pills are pushed in all plants with assembly-line operations. Some executives blame today's fast production pace and excessive moonlighting for driving workers to stimulants. One detective says that employers don't want to attack the problem for fear of stirring unfavorable publicity."[4]

The increased use of speedup methods in industry now threatens

[4]*Wall Street Journal,* November 22, 1966, p. 1.

the safety and health of workers in the most literal sense. According to the National Safety Council's 1966 report on U.S. industry, "14,500 workers died and another 2.2 million were temporarily or permanently disabled in 1966." The U.S. Public Health Service recognizes the crisis is greater than at any time in the nation's history and is spending a record $6.6 million on occupational health this year. Syndicated columnist Sylvia Porter recently discussed a "top level" report to the U.S. Surgeon General that argued that $50 million a year is needed to reduce hazards by 20 percent; she further argued that doing so "would add $11 billion a year to our production."[5]

The problems of speedup and increased safety hazards have been largely ignored by the official union leaders. Workers have been forced to seek solutions outside official union grievance machinery. Production, particularly in heavy industry, is plagued by slowdowns and minor acts of sabotage. Bolts are dropped into the slots in which the chains travel that pull the assembly lines; machinery is not maintained or is handled in a way that will hasten its breakdown. The quality of the product is harmed by shortcuts that allow a momentary breathing spell; creativity and efficiency are withheld. The object is revenge, release from boredom, and the rest that results while repairs are awaited.

For brief periods after each guerrilla victory (and under management's increased surveillance) the glee is limitless though no trace of it can be found on the facial expressions of the participants. Nevertheless it is a difficult war. Victories are short-lived. The tension saps energies and the speedup continues. In many plants employees hired as spies openly take notes. While there are few mortalities (firings), there are many casualties. Suspected trouble-makers are sometimes temporarily laid-off for real or for alleged infractions of rules unrelated to the actual charge. Most often they are transferred to other departments of the shop. They sustain no loss in pay, but must accustom themselves to new foremen, new repetitive tasks and undergo a period of initiation in their new work groups.

The widespread introduction of automated machinery since World War II has increased the existing alienation of American workers. When new machines and methods are substituted for the old, new job classifications and rates must be defined. The employers make every attempt to reclassify jobs so as to downgrade wages. Then too, they sometimes meet outbreaks of worker militancy with threats of automating jobs out of existence. It is impossible to measure the anger that results.

[5] *San Francisco Chronicle,* April 13, 1967.

Automation qualitatively increases nervous tension on-the-job. A worker at a machine on which he or she can produce one hundred pieces a day, is placed at a machine that can be made to turn out five hundred. A mistake that previously made it necessary to scrap one piece becomes one that necessitates the scrapping of five. At the same time, the new machine cheats the worker of the opportunity to use the skills needed to operate the old one. The deskilled worker loses individual bargaining power, freedom in the job market and a daily loss of work gratification—a damage to self-image.

Even though armament production has absorbed the jobs lost because of automation, workers bitterly hate the automation process. In it they see future joblessness. They reject all claims that it represents progress. They are aware of the human price. It uproots them and requires that they transplant themselves to another workplace and often to another geographic area. If their work area is automated and they are lucky enough to retain their employment, they may face an even more dismal prospect: an on-the-job loneliness for which there is no compensation. The friends that once surrounded them, providing an on-the-job family, disappear or no longer work within earshot. Increased absenteeism and loss of morale are inevitable. What once made the job just bearable has been eliminated. Also, the fighting weapon, the informal work group, has been destroyed; new ones must be built.

The final indignity of the process for the workers is that they and their leaders are seldom if ever consulted before automated change is introduced. They are presented with an accomplished fact—change designed by humans who have no conception of an industrial worker's life experience, on the job or off.

But the consequences of automation give workers weapons they did not previously have. Probably, like the British workers during the beginnings of Luddism in the late eighteenth century, American workers now note the demoralization of industry's middle class. Computerization, automation's companion, is stripping middle executives and immediate management of their power to make decisions. Meaningful decisions are increasingly made at the top.

Automation creates problems for management in still other ways. Automated machines represent a far larger capital investment than their predecessors. They are far more vulnerable to neglectful treatment. Their complexity provides increased opportunities for the minor acts of sabotage that are already widespread and difficult to detect. A slowdown or stoppage of an automated machine causes a production loss several times over the loss caused by a similar crisis involving the machines it replaced. One worker is able to restrict production to a degree that earlier would have involved a half dozen.

The rapid disappearance of family-owned companies and the growing number of corporate mergers contribute to the rank-and-file revolts in a manner similar to that of automation. In industries run from the top by professionals for multi-absentee owners, the symbol of authority is no longer human, with a consequent effect on the contents and enforcement of directives from the main office. Embattled from above and below, the vise on middle and lower management twists tighter. The problem is exaggerated in corporations of the conglomerate type owning factories of productive units in a number of non-related industries. Top managers directing units making steel, candy, silk stockings and chemicals lose contact with the production processes. They are in the business of managing.

The unique character of the conglomerate gives their managers a new weapon in their dealings with organized labor. If a particular union strikes in one of their industries, the others—in different industries under contract to different unions—are free to operate and profit. It is much easier to pit union against union.

According to Federal Trade Commission figures, over 70 percent of all important mergers and acquisitions (involving $10 million in assets) between 1960 and 1965 were conglomerate. Only 13 percent of the mergers were with firms producing similar or related products. The same trend continued into 1967. (The FTC estimates that at the current merger pace, 75 percent of all corporate assets in the nation will be in the hands of 200 corporations by 1975.) International unions (so called because they include Canadians) are thus forced to negotiate contracts for larger and larger numbers of their members. By their very nature, these negotiations become more and more attentive to wage and economic fringe benefit payment patterns, less and less concerned with the working conditions that vary so widely from workplace to workplace. The condition of daily life in industry degenerates. It is absolutely necessary and proper that American workers permit the top leaders of their international unions more centralized power. There is no other way to challenge growing corporate power during the negotiation of master collective bargaining agreements. At the same time, the ranks want to determine the goals of those negotiations and to use their power in the workplace to increase their control over the nature of work. How to simultaneously centralize labor's total power on the one hand and decentralize it on the other is a decisive issue of the revolts. No sense can be made of them unless this is recognized.

There is another objective condition in industrial society that affects the revolts and must be mentioned briefly: the labor shortage. It became a major problem for industry in 1966, or after the revolts began, but this is not to downgrade its effect. It allowed a greater degree of independence for those already in the workforce when it began. Probably more important, however, it caused industry to hire hundreds of thousands of youths who would in the past have had to wait years longer to get what has long been considered "adult employment." The attitudes of the new young workers have been a revelation to the older workers. They, like their middle class counterparts in the universities, are free of the wounds that the Depression inflicted on previous generations. For large numbers of them a good self-image is not dependent upon having a reverent attitude toward employment. They rebel against doing what has dulled and shortened the lives of their parents. The following experience in today's factories is not uncommon: A young worker is offered a higher paying job, discovers it requires a faster pace or involves an onerous condition and turns it down—preferring to live easier at less pay. The older workers observe such an action in shocked respect. They would not have dreamed of taking such a step. It reveals to them the sacrifices they have long endured. The experience can widen but more often helps to narrow gaps. Today's young are armed with mirrors.

The revolt of university students has had a radicalizing effect on the entire society. This includes industrial workers. Many of them are repulsed by the attire and conduct of some of the students, but dissent of any kind has a contagion. Besides, the repulsion is an initial and surface reaction. The workers' rebellion creates tolerances and even feelings of kinship for others doing the same.

Will the students develop new alliances now that they have lost a base in the civil rights movement? Already, radical students have begun to re-evaluate their attitudes toward unions. They have been taught, often by formerly radical social scientists, that American workers are now fat on beer, barbecue and television, and no longer capable of struggle for social progress. The rank-and-file revolts are destroying the cynical myth and providing opportunity for alliances. The initiative will not always be from the students. It must not be forgotten that during the Free Speech Movement's revolt on the Berkeley campus in December, 1964, it was the San Francisco local of the Service Employees International Union that provided the FSM with its first public support in the Bay Area and paved the way for public support from the powerful San Francisco Central Labor Council. During the FSM strike that in the same month closed that campus, rank-and-file Teamsters respected the students picket lines until ordered to cross them by their leadership. The Cement Truck Drivers East Bay Teamsters local, however, officially honored the strike. Early in 1965, when Mario Savio and the other FSM leaders were under attack from the entire establishment in the state, Paul Schrade, the west coast director of the United Automobile Workers visited the Berkeley campus and before press and public declared that he would greet the presence of students like Savio inside his union.

The most decisive crisis for American unions is the alienation that lies between them and members of the black community: particularly the black youth, but also the black union members. The main cause of the crisis is twofold: White rank-and-file workers are, in the main, but to varying degrees, racially prejudiced; the leadership of labor has generally failed to provide the leadership that could solve the crisis. In the broadest sense of the term the crisis is one of leadership. The top officials of labor have failed to provide adequate leadership for any of the major problems facing workers. Walter Reuther provides a good example. He has many times provided segments of the civil rights movement with valuable aid. Those admirable actions are cheated of their full educational value for the UAW ranks—both white and black. "He is helping them, but what about us?" A Reuther who conducted a more than rhetorical battle against the speedup in the auto plants could increase his union's support of the black revolution tenfold without incurring the wrath of the white workers in his ranks. At first they would forgive him his trespasses because he was also delivering for them. Only then could there be the receptivity that allows for education in the best sense. Also, the black UAW members, who suffer from the speedup as much as do the white workers, could begin to take Reuther seriously.

Almost invariably, when labor leaders make speeches asking that their white ranks champion the rights of blacks in industry, they are asking the whites to give up something without offering them anything in return. White workers involved in the formation of the CIO welcomed the presence of blacks because it won an industrial union for them. For that time, the appearance of substantial numbers of blacks in mass production industries with full union membership was progress. As a result, the prejudice of the whites who experienced it was diminished. As always, morality followed necessity. Tragically, the initial progress was not built upon. The CIO bureaucratized and lost its momentum. The blacks lost a vehicle for major progress and organized labor lost a natural ally.

The momentum of the movement for black liberation and labor's lack of responsiveness dictate that black workers will organize, as such, within industry and unions. If this attempt at organization is grounded in demands for an improvement of work life as well as black freedom it will find sympathies among white workers. The organizations they form will help stimulate the formation of internal union opposition movements in general. The present weakness of the rank-

and-file revolts is that they are localized and isolated from one another. If the revolts continue to grow in scope, it is likely that it will mean the beginning of the end of labor's leadership crisis. Only the failure of the revolts and the consequent demoralization can create the basis for the development of a major racist movement among white industrial workers.

The isolation of labor from its natural allies is closely related to its political failures. The politics which join the official labor leadership to the Democratic party contribute to its impotency in serving its membership. There is hardly a major labor negotiation that fails to demonstrate this fact. There is not one aspect of labor's leadership crisis that has not contributed to the cause of the rank-and-file revolts. . . .

What of the future of the rank and file union revolts occurring mainly in the mass production and transportation industries? They have several major strengths to build upon. One of their principal powers arises from the subjective consciousness that motivates them: large numbers of industrial workers are simply no longer willing to tolerate the conditions under which they are expected to produce the goods and services that in major part maintain this society. Their major strength, however, lies in the organizational base on which they are founded, the primary or informal work groups. The groups are created by production technology which puts from three to ten workers in regular face to face communication with one another during each work turn. They have naturally selected informal leadership. They are able to maintain control and discipline over their members through use of the social weapon, first by the "chill" treatment, then ridicule, then worse. They can effect the speed and efficiency of production of goods or services. They are the micro-organizational units which create the phantom unions that are behind all wildcat strikes, slowdowns and withdrawals of efficiency. They are the only organizations which cannot be taken away from the ranks and that cannot be bureaucratized.

A third strength of the revolts exists because they have broken out at a time when there is deep dissatisfaction in other large specific segments of the labor force and in the population generally. This was far less true in the 1930s. At that time there were no large scale radicalizations as such among racial or ethnic minorities, students and professionals—that is, that had very definite independent and separate identities of their own. There were no hints of a growing radicalization among women. Public workers were not ignoring anti-strike laws and forming massive unions. In short, the CIO revolution did not occur in as widespread a momentum for societal change. Even though it has yet to manifest itself as dramatically, today's struggle against the "life that is" is far more general than in the 1930s.

The fourth major strength is a historical first, intellectuals now have potential means for building their own independent base inside organized labor. The opportunity exists due to the unions being organized by teachers, social workers and professionals in many career categories. During the 1930s, intellectuals obtained access to the labor movement mainly by invitation from union officials in need of assistance. They came as outsiders. Paid and unpaid they worked as staffers and consultants. They remained until they were no longer of use or until they differed openly with their employers or sponsors on serious policy issues. They can now participate as equals, as card carrying members, in large numbers and with memberships of their own to back them. And because professionals are now getting their own unions, blue-collar workers are in position to give direct and immediate aid to a large segment of the new middle class. In return, and not as a gift, blue-collar workers can have available to them by a much more direct process, the cultural sophistication and technical and intellectual skills that a class conscious economic, social and educational system denies so many of them and which are so necessary to their struggle.

The rank-and-file revolts have one overall and general weakness. They have thus far been waged mainly around immediate issues within separate workplaces that involve large numbers of supporters for only brief crisis periods. Between those periods their active supporters tend to dwindle to a small number of militants who are then faced with the problem of defending themselves from their employers and top union officials while seeking to maintain a core of key rebel leaders in wait for the next crisis issue that will enable them to again put large numbers into motion. The problem of how to attract the support of a critical mass in each place of work and then retain it reveals three major and specific weaknesses of the rebel movements. First of all, and not necessarily in order of importance, the revolts have been unable to overcome their organizational isolation, one from another. The sense of isolation in itself has a demoralizing effect upon the rebels. And because the revolts have been conducted within separate local unions representing separate workplaces, their opponents have been allowed to deal with them in the same way, thereby avoiding the necessity of making major concessions. There are no large rebel caucuses or committees. There are no organizational vehicles to unite rebelling local unions in different workplaces owned by the same employer, to unite locals in the U.S. and Canada within the same industry or international union, or to unite rebel groups across industrial lines within the same city or region. Among other things, this makes it impossible for the rebels to directly challenge the offices of top union officials who are unresponsive to the needs of the ranks.

The second specific and major weakness of the revolts is directly related to the fact that their stated demands have thus far been limited to a series of slogans for single and relatively immediate goals. No rank and file group has yet come forth with an overall program or long range perspective statement. Thus, to those not involved in their groups, either in or outside industry, it appears that they seek only piecemeal democratic reform of their unions and the present institution of collective bargaining. But to obtain, for example, any one or more of the following demands: funded pensions after thirty years of labor regardless of age, a thirty hour week with forty hours pay, the right to place limitations on production paces and work loads, the right of the ranks to choose collective bargaining goals as well as to ratify what has been negotiated by union negotiators, increased job and skill upgrading opportunities for black and brown workers —requires far more than a concerted drive to rally the ranks around just the slogans. In the first place, drives that are limited to the winning of one or a series of popular demands seldom produce a stable organization, if they produce one at all. As a result the drives are unable to sustain themselves at the needed momentum and force for more than brief periods. They do not develop broad divisions of labor. They are unable to bank the change in consciousness level of the participants. Too often, rank-and-file militants find themselves facing a new outbreak of mass militancy in their workplaces with little more organizational development to handle it than existed at the beginning of the previous outbreak.

Ongoing organizations with any kind of mass participation and following are those that have developed a "world view" or context that supports their popular demands. They have been able to attract larger than elite core numbers because they have been able to overcome the skepticism and pessimism that exists in the majority because of their inability to see a successful alternative to doing things as they are done presently. In most instances, today's outbreaks of mass dissatisfaction whether in ghettoes, on campuses, or inside industrial workplaces are momentary acts of desperation against "things as they are." The sense of hopelessness about accomplishing progressive change is only temporarily overcome. Failure to obtain quick success for popular demands brings a return of the feeling that it is hopeless to try to win the demands because the powerful employers are opposed to them and the union officials aren't interested in making the fight necessary to win them. In the main, this demoralization is fed by two things: (1) the failure of the rank and file leadership to project a vision of union democracy wherein bureaucratic officials could not so easily frustrate rank-and-file drives for work life improvements and (2) the failure to propose the concrete democratic structural-governmental union reforms necessary for fulfillment of the vision. The present crisis in the auto workers union provides an excellent example to clarify and amplify on the above. The ranks of that union are now, as they have been for years, interested in exercising limitations on the production speeds set by the employers. They are able to use a formalized grievance process in order to protest the speedup, but have found it ineffective in stopping it. In addition to poor collective bargaining contract language, the ratio of union representatives to workers on the shop floor is as high as one to four hundred. Grievance committee men and women are unable to give ample representation to the workers they are supposed to represent and moreover, are strangers to most of them. In the face of this problem, leaflets have recently been distributed by rebel groups in Detroit General Motors UAW locals calling for union representation on the shop floor equal to that of management's, which is often as low as one to fifteen. Such a ratio for the union would mean that every worker would work within eyesight of his or her union representative who also labors "on the line." What if working shop stewards of this sort formed plant for plant committees and city, regional, and national councils based upon the committees? Pyramiding of this sort from elementary units of representation that are based in the work process, might well be an alternative basis for UAW government, far superior to the present elite executive board elected at bi-annual conventions held in places and atmospheres far removed from the places of work. The demand for a better union representation ratio is a good one, but it is improbable that large numbers in the ranks will mobilize around it until they see it as more than a simple and immediate reform of the grievance handling process.

To be able to envisage a new union structure that does not immediately and bureaucratically conservatize new militants who are elected to official positions is prerequisite for successful rank-and-file rebel mobilization. The present union governmental structures and practices cause new leaders to immediately lose direct contact with the people who elected them. The institution of the monthly local union meeting has failed as the method of maintaining that contact. The automobile population explosion and the disappearance of cohesive neighborhoods of industrial workers nearby the factories makes attendance at local meetings too great a chore. Few locals get attendances of over five percent of their membership. This factor alone cuts the vast majority out of the union decision making process. It is difficult to arouse sustained enthusiasm for immediate reforms if the system that has frustrated the fulfillment of previous reforms continues to operate unchanged.

The third major weakness of the rank-and-file revolts also results from the limitations of the stated goals held forth by those that lead them. Between 1937 and 1940, five million semi-skilled American workers established industrial unions. The momentum which made the CIO possible was developed on far more than a desire for union recognition and collective bargaining contracts. Over and above the practical demands was the dream of a whole new life expressed in idealistic terms. The momentum was lost during World War II and the bureaucratized unions that emerged from that war make demands that, if won, do no more than provide workers with the material wealth necessary to enable them to continue to produce, and under conditions that are deteriorating rather than improving. It is not that the vision of a new and better life is dead. In themselves, the revolts are proof that the dream still exists. A generation long period of relative full employment has meant that millions have spent adult lifetimes doing murderously repetitive work tasks without interruption or relief. They have found that work whose only reward is the ability to pay bills has no meaning; that work to create products that cannot be identified with also brings a quality of meaninglessness to their entire existences. They want to make quality products in which they can take pride, which are built to last rather than to be "hawked" on television. They want to produce quality services without sacrifice of what is creative in their personalities. The older workers do not want to finish out their work lives in monotony and boredom. The young do not want to be shuffling drudges by the time they reach forty, sapped to a point where nightly there is little energy left for more than activities of momentary escape. The general public will one day be shocked to learn that there is not an auto or rubber worker who doesn't curse or look the other way when they see their products rolling down the street; that there is not an electrical appliance worker who likes to have at home one of the products he or she helps to make; and that there is not a steel worker who is not angered by employer imposed conditions that cheats a run of steel of its potential quality. It is the same for all workers regardless of industry. Break through the crust of cynicism created by work done under conditions that denies responsibility and the dream is there. Workers want to be able to participate in the making of the decisions that affect their work lives. But until they make their angers and desires known beyond the areas behind the timeclocks, the public will continue to believe that the official pronouncements of the unions represent the true feelings of the workers and that their major interests do not go beyond the purely economic. But how is it possible to break away from the limitations of present official union practices and ideologies without open presentation of alternatives to their equally narrow goals? This is the biggest of the tasks that history has placed upon the rank-and-file unionists who lead the revolts.

Part Four
PROPHECIES

1

Ernest Mandel
WHERE IS AMERICA GOING?

What American working people do in the foreseeable future will depend on two things: the course of the American economy and the spirit of the workers themselves. Ernest Mandel (1923–), a Belgian Marxist economist, predicts hard times for American capitalism and a consequent revival of working-class militancy. The factor he stresses most is the ability of European and Japanese firms to undersell American companies. This competition from abroad, Mandel believes, will compel American capitalists to push American workers harder, to attack the standard of living that unionized workers have come to take for granted, and thus, perhaps, to breath new life into the unions themselves.

Today, profound forces are working to undermine the social and economic equilibrium which has reigned in the United States for more than 25 years, since the big depressions of 1929–32 and of 1937–38. Some of these are forces of an international character, linked with the national liberation struggles of the peoples exploited by American imperialism—above all the Vietnamese Revolution. But from the point of view of Marxist method, it is important in the first place to stress those forces which are at work inside the system itself. This essay will attempt to isolate six of these forces—six historic contradictions which are now destroying the social equilibrium of the capitalist economy and bourgeois order of the United States.

THE DECLINE OF UNSKILLED LABOUR AND THE SOCIAL ROOTS OF BLACK RADICALIZATION

American society, like every other industrialized capitalist country, is currently in the throes of an accelerated process of technological

SOURCE. *New Left Review*, March–April 1969, pp. 3–15. Reprinted with permission.

change. The third industrial revolution—summarized in the catchword 'automation'—has by now been transforming American industry for nearly two decades. The changes which this new industrial revolution have brought about in American society are manifold. During the fifties, it created increased unemployment. The annual growth-rate of productivity was higher than the annual growth-rate of output, and as a result there was a tendency to rising structural unemployment even in times of boom and prosperity. Average annual unemployment reached 5,000,000 by the end of the Republican administration.

Since the early sixties, the number of unemployed has, however, been reduced somewhat (although American unemployment statistics are very unreliable). It has probably come down from an average of 5,000,000 to an average of 3,500,000 to 4,000,000: these figures refer to structural unemployment, and not to the conjunctural unemployment which occurs during periods of recession. But whatever may be the causes of this temporary and relative decline in structural unemployment, it is very significant that one sector of the American population continues to be hit very hard by the development of automation: the general category of unskilled labour. Unskilled labour jobs are today rapidly disappearing in US industry. They will in the future tend to disappear in the economy altogether. In absolute figures, the number of unskilled labour jobs in industry has come down from 13,000,000 to less than 4,000,000, and probably to 3,000,000, within the last 20 years. This is a truly revolutionary process. Very rarely has anything of the kind happened with such speed in the whole history of capitalism. The group which has been hit hardest by the disappearance of unskilled jobs is, of course, the black population of the United States.

The rapid decline in the number of unskilled jobs in American industry is the nexus which binds the growing negro revolt, especially the revolt of negro youth, to the general socio-economic framework of American capitalism. Of course it is clear, as most observers have indicated, that the acceleration of the negro revolt, and in particular the radicalization of negro youth in the fifties and early sixties, has been closely linked to the development of the colonial revolution. The appearance of independent states in Black Africa, the Cuban Revolution with its radical suppression of racial discrimination, and the development of the Vietnam War, have been powerful subjective and moral factors in accelerating the Afro-American explosion in the USA. But we must not overlook the objective stimuli which have grown out of the inner development of American capitalism itself. The long post-war boom and the explosive progress in agricultural productivity were the first factors in the massive urbanization and proletarization of the Afro-Americans: the Northern ghettoes grew by leaps and bounds. Today, the average rate of unemployment among the black population is double what it is among the white population, and the average rate of unemployment among *youth* is double what it is among adults, so that the average among the black youth is nearly four times the general average in the country. Up to 15 or 20 per cent of young black workers are unemployed: this is a percentage analogous to that of the Great Depression. It is sufficient to look at these figures to understand the social and material origin of the black revolt.

It is important to stress the very intimate inter-relationship between this high rate of unemployment among black youth and the generally scandalous state of education for black people in the ghettoes. This school system produces a large majority of drop-outs precisely at the moment when unskilled jobs are fast disappearing. It is perfectly clear under these conditions why black nationalists feel so strongly about the problem of community control over black schools—a problem which in New York and elsewhere has become a real crystallizing point for the black liberation struggle.

THE SOCIAL ROOTS OF THE STUDENT REVOLT

The third industrial revolution can be seen at one and the same time as a process of *expulsion* of human labour from traditional industry, and of tremendous *influx* of industrial labour into all other fields of economic and social activity. Whereas more and more people are replaced by machines in industry, activities like agriculture, office administration, public administration and even education become industrialized—that is, more and more mechanized, streamlined and organized in industrial forms.

This leads to very important social consequences. These may be summed up by saying that, in the framework of the third industrial revolution, manual labour is expelled from production while intellectual labour is reintroduced into the productive process on a gigantic scale. It thereby becomes to an ever-increasing degree alienated labour—standardized, mechanized, and subjected to rigid rules and regimentation, in exactly the same way that manual labour was in the first and second industrial revolutions. This fact is very closely linked with one of the most spectacular recent developments in American society: the massive student revolt, or, more correctly, the growing radicalization of students. To give an indication of the scope of this transformation in American society, it is enough to consider that the

United States, which at the beginning of this century was still essentially a country exporting agricultural products, today contains fewer farmers than students. There are today in the United States 6,000,000 students, and the number of farmers together with their employees and family-help has sunk below 5,500,000. We are confronted with a colossal transformation which upsets traditional relations between social groups, expelling human labour radically from certain fields of activity, but reintroducing it on a larger scale and at a higher level of qualification and skill in other fields.

If one looks at the destiny of the new students, one can see another very important transformation, related to the changes which automation and technological progress have brought about in the American economy. Twenty or thirty years ago, it was still true that the students were in general either future capitalists, self-employed or agents of capitalism. The majority of them became either doctors, lawyers, architects, and so on or functionaries with managerial positions in capitalist industry or the State. But today this pattern is radically changed. It is obvious that there are not 6,000,000 jobs for capitalists in contemporary American society: neither for capitalists or self-employed professionals, nor for agents of capitalism. Thus a great number of present-day students are not future capitalists at all, but future salary-earners, in teaching, public administration and at various technical levels in industry and the economy. Their status will be nearer that of the industrial worker than that of management. For meanwhile, as a result of automation, the difference of status between the technician and the skilled worker is rapidly diminishing. US society is moving towards a situation in which most of the skilled workers for whom there remain jobs in industry will have to have a higher or semi-higher education. Such a situation already exists in certain industries even in countries other than the United States —Japanese shipbuilding is a notorious example.

The university explosion in the United States has created the same intense consciousness of alienation among students as that which is familiar in Western Europe today. This is all the more revealing, in that the material reasons for student revolt are much less evident in the United States than in Europe. Overcrowding of lecture halls, paucity of student lodgings, lack of cheap food in restaurants and other phenomena of a similar kind play a comparatively small role in American universities, whose material infrastructure is generally far superior to anything that we know in Europe. Nevertheless, the consciousness of alienation resulting from the capitalist form of the university, from the bourgeois structure and function of higher education and the authoritarian administration of it, has become more and more widespread. It is a symptomatic reflection of the changed social position of the students today in society.

American students are thus much more likely to understand general social alienation, in other words to become at least potentially anti-capitalist, than they were 10 or 15 years ago. Here the similarity with developments in Western Europe is striking. As a rule, political mobilization on the US campus started with aid to the black population within the United States, or solidarity with liberation movements in the Third World. The first political reaction of American students was an anti-imperialist one. But the logic of anti-imperialism has led the student movement to understand, at least in part, the necessity of anti-capitalist struggle, and to develop a socialist consciousness which is today widespread in radical student circles.

AUTOMATION, TECHNICIANS AND THE HIERARCHICAL STRUCTURE OF THE FACTORY

The progress of automation has also had another financial and economic result, which we cannot yet see clearly in Europe, but which has emerged as a marked tendency in the United States during the sixties. Marxist theory explains that one of the main special effects of automation and the present technological revolution is a shortening of the life-cycle of fixed capital. Machinery is now generally replaced every four or five years, while it used to be replaced every ten years in classical capitalism. Looking at the phenomenon from the perspective of the operations of big corporations, this means that there is occurring a shift of the centre of their gravity away from problems of *production* towards problems of *reproduction*.

The real bosses of the big corporations no longer mainly discuss the problems of how to organize production: that is left to lower-echelon levels of the hierarchy. The specific objective in which they are interested is how to organize and to ensure reproduction. In other words, what they discuss is future plans: plans for replacing the existing machinery, plans for financing that replacement, new fields and locations for investment, and so on. This has given the concentration of capital in the United States a new and unforeseen twist. The process of amalgamation during the last few years has not predominantly consisted in the creation of monopolies in certain branches of industry, fusing together automobile, copper or steel trusts, or aviation factories. It has instead been a movement towards uniting apparently quite *unconnected* companies, operating in completely heteroclite fields of production. There are some classical examples of this process, widely discussed in the American financial press, such as the Xerox-CIT merger, the spectacular diversification of the International Telephone and Telegraph Corporation, or the Ling-Temco-Vought empire, which recently bought up the Jones and Laughlin Steel Corporation.

What this movement really reflects is the growing pre-occupation with "pure" problems of accumulation of capital. That is to say, the imperative today is to assemble enough capital and then to diversify the investment of that capital in such a way as to minimize risks of structural or conjunctural decline in this or that branch—risks which are very great in periods of fast technological change. In other words, the operation of the capitalist system in the United States today shows in a very clear way what Marxists have always said (and what only economists in the Soviet Union and some of their associates in East European countries and elsewhere are forgetting today), namely that real cost reduction and income maximization is impossible if profitability is reckoned only at plant level. In fact, it is a truth which every big American corporation understands, that it is impossible to have maximum profitability and economic rationality at plant level, and that it is even impossible to achieve it at the level of a *single branch of industry*. That is why the prevailing capitalist tendency in the USA is to try to combine activities in a number of branches of production. The type of financial empire which is springing up as a result of this form of operation is a fascinating object of study for Marxists.

But the more Big Capital is exclusively pre-occupied with problems of capital accumulation and reproduction, the more it leaves plant management and organization of production to lower-echelon experts, and the more the smooth running of the economy must clash with the survival of private property and of the hierarchical structure of the factory. The absentee factory-owners and money-juggling financiers divorced from the productive process are not straw men. They retain ultimate power—the power to open or to close the plant, to shut it in one town and relaunch it 2,000 miles away, to suppress by one stroke of their pens 20,000 jobs and 50 skills acquired at the price of long human efforts. This power must seem more and more arbitrary and absolute in the eyes of the true technicians who precisely do *not* wield the decisive power, that of the owners of capital. The higher the level of education and scientific knowledge of the average worker-technician, the more obsolete must become the attempts of both capitalists and managers to maintain the hierarchical and authoritarian structure of the plant, which even contradicts the logic of the latest techniques—the need for flexible co-operation within the factory in the place of a rigid chain of command.

THE EROSION OF REAL WAGE INCREASES THROUGH INFLATION

Since the beginning of the sixties and the advent of the Kennedy Administration, structural unemployment has gone down and the rate of growth of the American economy has gone up. This shift has been generally associated with an increased rate of inflation in the American economy. The concrete origins and source of this inflation are to be located not only in the huge military establishment—although, of course, this is the main cause—but also in the vastly increased indebtedness of the whole American society. Private debt has accelerated very quickly; in the last 15 years it has gone up from something like 65 per cent to something like 120 per cent of the internal national income of the country, and this percentage is rising all the time. It passed the $1,000,000,000 (thousand billion) mark a few years ago, in 1966, and is continually rising at a quicker rate than the national income itself. The specific price behaviour of the monopolistic and oligopolistic corporations, of course, interlocks with this inflationary process.

This is not the place to explore the technical problems of inflation. But it should be emphasized that the result of these inflationary tendencies, combined with the Vietnam war, has been that, for the first time for over three decades the growth of the real disposable income of the American working class has stopped. The highest point of that disposable real income was reached towards the end of 1965 and the beginning of 1966. Since then it has been going down. The downturn has been very slow—probably less than 1 per cent per annum. Nevertheless it is a significant break in a tendency which has continued practically without interruption for the last 35 years. This downturn in the real income of the workers has been the result of two processes: on the one hand inflation, and on the other a steep increase in taxation since the beginning of the Vietnamese war. There is a very clear and concrete relation between this halt in the rise of the American working class's real income, and the growing impatience which exists today in American working class circles with the US Establishment as such, whose distorted reflection was partly to be seen in the Wallace movement.

It is, of course, impossible to speak at this stage of any political opposition on the part of the American working class to the capitalist system as such. But if American workers accepted more or less easily and normally the integration of their trade union leadership into the Democratic Party during the long period which started with the Roosevelt Administration, this acceptance was a product of the fact that their real income and material conditions, especially their social security, improved during that period. Today that period seems to be coming to an end. The current stagnation of proletarian real income means that the integration of the trade union bureaucracy into the bourgeois Democratic Party is now no longer accepted quite so easily as it was even four years ago. This was evident during the Presidential Election campaign of 1968. The UAW leadership organized their usual special convention to give formal endorsement to the Democratic candidates, Humphrey and Muskie. This time they got a real shock. Of the thousand delegates who normally come to these conventions, nearly one half did not show up at all. They no longer supported the Democratic Party with enthusiasm. They had lost any sense of identification with the Johnson Administration. All the talk about welfare legislation, social security, medicare and the other advantages which the workers had gained during the last four years was largely neutralized in their eyes by the results of inflation and of increased taxation on their incomes. The fact was that their real wages had stopped growing and were even starting to decline a little.

It is well known that dollar inflation in the United States has created major tensions in the world monetary system. Inside the USA, there is now a debate among different circles of the ruling class, the political personnel of the bourgeoisie, and the official economic experts, as to whether to give priority to restoring the US balance of payments, or to maintaining the present rate of growth. These two goals seem to be incompatible. Each attempt to stifle inflation completely, to re-establish a very stable currency, can only be ensured by deflationary policies which create unemployment—and probably unemployment on a considerable scale. Each attempt to create full employment and to quicken the rate of growth inevitably increases inflation and with it the general loss of power of the currency. This is the dilemma which confronts the new Republican administration today as it confronted Johnson yesterday. It is impossible to predict what course Nixon will choose, but it is quite possible that his economic policy will be closer to that of the Eisenhower Administration than to that of the Kennedy-Johnson Administrations.

A group of leading American businessmen, who form a council of business advisors with semi-official standing, published a study two weeks before the November 1968 election which created a sensation in financial circles. They stated bluntly that in order to combat inflation, at least 6 per cent unemployment was needed. These American businessmen are far more outspoken than their British counterparts, who are already happy when there is talk about 3 per cent unemployment. Unemployment of 6 per cent in the United States means about 5,000,000 permanently without work. It is a high figure compared to the present level, to the level under "normal" conditions, outside of recessions. If Nixon should move in that direction, in which the international bankers would like to push him, the American bourgeoisie will encounter increased difficulty in keeping the trade-union movement quiescent and ensuring that the American workers continue to accept the integration of their union bureaucracy into the system, passively submitting to both bosses and union bureaucrats.

THE SOCIAL CONSEQUENCES OF PUBLIC SQUALOR

There is a further consequence of inflation which will have a growing impact on the American economy and especially on social relations in the United States. Inflation greatly intensifies the contradiction between "private affluence" and "public squalor." This contradiction has been highlighted by liberal economists like Galbraith, and is today very striking for a European visiting the United States. The extent to which the public services in that rich country have broken down is, in fact, astonishing. The huge budget has still not proved capable of maintaining a minimum standard of normally functioning public services. In late 1968, the *New York Times Magazine*, criticizing the American postal services, revealed that the average letter travels between Washington and New York more slowly today than it did a hundred years ago on horseback in the West. In a city like New York street sweeping has almost entirely disappeared. Thoroughfares are generally filthy: in the poorer districts, streets are hardly ever cleaned. In the richer districts, the burgers achieve clean streets only because they pay private workers out of their own pockets to sweep the streets and keep them in more or less normal conditions. Perhaps the most extraordinary phenomenon, at any rate for the European, is that of certain big cities in the South-West which do not have any public transport system *whatsoever*: not a broken-down system—just no system at all. There are private cars and nothing else—no buses, no trams, no subways, nothing.

The contradiction between private affluence and public squalor has generally been studied from the point of view of the consumer, and of the penalties or inconveniences that it imposes on the average citizen. But there is another dimension to this contradiction which will become more and more important in the years to come. This is its impact on what one could call the "producers," that is to say of the people who are employed by public administration.

The number of these employees is increasing very rapidly. Public administration is already the largest single source of employment in the United States, employing over 11,000,000 wage earners. The various strata into which these 11,000,000 can be divided are all chronically underpaid. They have an average income which is lower than the income of the equivalent positions in private industry. This is not exceptional; similar phenomena have existed or exist in many European countries. But the results—results which have often been seen in Europe during the last 10 or 15 years—are now for the first time appearing on a large scale in the United States.

Public employees, who in the past were outside the trade-union movement and indeed any form of organized social activity, are today becoming radicalized at least at the union level. They are organizing, they are agitating, and they are demanding incomes at least similar to those which they could get in private industry. In a country like the United States, with the imperial position it occupies on a world scale, the vulnerability of the social system to any increase in trade-union radicalism by public employees is very great. A small example will do as illustration. In New York recently both police and firemen were, not officially but effectively, on strike—at the same time. They merely worked to rule, and thereby disorganized the whole urban life of the city. Everything broke down. In fact, for six days total traffic chaos reigned in New York. Drivers could park their cars anywhere without them being towed away. (Under normal conditions, between two and three thousand cars are towed away by the police each day in New York.) For those six days, with motorists free to park where they liked, the town became completely blocked after an hour of morning traffic—just because the police wanted a 10 per cent rise in wages.

The economic rationale of this problem needs to be understood. It is very important not to see it simply as an example of mistaken policy on the part of public administrators or capitalist politicians, but rather as the expression of basic tendencies of the capitalist system. One of the main trends of the last 25 or 30 years of European capitalism has been the growing socialization of all indirect costs of production. This constitutes a very direct contribution to the realization of private profit and to the accumulation of capital. Capitalists increasingly want the State to pay not only for electrical cables and roads, but also for research, development, education, and social insurance. But once this tendency towards the socialization of indirect costs of production gets under way, it is obvious that the corporations will not accept large increases in taxation to finance it. If they were to pay the taxes needed to cover all these costs, there would in fact be no "socialization." They would continue to pay for them privately, but instead of doing so directly they would pay indirectly through their taxes (and pay for the administration of these payments too). Instead of lessening the burden, such a solution would in fact increase it. So there is an inevitable institutionalized resistance of the corporations and of the capitalist class to increasing taxes up to the point where they would make possible a functional public service capable of satisfying the needs of the entire population. For this reason, it is probable that the gap between the wages of public employees and those of private workers in the United States will remain, and that the trend towards radicalization of public employees—both increased unionization and even possibly political radicalization—will continue.

Moreover, it is not without importance that a great number of university students enter public administration—both graduates and so-called drop-outs. Even today, if we look at the last four or five years, many young people who were student leaders or militants three or four years ago are now to be found teaching in the schools or working in municipal social services. They may lose part of their radical consciousness when they take jobs; that is the hope not only of their parents but also of the capitalist class. But the evidence shows that at least part of their political consciousness is preserved, and that there occurs a certain infiltration of radicalism from the student sector into the teaching body—especially in higher education—and into the various strata of public administration in which ex-students become employed.

THE IMPACT OF FOREIGN COMPETITION

The way in which certain objective contradictions within the United States economy have been slowly tending to transform the subjective consciousness of different groups of the country's population —negroes, especially negro youth; students; technicians; public employees—has now been indicated. Inflation has begun to disaffect growing sections of the working class. But the final, and most important, moment of a Marxist analysis of US imperial society today has not yet been reached—that is the threat to American capitalism now posed by international competition.

Traditionally, American workers have always enjoyed much higher real wages than European workers. The historical causes for this phenomenon are well known. They are linked with the shortage of labour in the United States, which was originally a largely empty country. Traditionally, American capitalist industry was able to absorb these higher wages because it was practically isolated from international competition. Very few European manufactured goods reached the United States, and United States industry exported only a small part of its output. Over the last 40 years, of course, the situation has slowly changed. American industry has become ever more integrated into the world market. It participates increasingly in international competition, both because it exports more and because the American domestic market is rapidly itself becoming the principal sector of the world market, since the exports of all other capitalist countries to the United States have been growing rapidly. Here a major paradox seems to arise. How can American workers earn real wages which are between two and three times higher than real wages in Western Europe, and between four and five times higher than real wages in Japan, while American industry is involved in international competition?

The answer is, of course, evident. These higher wages have been possible because United States industry has operated on a much higher level of productivity than European or Japanese industry. It has enjoyed a productivity gap, or as Engels said of British industry in the 19th century, a *productivity monopoly* on the world market. This productivity monopoly is a function of two factors: higher technology, and economy of scale—that is a much larger dimension of the average factory or firm. Today, both of these two causes of the productivity gap are threatened. The technological advance over Japan or Western Europe which has characterized American imperialism is now disappearing very rapidly. The very trend of massive capital export to the other imperialist countries which distinguishes American imperialism, and the very nature of the so-called "multi-national" corporation (which in nine cases out of ten is in reality an American corporation), diffuses American technology on a world scale, thus equalizing technological levels at least among the imperialist countries. At the same time, it tends, of course, to increase the gap between the imperialist and the semi-colonial countries. Today, one can say that only in a few special fields such as computers and aircraft does American industry still enjoy a real technological advantage over its European and Japanese competitors. But these two sectors, although they may be very important for the future, are not decisive for the total export and import market either in Europe or in the United States, nor will they be decisive for the next 10 or 20 years. So this advantage is a little less important than certain European analysts have claimed.

If one looks at other sectors, in which the technological advantage is disappearing or has disappeared—such as steel, automobiles, electrical appliances, textiles, furniture, or certain types of machinery—it is evident that a massive invasion of the American market by foreign products is taking place. In steel, something between 15 and

20 per cent of American consumption is today imported from Japan and Western Europe. The Japanese are beginning to dominate the West Coast steel market, and the Europeans to take a large slice of the East Coast market. It is only in the Mid-West, which is still the major industrial region of the United States, that imported steel is not widely used. But with the opening of the St. Lawrence seaway, even there the issue may be doubtful in the future. Meanwhile, automobiles are imported into the United States today at a rate which represents 10–15 per cent of total annual consumption. This proportion too could very quickly go up to 20–25 per cent. There is a similar development in furniture, textiles, transistor radios and portable television sets; shipbuilding and electrical appliances might be next.

So far, the gradual disappearance of the productivity differential has created increased competition for American capitalism in its own home market. Its foreign markets are seriously threatened or disappearing in certain fields like automobiles and steel. This, of course, is only the first phase. If the concentration of European and Japanese industry starts to create units which operate on the same scale as American units, with the same dimensions as American corporations, then American industry will ultimately find itself in an impossible position. It will then have to pay three times higher wages, with the same productivity as the Europeans or the Japanese. That would be an absolutely untenable situation, and it would be the beginning of a huge structural crisis for American industry.

Two examples should suffice to show that this is not a completely fantastic perspective. The last merger in the Japanese steel industry created a Japanese corporation producing 22,000,000 tons of steel a year. In the United States, this would make it the second biggest steel firm. On the other hand, in Europe the recent announcement that Fiat and Citroen are to merge by 1970 has created an automobile corporation producing 2,000,000 cars a year; this would make it the third largest American automobile firm, and it would move up into second place, overtaking Ford, if the momentum of its rate of growth, compared with the current rate of growth in the American industry, were maintained for another three or four years.

These examples make it clear that it is possible for European and Japanese firms, if the existing process of capital concentration continues, to attain not only a comparable technology but also comparable scale to that of the top American firms. When they reach that level, American workers' wages are certain to be attacked, because it is not possible in the capitalist world to produce with the same productivity as rivals abroad and yet pay workers at home two or three times higher wages.

THE WAGE DIFFERENTIALS ENJOYED BY AMERICAN WORKERS

The American ruling class is becoming increasingly aware that the huge wage differential which it still grants its workers is a handicap in international competition. Although this handicap has not yet become a serious fetter, American capitalists have already begun to react to it in various ways over the past few years.

The export of capital is precisely designed to counteract this wage differential. The American automobile trusts have been investing almost exclusively in foreign countries, where they enjoy lower wages and can therefore far more easily maintain their share of the world market, with cars produced cheaply in Britain or Germany, rather than for higher wages inside the United States. Another attempt to keep down the growth of real wages was the type of incomes policy advocated by the Kennedy and Johnson administrations—until 1966, when it broke down as a result of the Vietnam war. A third form of counteraction has been an intensification of the exploitation of labour—in particular a speed-up in big industry which has produced a structural transformation of the American working class in certain fields. This speed-up has led to a work rhythm that is so fast that the average adult worker is virtually incapable of keeping it up for long. This has radically lowered the age structure in certain industries, such as automobiles or steel. Today, since it is increasingly difficult to stay in plants (under conditions of speed-up) for 10 years without becoming a nervous or physical wreck, up to 40 per cent of the automobile workers of the United States are young workers. Moreover, the influx of black workers in large-scale industry has been tremendous as a result of the same phenomenon, since they have fewer job opportunities outside the factories. Today, there are percentages of 35, 40 or 45 per cent black workers in some of the key automobile factories. In Ford's famous River Rouge plant, there are over 40 per cent black workers; in the Dodge automobile plant in Detroit, there are over 50 per cent. These are still exceptional cases—although there are also some steel plants with over 50 per cent black workers. But the average employment of black workers in United States industry as a whole is far higher than the demographic average of 10 per cent: it is something like 30 per cent.

None of these policies has so far had much effect. However, if the historic moment arrives when the productivity gap between American and West European and Japanese industry is closed, American capitalism will have absolutely no choice but to launch a far more ruthless attack on the real wage levels of American workers than has occurred hitherto in Western Europe, in the various countries where a small wage differential existed (Italy, France, West Germany, England and Belgium, at different moments during the sixties). Since the wage differential between Europe and America is not a matter of 5, 10, or 15 per cent, as it is between different Western European countries, but is of the order of 200–300 per cent, it is easy to imagine what an enormous handicap this will become when productivity becomes comparable, and how massive the reactions of American capitalism will then be.

It is necessary to stress these facts in order to adopt a Marxist, in other words a materialist and not an idealist approach to the question of the attitudes of the American working class towards American society. It is true that there is a very close inter-relation between the anti-communism of the Establishment, the arms expenditure which makes possible a high level of employment, the international role of American imperialism, the surplus profits which the latter gets from its international investments of capital, and the military apparatus which defends these investments. But one thing must be understood. The American workers go along with this whole system, not in the first place because they are intoxicated by the ideas of anti-communism. They go along with it because it has been capable of delivering the goods to them over the last 30 years. The system has been capable of giving them higher wages and a higher degree of social security. It is this fact which has determined their acceptance of anti-communism, and not the acceptance of anti-communism which has determined social stability. Once the system becomes less and less able to deliver the goods, a completely new situation will occur in the United States.

Trade-union consciousness is not only negative. Or, to formulate this more dialectically, trade-union consciousness is in and by itself socially neutral. It is neither reactionary nor revolutionary. It becomes reactionary when the system is capable of satisfying trade-union demands. It creates a major revolutionary potential once the system is no longer capable of satisfying basic trade-union demands. Such a transformation of American society under the impact of the international competition of capital is today knocking at the door of US capitalism.

The liberation struggles of the peoples of the Third World, with their threat to American imperialist investment, will also play an important role in ending the long socio-economic equilibrium of American capitalism. But they do not involve such dramatic and immediate economic consequences as the international competition of capital could have, if the productivity gap were filled.

As long as socialism or revolution are only ideals preached by militants because of their own convictions and consciousness, their social impact is inevitably limited. But when the ideas of revolutionary socialism are able to unite faith, confidence and consciousness with the immediate material interest of a social class in revolt—the working class, then their potential becomes literally explosive. In that sense, the political radicalization of the working class, and therewith socialism, will become a practical proposition in the United States within the next 10 or 15 years, under the combined impact of all these forces which have been examined here. After the black workers, the young workers, the students, the technicians and the public employees, the mass of the American workers will put the struggle for socialism on the immediate historical agenda in the United States. The road to revolution will then be open.

2

Barbara Garson
A STRIKE FOR HUMANISM

Barbara Garson, the young playwright whose first work, MacBird, *was a satiric attack on American policy in Vietnam, offers a microcosm of the process forecast by Mandel in her description of a strike of automobile workers in Lordstown, Ohio, during the spring of 1972. The Lordstown plant was built by General Motors in response to the increased sales in the United States of imported compact cars. When costs failed to drop as rapidly as expected, management speeded up the assembly line and imposed harsher discipline. The workers rebelled. As Garson portrays them—they were young, many of them veterans of the Vietnam war, more interested in working conditions and less interested in wages than their fathers, remarkably similar to the student radicals of the 1960s in their style of life—the rebellious workers of Lordstown may be the forerunners of many more rebels to come.*

"Is it true," an auto worker asked wistfully, "that you get to do fifteen different jobs on a Cadillac?" "I heard," said another, "that with Volvos you follow one car all the way down the line."

Such are the yearnings of young auto workers at the Vega plant in Lordstown, Ohio. Their average age is twenty-four, and they work on the fastest auto assembly line in the world. Their jobs are so subdivided that few workers can feel they are making a car.

The assembly line carries 101 cars past each worker every hour. Most GM lines run under sixty. At 101 cars an hour, a worker has thirty-six seconds to perform his assigned snaps, knocks, twists, or squirt on each car. The line was running at this speed in October when a new management group, General Motors Assembly Division (GMAD or Gee-Mad), took over the plant. Within four months they fired 500 to 800 workers. Their jobs were divided among the remaining workers, adding a few more snaps, knocks, twists, or squirts to

SOURCE. *Harpers Magazine*, June 1972, under title "Luddites In Lordstown." Reprinted with the permission of the author.

each man's task. The job had been boring and unbearable before. When it remained boring and became a bit more unbearable there was a 97 per cent vote to strike. More amazing—85 per cent went down to the union hall to vote.[1]

One could give a broad or narrow interpretation of what the Lordstown workers want. Broadly they want to reorganize industry so that each worker plays a significant role in turning out a fine product, without enduring degrading supervision. Narrowly, they want more time in each thirty-six-second cycle to sneeze or to scratch.

John Grix, who handles public relations at Lordstown, and Andy O'Keefe for GMAD in Detroit both assured me that work at Lordstown is no different than at the older assembly plants. The line moves faster, they say, but then the parts are lighter and easier to install. I think this may be true. It is also true of the workers. These young people are not basically different from the older men. But they are faster and lighter. Because they are young they are economically freer to strike and temperamentally quicker to act. But their yearnings are not new. The Vega workers are echoing a rank-and-file demand that has been suppressed by both union and management for the past twenty years: HUMANIZE WORKING CONDITIONS.

Hanging around the parking lot between shifts, I learned immediately that to these young workers, "It's not the money."

"It pays good," said one, "but it's driving me crazy."

"I don't want more money," said another. "None of us do."

"I do," said his friend. "So I can quit quicker."

"It's the job," everyone said. But they found it hard to describe the job itself.

"My father worked in auto for thirty-five years," said a clean-cut lad, "and he never talked about the job. What's there to say? A car comes, I weld it. A car comes, I weld it. A car comes, I weld it. One hundred and one times an hour."

I asked a young wife, "What does your husband tell you about his work?"

[1]The union membership voted to settle the twenty-two-day strike in late March, but the agreement appeared to be somewhat reluctant; less than half of the members showed up for the vote, and 30 per cent of those voted against the settlement. The union won a number of concessions, among them full back pay for anybody who had been disciplined in the past few months for failure to meet work standards. Meanwhile, however, UAW locals at three other GM plants around the country threatened to strike on grounds similar to those established at Lordstown. In early April GM recalled 130,000 Vegas of the 1972 model because of a possible fire hazard involving the fuel and exhaust systems.

"He doesn't say what he does. Only if something happened like, 'My hair caught on fire,' or, 'Something fell in my face.' "

"There's a lot of variety in the paint shop," said a dapper twenty-two-year-old up from West Virginia. "You clip on the color hose, bleed out the old color, and squirt. Clip, bleed, squirt, think; clip, bleed, squirt, yawn; clip, bleed, squirt, scratch your nose. Only now the Gee-Mads have taken away the time to scratch your nose."

A long-hair reminisced, "Before the Go-Mads, when I had a good job like door handles, I could get a couple of cars ahead and have a whole minute to relax."

I asked about diversions. "What do you do to keep from going crazy?"

"Well, certain jobs like the pit you can light up a cigarette without them seeing."

"I go to the wastepaper basket. I wait a certain number of cars, then find a piece of paper to throw away."

"I have fantasies. You know what I keep imagining? I see a car coming down. It's red. So I know it's gonna have a black seat, black dash, black interiors. But I keep thinking what if somebody up there sends down the wrong color interiors—like orange, and me putting in yellow cushions, bright yellow!"

"There's always water fights, paint fights, or laugh, talk, tell jokes. Anything so you don't feel like a machine."

But everyone had the same hope: "You're always waiting for the line to break down."

The Vegas plant hires about seven thousand assembly-line workers. They commute to Lordstown from Akron, Youngstown, Cleveland, even as far as Pittsburgh. Actually, there is no Lordstown—just a plant and some trailer camps set among farmhouses. When the workers leave, they disperse throughout southern Ohio. GM presumably hoped that this location would help minimize labor troubles.

The nearest real town, Warren, contributes many workers from each high school graduating class. There are men up from western Pennsylvania and West Virginia camping in rooming houses waiting to send for their families back home or start new ones in Ohio. There are sons of steel and auto workers still living at home or with their wives and children. There's a bright sprinkling of women and local hippies on the line. The plant personnel manager estimates that 12 per cent of the workers come straight out of the Army.

I took the guided tour of the plant. It's new, it's clean, it's well lit without windows, and it's noisy. Hanging car bodies move past at the speed of a Coney Island ride slowing down. Most men work alongside the line but some stand in a man-sized pit craning their necks to work on the undersides of the cars.

MILITARISM IN THE INDUSTRIAL COMPLEX

I stopped to shout at a worker drinking coffee, *"Is there any quiet place to take a break?"* He shouted back, *"Can't hear you, ma'am. Too noisy to chat on a break."* As a plant guard rushed over to separate us I spotted Duane,[2] from Fort Lewis, shooting radios into a car with an air gun. Duane had been in the Army while I was working at a GI coffeehouse. He slipped me a note with his address.

When I left the plant there were leafleteers at the gate distributing *Workers' Power.* Guards with binocular cameras closed in snapping pictures; Lieutenant James V. Cunningham of plant protection checked everyone's ID. He copied down the names of leafleteers and workers who took papers. He took my name too.

That evening I visited Duane. He had rented a two-bedroom bungalow on the outskirts of a town that had no center. He had grown his hair a bit but, in fact, he looked neater and trimmer than when he'd been in the Army. Duane had a way of stymieing officers because he adhered strictly to Army regulations about dress, and yet somehow he managed to look like a shaggy hippie. He was always being stopped and sputtered at by officers who could never find anything specific to order him to trim or polish.

I told him about the incident at the gate. "Just like the Army," he said. He summarized life since his discharge: "Remember you guys gave me a giant banana split the day I ETSed [got out on schedule]? Well, it's been down hill since then. I came back to Cleveland; stayed with my dad, who was unemployed. Man, was that ever a downer. But I figured things would pick up if I got wheels, so I got a car. But it turned out the car wasn't human and that was a problem. So I figured, 'What I need is a girl.' But it turned out the girl *was* human and *that* was a problem. So I wound up working at GM to pay off the car and the girl." And he introduced me to his lovely pregnant wife, of whom he seemed much fonder than he sounds.

A couple of Duane's high-school friends, Stan and Eddie, wound up at Lordstown too. Stan at twenty-one was composed and placid, a married man with a child. Eddie at twenty-two was an excitable

[2]Since many workers were afraid of losing their jobs, I have changed names, juggled positions on the line, and given reasonable facsimiles for identifying details.

youth. Duane had invited them over to tell me what it's like working at the plant.

"I'll tell you what it's like," said Duane. "It's like the Army. They even use the same words like *direct order.* Supposedly you have a contract so there's some things they just can't make you do. Except, if the foreman gives you a direct order, you do it, or you're out."

"Out?" I asked.

"Yeah, fired—or else they give you a DLO."

"DLO?"

"Disciplinary layoff. Which means you're out without pay for however long they say. Like maybe it'll be a three-day DLO or a week DLO."

Eddie explained it further: "Like this new foreman comes up to me and says, 'Pick up that piece of paper.' Only he says it a little nastier, with a few references to my race, creed, and length of hair. So I says, 'That's not my job.' He says, 'I'm giving you a direct order to pick up that piece of paper.' Finally he takes me up to the office. My committeeman comes over and tells me I could of lost my job because you can't refuse a direct order. You do it, and then you put in a grievance—ha!"

"Calling your committeeman," says Duane. "That's just like the Army too. If your CO [commanding officer] is harassing you, you can file a complaint with the IG [inspector general]. Only thing is you gotta go up to your CO and say, 'Sir, request permission to see the inspector general to tell him my commanding officer is a shit.' Same thing here. Before you can get your committeeman, you got to tell the foreman exactly what your grievance is in detail. So meantime he's working out ways to tell the story different."

Here Stan took out an actual DLO form from his wallet. "Last week someone up the line put a stink bomb in a car. I do rear cushions, and the foreman says, 'You get in that car.' We said, 'If you can put your head in that car we'll do the job.' So the foreman says, 'I'm giving you a direct order.' So I hold my breath and do it. My job is every other car so I let the next one pass. He gets on me, and I say, 'It ain't my car. Please, I done your dirty work and the other one wasn't mine.' But he keeps at me, and I wind up with a week off. Now I got a hot committeeman who really stuck up for me. So you know what? They sent *him* home too. Gave the committeeman a DLO!" At most plants management realizes that the committeeman—even a zealous committeeman—plays a role in channelling anger into a long and complex grievance procedure. Eddie explained the co-optive function of the grievance process to me:

"Guy next to me, this boob Larry, he puts in alternators and they changed it to a one man job. So he lets half the cars get away. Then he calls the committeeman and files a 78 [A grievance claiming that the job can't be done in the allotted time. About 1000 78's had piled up by the time of the strike]. Soon as he's got those forms filled out he's back to work. I walk up to him afterwards and say, "Look at you. Now you're smiling and you're doing the god damn job. You can wipe your ass with that grievance." Two months later he's still doing the job just like GM wants him to. The union is saying 'Hang on Fellah, we'll help you' and he's still on the line like a fucking machine."

"See, just like the Army," Duane repeats. "No, it's worse 'cause you're welded to the line. You just about need a pass to piss."

"That ain't no joke," says Eddie. "You raise your little hand if you want to go wee-wee. Then wait maybe half an hour till they find a relief man. And they write it down every time too. 'Cause you're supposed to do it on your own time, not theirs. Try it too often, and you'll get a week off."

"I'd rather work in a gas station," said Stan wistfully. "That way you pump gas, then you patch a tire, then you go to the bathroom. You do what needs doing."

"Why don't you work in a gas station?" I asked.

"You know what they pay in a gas station? I got a kid. Besides, I couldn't even get a job in a gas station. Before I got in here I was so hard up I wound up selling vacuum cleaners—$297 door to door. In a month I earned exactly $10 selling one vacuum cleaner to a laid-off steel worker for which I'll never forgive myself."

"No worse than making cars," Eddie said. "Cars are your real trap, not vacuum cleaners. You need the car to keep the job and you need the job to keep the car. And don't think they don't know it. They give you just enough work to keep up the payments. They got it planned exactly, so you can't quit."

"He's a little paranoid," Duane said.

"Look it," says the paranoid reasonably. "They give you fifty, fifty-five hours' work for a couple of weeks. So your typical boob buys a color TV. Then they cut you back to thirty hours. There's not a married man who doesn't have bills. And the company keeps it like that so there's no way out. You're stuck for life."

I asked about future plans.

Eddie was getting out as soon as he saved enough money to travel. He thought he might work for three more months. He'd said three months when he started, and it was nine months already, but "things came up."

Duane figured he'd stay till after his wife had the baby. That way he could use the hospital plan. After that? "Maybe we'll go live on the land. I don't know. I wish someone would hand me a discharge."

Stan was a reasonable man—or a boob, as Eddie might have it. He knew he was going to stay. "If I'm gonna do some dumb job the rest of my life, I might as well do one that pays."

Though none of them could afford to quit, they were all eager for a strike. They'd manage somehow. For Stan it was a good investment in his future job. The others just liked the idea of giving GM a kick in the ass from the inside.

THE BLUE-COLLAR COMMUNE

Later in the week I stayed at an auto-workers' commune. Like so many other young people, they were trying to make a one-generational family—a homestead. Life centered, as of old, around the hearth, which was a water pipe bubbling through bourbon. The family Bibles were the Books of the Dead—both Tibetan and Egyptian. Throughout the evening, six to twelve people drifted through the old frame house waiting for Indian Nut (out working night shift at Lordstown) and his wife Judy (out babysitting).

Judy returned at midnight to prepare dinner for her husband. By 2:00 A.M. she complained: "They can keep them two, three, four hours over." Overtime is mandatory for auto workers, but it's not as popular at Lordstown as it is among older workers at other plants.

At two-thirty the Nut burst in, wild-haired, wild-eyed and sweet-smiled. He had a mildly maniacal look because his glasses were speckled with welding spatter.

"Got a new foreman, a real Gee-mad-man. Sent a guy home for farting in a car. And another one home for yodeling."

"Yodeling?" I asked.

"Yeah, you know." (And he yodeled.)

(It's common in auto plants for men to break the monotony with noise, like the banging of tin cans in jail. Someone will drop something, his partner will yell "Whaa," and then "Whaa" gets transmitted all along the line.)

"I bet there's no shop rule against farting," the Nut conjectured. "You know those porkers have been getting their 101 off the line again, and not that many of them need repairs. It's the hillbillies. Those cats have no stamina. The union calls them to a meeting, says, 'Now don't you sabotage, but don't you run. Don't do more than you can do.' And everybody cheers. But in a few days it's back to where it was. Hillbillies working so fast they ain't got time to scratch their balls. Meantime these porkers is making money even faster than they're making cars."

I ask who he means by the hillbillies. "Hillbillies is the general

Ohio term for assholes, except if you happen to be a hillbilly. Then you say Polack. Fact is everybody is a hillbilly out here except me and two other guys. And they must work day shift cause I never see them.

"Sabotage?" says the Nut. "Just a way of letting off steam. You can't keep up with the car so you scratch it on the way past. I once saw a hillbilly drop an ignition key down the gas tank. Last week I watched a guy light a glove and lock it in the trunk. We all waited to see how far down the line they'd discover it. . . . If you miss a car, they call that sabotage. They expect the sixty-second minute. Even a machine has to sneeze. Look how they call us in weekends, hold us extra, send us home early, give us layoffs. You'd think we were machines the way they turn us on and off."

I apologized for getting Indian Nut so steamed up and keeping him awake late. "No," sighed Judy. "It always takes a couple of hours to calm him down. We never get to bed before four."

Later that day, about 1:00 P.M., Indian Nut cooked breakfast for all of us (about ten). One nice thing about a working-class commune: bacon and eggs and potatoes for breakfast—no granola.

It took about an hour and a half to do the day's errands—mostly dope shopping and car repair. Then Indian Nut relaxed for an hour around the hearth.

As we talked some people listened to Firesign Theatre while others played Masterpiece or Monopoly. Everyone sucked at the pipe from time to time.

A college kid came by to borrow records. He was the editor of the defunct local underground paper called *Anonymity*. (It had lived up to its title before folding.)

"I've been trying to get Indian Nut to quit working there," he said.

"Why?" I asked.

"Don't you know? GM makes M-16s."

"Yeah, well, you live with your folks," said one of the Monopolists.

"You can always work some kind of rip-off," replied the ex-editor.

Everyone joined the ensuing philosophical inquiry about where it was moral to work and whom it was moral to rip-off.

"Shit," sighed Indian Nut. "It's four-thirty. Someone help Judy with the dishes." Taking a last toke, the Nut split for the plant.

"HATE THEM, HATE THEIR CAR"

As I proceeded with my unscientific survey, I found that I couldn't predict a man's militancy from his hair length, age, or general freakiness. But you could always guess a man's attitudes by his comments on the car.

When someone said, "I wouldn't even buy a Vega, not a '71 or a '72," then he would usually say, "General Motors—all they care about is money. Not the worker, not the car, just the goddamn money."

A nineteen-year-old told me bitterly: "A black guy worked next to me putting sealer into the cracks. He used to get cut all the time on sharp edges of metal. One day his finger really got stuck and he was bleeding all over the car. So I stopped the line. [There's a button every so many feet.] Sure they rushed him to the hospital, but boy did they get down on me for stopping the line. That line runs no matter what the cost."

One youth spontaneously kicked the car (I was driving a Vega) and shouted, "What'd you buy this piece of shit for?" He referred to General Motors as "Capitalist Pigs." He was the only man I heard use such language, and he was the short-haired son of a foundry worker.

The mildest man I met was driving a Vega. He was a long-haired, or at least shaggy-haired, twenty-one-year-old. He thought the Vega was a "pretty little thing." When I asked about his job he said, "It's a very important job. After all, everybody's got to have a car." Yes, he had voted for the strike. "Myself, I'd rather work, but if they're gonna keep laying people off, might as well strike now and get it over with." Anyway, he figured the strike would give him time to practice: he was second guitarist in a band, and if his group could only "get it together," maybe he could quit GM. He had other hopes too. For instance: "The company lets you put in suggestions, and you get money if they use your suggestions." He was a cheerful, good-natured lad, and, as I say, he liked the Vega.

There's a good reason why attitudes toward the car correlate with attitudes toward the company. It's not just "hate them, hate their car." It's also hate your job and hate yourself when you think you're making a hunk of junk, or when you can't feel you've made anything at all. I was reminded of this by a worker's mother.

While her son and his friends talked shop—DLOs, strike, rock bands—I talked to her in the kitchen. Someone in the supermarket where she worked had said that these kids were just lazy. "One thing, Tony is not lazy. He'll take your car apart and put it together any day. Ever since he's been in high school we haven't had to worry about car trouble. The slightest knock and he takes care of it. And he never will leave it half done. He even cleans up after himself.

"And I'm not lazy either. I love to cook. But supposing they gave me a job just cracking eggs with bowls moving past on a line. Pretty soon I'd get to a point where I'd wish the next egg was rotten just to spoil their whole cake."

At the Pink Elephant Bar I met a man who'd voted against the strike, one of the rare 3 per cent. He was an older man who'd worked in other auto plants. "I seen it before. The international [union] is just giving them enough rope to hang themselves. They don't ever take on speed-up or safety. And they don't ever help with any strike *they* didn't call.

"Meany and his silk shirts . . . Reuther's daughter hob-nobbed with Miss Ford, but at least he didn't wear silk shirts . . . Woodcock? Who cares what he wears.

"Like I was saying, they see a kicky young local so they go along. They authorize the strike. But it's just giving you enough rope to hang yourself. They see you got young inexperienced leadership—I'm not saying our leadership is young and inexperienced but what it is, is—young and inexperienced.

"So they let 'em go ahead. But they don't give 'em no help. They don't give 'em no funds. They don't even let the other locals come out with you. When it comes to humanizing working conditions you might as well be back before there was any unions.

"So the strike drags on, it's lost, or they 'settle' in Detroit. Everybody says, 'There, it didn't pay.' And the next time around the leadership gets unelected. See, they gave 'em enough rope to hang 'emselves."

Other GM plants are having labor troubles, but no coordinated union action has been authorized. It is difficult for an outsider to tell when the UAW International is giving wholehearted help. But with or without the international, workers will continue to agitate for better working conditions.

The members of local 1112 at Lordstown have defined their demands as narrowly as possible. They want GM to hire more men. They do not, they hasten to explain, want to limit the speed of the line. Gary Bryner, president of the local (an elder statesman at twenty-nine), said, "We recognize that it's management's prerogative to run the plant. But all we've got is our labor, so we want to see that our conditions of labor are okay."

Despite this humble goal, local 1112 is undertaking a fight that the international union has backed away from, even suppressed, in the past.

Every three years for the past fifteen, Walter Reuther bargained with auto manufacturers for higher wages and better benefits—off the job. And every three years for the past fifteen, auto workers rejected Reuther's contracts, demanding, in addition, better conditions—on the job.

The underlying assumption in an auto plant is that no worker wants to work. The plant is arranged so that employees can be controlled, checked, and supervised at every point. The efficiency of an assembly line is not only in its speed but in the fact that the workers are easily replaced. This allows the employer to cope with high turnover. But it's a vicious cycle. The job is so unpleasantly subdivided that men are constantly quitting and absenteeism is common. Even an accident is a welcome diversion. Because of the high turnover, management further simplifies the job, and more men quit. But the company has learned to cope with high turnover. So they don't have to worry if men quit or go crazy before they're forty.

The UAW is not a particularly undemocratic union. Still, it is as hard for the majority of its members to influence their international as it is for the majority of Americans to end the war in Vietnam. The desire to reduce alienation is hard to express as a union demand, and it's hard to get union leaders to insist upon this demand. Harder still will be the actual struggle to take more control over production away from corporate management. It is a fight that questions the right of private ownership to the means of production.

In the first half of this century workers fought for union recognition and higher wages. The older workers in auto plants fought for and won those demands. The younger workers accept these victories, but they add: "It's not just the money: it's the job." Whether inside or outside the present union structure, the movement to humanize working conditions will dominate the next half of this century.

SUGGESTIONS FOR FURTHER READING

These suggestions for further reading are in addition to books and pamphlets cited in the introduction, or excerpted for this volume. Paperbacks readily available from commercial publishers and listed in *Paperbound Books in Print* are simply designated "paperback." In a few cases, when the publisher is a radical press or a trade union, an address has been added.

Accounts by or about individual labor radicals are the best place to begin. Eugene Victor Debs and Samuel Gompers exemplify the radical and conservative labor leaders at the turn of the century. The best approach to Debs' life is a biography by Ray Ginger, *Eugene V. Debs: The Making of an American Radical* (paperback). Gompers speaks for himself in *Seventy Years of Life and Labour: An Autobiography*, two volumes (New York: E. P. Dutton, 1925, reprinted by Augustus M. Kelley, New York, 1967). A remarkable autobiography of a man whose father was a coal miner, who became a socialist after hearing Debs speak in 1908, and who lived to be the lead organizer for the UAW in Flint, Michigan, in 1936, is Wyndham Mortimer, *Organize! My life as a Union Man* (Boston: Beacon Press, 1971).

Other outstanding books in this category are Lucy Parsons, *Life of Albert R. Parsons: With Brief History of the Labor Movement in America* (Chicago: Lucy E. Parsons, 1889), a biography of the Haymarket martyr, which his wife sold on the streets of Chicago; *Bill Haywood's Book: The Autobiography of William D. Haywood* (paperback); the autobiography of the author of "Solidarity Forever," Ralph Chaplin, *Wobbly: The Rough-and-Tumble Story of an American Radical* (Chicago: University of Chicago Press, 1948); and Saul D. Alinsky, *John L. Lewis: An Unauthorized Biography* (New York: Putnam's, 1949).

Labor's Untold Story, by Richard O. Boyer and Herbert M. Morais, is a one-volume survey of American labor history that has been reprinted in paperback by the United Electrical, Radio and Machine Workers of America, 11 East 51 Street, New York, N.Y. 10022. It has a useful bibliography and offers a more positive view of the CIO than does the present volume. Philip S. Foner, *History of the Labor Movement in the United States*, four volumes (New York: International Publishers, 1947–), is more detailed but at this writing carries the story only through World War I. The story of the CIO is told from a liberal, scholarly standpoint by Walter Galenson, *The CIO Challenge to the AFL: A History of the American Labor Movement, 1935–1941* (Cambridge, Mass.: Harvard University Press, 1960) and by Irving Bernstein, *Turbulent Years: A History of the American Worker, 1933–1941* (paperback). A radical journalist who personally witnessed many of the events he describes goes over the same ground, but from a different point of view, in Art Preis, *Labor's Giant Step: Twenty Years of the CIO*, available in paperback from Pathfinder Press, 410 West Street, New York, N.Y. 10014.

Among many accounts of individual strikes are Henry David, *The History of the Haymarket Affair* (paperback); Almond Lindsay, *The Pullman Strike* (paperback); William Z. Foster, *The Great Steel Strike and Its Lessons* (New York: B.W. Huebsch, 1920); Farrell Dobbs, *Teamster Rebellion*, available in paperback from Pathfinder Press; Mike Quin [Paul William Ryan], *The Big Strike* (Olema, California: Olema Publishing Company, 1949), a participant's story of the San Francisco general strike of 1934; Ruth McKenney, *Industrial Valley* (New York: Harcourt, Brace, 1939), an account of the Akron sitdown strikes; and a scholarly, exhaustive, but not unbiased work, Sidney Fine, *Sit-Down: The General Motors Strike of 1936–1937* (Ann Arbor, Mich.: University of Michigan Press, 1969).

Periodicals which regularly present material on American labor radicalism include *Labor History*, and *Radical America*, 5 Upland Road, Cambridge, Mass., 02140. James Green, "Working Class Militancy in the Depression," *Radical America*, November–December 1972, surveys studies of labor radicalism in the 1930s.

American fiction about working-class life has been unjustly denigrated. Upton Sinclair, *The Jungle* (paperback), about packinghouse workers in Chicago, and John Steinbeck, *In Dubious Battle* (paperback), about farm laborers in California, are classics. Other striking novels are Thomas Bell, *Out of this Furnace* (New York: Liberty Book Club, 1941), which tells the story of three generations of steelworkers in the Monongahela Valley; and K. B. Gilden, *Between the Hills and the Sea* (Garden City, N.Y.: Doubleday, 1971), which, in part, provides a shop steward's view of the McCarthy period and its aftermath.

The best resources for further study are surviving participants in the labor radicalism of the 1930s. Studs Terkel's *Division Street* and *Hard*

Times (both in paperback) will put the reader in the right mood for this kind of work. My wife, Alice Lynd, and I have edited a collection of interviews entitled *Rank and File: Personal Accounts of Working-Class Organizing* (Boston: Beacon Press, 1973).